D1831626

THE CONGRESS INDIRA TO SONIA GANDHI

VIJAY SANGHVI

KALPAZ PUBLICATIONS

DELHI-110052

The Congress Indira to Sonia Gandhi

© Vijay Sanghvi

ISBN: 81-7835-340-7

All rights Reserved. No Part of this book may be reproduced in any manner without written permission

Published in 2015 in India by:
Kalpaz Publications
C-30, Satyawati Nagar,
Delhi-110052
E-mail: kalpaz@hotmail.com

Lassertype Setting by: Rudra Computer Graphics, Delhi
Printed at : Salasar Imaging System, Delhi

Contents

Preface

The steady dilution of the Indian National Congress, as pithily demonstrated in the state assembly elections where the party ended up as a lame 'B' team of its rival, is essentially the story of a personality-driven party which over the years has been denuded of leadership. The story can be told in terms of electoral reverses. The essential argument of this book is however different. At one level, this book describes how an essentially amorphous party has become an appendage to individuals and personalities, which in turn has reduced both its social base and ideological content. While that certainly remains the core concern of the book as it traverses forty years of a great political formation's decline, its primary aim is to locate the shift to specific conjunctures. Unless specific moments when the party made self-defeating compromises are identified, it will be impossible for any chronicle to detail its failures.

The book is premised on the fundamental belief that the rise of the Hindu Right and various other fundamentalist and sub-national offshoots is directly related to the Congress' failure to renew itself both politically and ideologically.

In a manner of speaking, the Congress has 'died' five times: the first death was manifested in the manner in which the all-encompassing character of the national movement got frittered away. But that was more of a consequence rather than an outcome of any transient failure. Gandhi's assassination meant the demise of mass-based mobilization. When Nehru died, it symbolized the end of seductive dreams and secular values. Indira Gandhi represented the last great hope for a people who had invested their trust and hope in a progressive, forward-looking, vibrant force. Indira Gandhi, even before her own tragic assassination, had killed the Congress as a living entity.

The downturn in Gujarat symbolized the fall of a suspect but still catchy enough Congress bastion—its protestations regarding secularism. By uncritically adopting a "me-too" kind of strategy, the Congress not only diluted its brand equity but has also perhaps authored the beginning of a political death foretold.

The last two decades, which roughly comprise half the period of our story, have reinforced this book's firm belief that the Congress advanced only when it had personalities strong enough to guide its destiny.

Today, the party means differently to vast sections of observers and analysts. Some regard it as a boneless hulk that could be held by an individual to keep it standing. Even the Congress rank and file has come to believe that only a single family could be its saviour. For others, it is like a corporate giant held firmly in hands of one family. Even corporate giants need a community that the masses would take fancy to. Its market can only then be enlarged by a beautifully packaging. For those is the business of politics and power seeking, only commodity they can market is a dream- a dream that would put aflame the imagination of masses and make them invest in the dream. The Congress lacks the ability to conjure the dream for the masses. That is its tragedy because it has come to rely more on personalities rather than on the dream that the masses are looking for.

Some great individuals built the Congress: several ordinary people have destroyed it. If they have not succeeded yet, the electorate will give them enough reason to be periodically reminded of their abject failure to meet the saffron onslaught politically. The attempt in this book is to remain objective and dispassionate, but is certainly sure on one count; most of the party's wounds are self-inflicted. It will be gross injustice to presume that a multi-cultural, pluralist democracy has been or can be hijacked by a primarily fascist conglomerate like the Rashtriya Swayamsewak

Sangh and its offshoots. The failure has been of those who want to restore the primacy of the secular order, and it is here where the Congress, charged with the responsibility of providing leadership in this task, finds itself so utterly clueless in a blunderland of its own making.

Vijay Sanghvi

1

In Transit

"There are those metaphysical moments in the life of empires when their sheer size and their overwhelming power become the reason for their loss of purpose, direction, flexibility. What follows is a gradual loss of public respect and- often before their collapse- a loss of power."

John Ralston Saul

With the sole intention of retaining hold on power, Indira Gandhi, the then Prime Minister in March 1967 to December 1970, had radically transformed the organizational structure of the Indian National Congress, not once but twice. She perceived a constant threat from potential rivals within the party. She had acquired the office not by virtue of popular mandate as the most acceptable choice of the electorate but by the machinations and manipulations of few entrenched leaders from different regions who had created their own state- and national-level networks. Control over this reticulate of power gave them extraordinary leverage to neutralize her even though she was the prime minister. She was installed by them but was denied direct access to the party apparatus by those who had preferred her to Morarji Desai. This insecurity preyed on her mind continuously.

She encouraged conflicts between sections of the party representing different ideological hues and opinions. This was in stark contrast to Nehru's approach. Though Nehru had for eighteen years tried to keep the party to the left of the centre, there was a strong rightist conservative camp in the party. Nehru did not attempt to get rid of them. Instead he occupied the middle ground between the left and right of the party and tried to expand that space by reducing frictions between the two poles not just in the party, but in the polity, by co-opting them. He could do this because of his unchallenged position and unassailable status in the party.

Indira Gandhi's compulsions were of a qualitatively different order of magnitude which forced her to adopt a more divisive approach. She encouraged left leaning individuals in the party like Chandrajit Yadav, Arjun Arora, KV Raghunath Reddy and K R Ganesh, who were formerly associated with the Communist movement but had gravitated to the Congress after the Fourth General Election, to form the Socialist Forum within the Congress. At the same time her trusted lieutenant, Uma Shankar Dikshit, the party treasurer, launched the Nehru Forum, led by RD Bhandare, a Dalit leader who had switched his allegiance from the Republican Party of India to the Congress Party in 1963. He had obviously drawn inspiration and blessings from Indira Gandhi. By encouraging polarized conflicts she reduced the middle ground of the party in size but increased its power by giving it the all important job of manipulating and managing differences. Party management took on a different meaning

She introduced changes to the party in phases, but her first blow inflicted maximum damage and laid the foundations for the subsequent modifications. This was in November 1969, when she precipitated a vertical split in the party. Through the preceding year she had successfully engineered the gradual marginalization of the old guard. In August 1969 she took them head-on during the controversial election of the President of India. The recrimination that followed her not-so-clandestine opposition to the official Congress candidate brought about the first serious organization rupture in the party. The defeat of the official candidate provoked the old men who had till then controlled the party apparatus to expel her for indiscipline. In this crisis she managed to hold her ground and the majority remained with her.

She then converted the organizational victory into a mass victory following the massive popular mandate that she secured in the election of 1971. By then she was so deeply entrenched as an independent player in the national polity that she reduced the party to a personal instrument since she no longer required it as a platform for communication to and staying in touch with the masses. This required eliminating all those leaders who had independent bases either at the mass level or in the organization. She deliberately drafted individuals without any individual standing as chief ministers and state Congress leaders. These men depended on her to survive and prosper and consequently had no autonomy since they had no hold over the legislature party or the electorate. Only one state leader challenged her authority to nominate the leader of the State Congress Legislature party and Chimanbhai Patel of Gujarat paid the heavy price for his defiance of her authority in December 1973. After brushing aside all possible challenge to her authority she was now talking directly to the people over and above the party structure.

Despite these radical changes she had not succeeded in fully eliminating all those who had their own standing and vote banks. Nor perhaps did she want to. She wanted some regional strongmen whose power she domesticated and managed through different means. One of these was to ensure that no single organized community acquired leverage over the institutional polity controlled by the Congress. Vasantrao Naik was for long retained as chief minister of Maharashtra only because he did not belong to the Maratha community. Marathas constitute a large, economically and political powerful community in Maharashtra and she was careful to ensure that they did not acquire the kind of hold that would pose a threat to her.

The process of purging the party of rivals was completed in January 1978 when she split the party for the second time, getting rid of leaders who felt emboldened to marginalize her after the electoral debacle of 1977. The new party, the current Indian National Congress (I) was now filled with individuals who could not win even a municipal election on their own strength. They existed in the party at her mercy and pleasure. Loyalty to the leader became the criterion for conferring the rewards of office. Their capacity, competence and experience had become entirely irrelevant qualifications. This set in motion a New Delhi-centric process of staying afloat. Aspirants to office constantly hovered in Delhi currying favours with patrons who had access to the party bosses who had access to the undisputed leader.

This led to the creation of a leadership layer in the party that had no time for political work in the moffusil towns and villages in the countryside. There was no premium on building foundations at the bottom. Rewards were now entirely contingent on access to the top, bringing in a culture of political entrepreneurship in which middle men, fixers, touts and agents thrived at the expense of the party worker at the base of the middle-heavy structure. This weakened the mobilizing capacity of the party as political energies were now shifted upwards to towns and cities from where access to patrons in New Delhi was easier. The sociology of the political class was altered as political families were reoriented culturally to metropolitan tastes and aspirations. This led to a total disconnect between the party and the people as succeeding generations of the kinship-based client network became densely packed with metropolis-driven sycophants.

This replacement of political personnel was accentuated by the command structure of the party. The party had always been deficient in a sound two-way system of communication that ensure proper mass feedback to the top that was far removed from the hurly burly of everyday life. This deficiency was made worse by the system under Indira Gandhi. Commands were issued from the top. Appointments were decided at the top. But feedback from the bottom was not entertained. The leader was not interested and the followers were afraid of communicating problems and the reality of the ground situation lest it offend the leader.

Even the Congress parliamentary party was crippled by this lack of real consultation. This tendency accelerated after Indira Gandhi's dramatic return to power in 1980. From then on she addressed the party in parliament at the beginning and at the conclusion of each session, but party members were not invited to present their case or articulate their problems. The parliamentary party forum was merely an audience of willing listeners since the culture of debate was discouraged. This same principle extended to the largest party organ, the All India Congress Committee sessions. Participants were carefully selected to ensure that no dissenting voice could sneak in and make itself heard.

The changes that took place after 1977-78 when the new party was founded had disastrous consequences. Even as the opposition at the national level remained disunited the party faced a severe setback when it lost the state legislature elections in Andhra Pradesh and Karnataka in January 1983. This was an unprecedented electoral disaster as both the states had voted for Indira Gandhi in both the 1977 and the1980 elections to the Lok Sabha. To make matters worse the party had lost the power in Andhra to a matinee idol who had floated his party only six months before the election. In Karnataka, the dispirited Janata Party won single handedly and without even a fraction of the resources that the Congress could command.

These developments provoked an uncharacteristic response. Jaideep Singh Baria, Lok Sabha member from Godhra, Gujarat wrote to Indira Gandhi asking her to shoulder the blame because she had closed all party forums for open debate. As members and workers could not apprise her of existing ground realities, she had led her party into the electoral fray in a state of complete ignorance about the realities on the ground. But the debacle and the criticism was not sufficient to provoke a change of thinking. The party forums continued to be sterile Even then she did not open the party forums for free debates.

The tendency was accelerated under Rajiv Gandhi. He condemned entrenched leaders of the party as power brokers when he delivered the inaugural presidential address to the Centenary Session of the party at Mumbai in December 1985. He was uncomfortable with many of the old-style leaders who had been put in place by his mother. However, he could not bring in wholesale changes immediately. Instead, he surrounded himself with an urban-based coterie. He appointed Kamlapati Tripathi as the working president of the party without giving him any authority to take decisions. He then embarrassed Tripathi by expelling Pranab Mukherji from the party in 1986 on the charge that Mukherji had drafted the letters for Tripathi to address to the Congress

President Rajiv Gandhi voicing his displeasure at the style of functioning adopted by Rajiv Gandhi. The Gandhi family style of leadership therefore witnessed no change even though the leader had changed. Rajiv Gandhi would not tolerate dissent even in private communications.

The most significant change under Rajiv Gandhi was lateral induction of a new generation of purely urban bred individuals who were till then outside the party. He began opening the party gates to them. Some bureaucrats from the Indian Foreign Service had easy access to him and could also get political offices both in the party and the government. The committee appointed to prepare a draft for the Panchayati Raj Bill was packed with men and women who had never lived in or even remotely encountered villages. At best they may have visited their ancestral homes in villages on exotic excursions.

He genuinely wanted to hold organizational elections but the coterie around him terrified him with tales of disastrous consequences. They deterred him from any such venture that could have put their own positions in jeopardy. But he was definitely made to act out the drama of populist rhetoric. When the government announced a steep hike in the prices of petroleum products in 1986 he had presided over the cabinet meeting that had approved the hike. Immediately thereafter he presided over the Congress Working Committee meeting that recommended the halving of the hike so as to reduce the burden on the masses. This drama was enacted only to create the impression that there was internal democracy in the Congress and that its senior most members had the welfare of the masses as the preeminent concern.

The rot had set in so deeply into the Congress party, the even when elections were held they were charades that had no relevance to democratic functioning. In the post-Rajiv Gandhi era, P V Narasimha Rao took the calculated risk of holding organizational elections at the Tirupati session in 1992 but was obviously terrified by the outcome when Sharad Pawar and Arjun Singh won the seats on the Working Committee with huge margins. That his advisors and strategists had bungled is clear from the fact that there was no dalit or woman among the ten elected members of the CWC. So he set in motion yet another political drama by seeking authority to re-nominate even the elected members to the Working Committee. Dubious methods of counting of votes was adopted at Kolkata when yet another election to the Working Committee was held two years later. This was done only to engineer the defeat of Rajesh Pilot, who had by then become a vociferous member of his Council of Ministers.

The entire history of organizational elections in the Congress only reflects the structure of a party that never really had any mechanism for two way-information flows. True Nehru and Indira Gandhi did make efforts to keep in touch with the masses directly by holding daily durbars at their residences early in the morning. Indira Gandhi could remember names and face of workers who she had met during her visits to states and greeted them by their names. In the political era that followed Indira Gandhi's departure even this method of being in direct touch with people ended. New systems began to emerge around the leader. The security cordon around the leader after the 1984 assassination of Indira Gandhi raised barriers between the ruler and the ruled which only compounded the problem posed by the absence of a feedback loop within the party.

By the mid-1980s the leaders of the Congress had become inaccessible not only to the masses but also to party workers. The situation degenerated even more because of the extraordinary control of access exercised by the personal staff of leaders. New men in the personal offices of the Congress president or the prime minister hardly knew old veterans who were still loyal to the party and still raised its flag in their villages. Their pleas for meeting fell on deaf ears. This was enough to complete the disconnect between the party and the people.

The Congress was, during the freedom struggle an all inclusive party. Every shade of opinion, ideology and interest was represented in the party. Even though there was no formal channel of communication, despite the underdeveloped state of communication and transport technology, the party could instantly mobilize masses for political actions because of its vast network of workers spread to every town and village. The nationalists had launched newspapers and journals that became vehicles for spread of word through out the country. The rank and file of the party could espouse causes and concerns of the people and ensure that their concerns reached the top through their networks with the regional leaders. The services to villagers and meeting their development demands helped the rank and file to mobilize the voters in election times.

These organizational assets were lost forever under the system introduced by Indira Gandhi and taken forward by Rajiv Gandhi. Since the Indian masses were entirely alien to Rajiv Gandhi's cultural ethos it became easier to introduce paradigm shifts in policy without bothering with the consequences. It was simply assumed that what was good for the urban masses must be good for the rural masses. The precedent established by Indira Gandhi, of retaining the posts of party chief and of the head of government, continued under Rajiv Gandhi and Narasimha Rao. No one dared to question Rajiv Gandhi but those who were interested in asserting their own authority within the party had questioned Narasimha Rao keeping two offices with himself. When they failed to move him to give up one office, even Sonia Gandhi's intervention proved to be futile and they split the party to set up a new party. But no one attended to the inherent and visible weakness from which the party structure was suffering for decades. The progressive decay of the party organization and the degeneration of its leadership capacities were to have profound consequences that manifested themselves in its debilitating alienation from substantial identity-based vote banks in the country.

The first of these was the other backward castes, significant sections of whom prospered due to policies followed by the Congress. Yet the party was not able to command their loyalties. Organizationally the party was unprepared for the future. The political consequences of the Green Revolution for instance, point to the clear failure of an inert party with entrenched leaderships to recruit new leaders from emerging classes. The High Yielding Variety Programme for introducing a Green Revolution that brought food self-sufficiency for the nation at the same time laid the foundations for the Congress party's eventual decline in the newly prosperous agricultural belts. The Green Revolution, launched on a moderate scale in the monsoon in 1966 turned out to be a grand success. The shift of the flow of new economic gains emanating from agriculture benefited the other backward classes who were engaged in agriculture and farm oriented activities. The new economic empowerment of the rich peasant unleashed a political consciousness commensurate with their new economic power and a desire for political power that would consolidate their power over the countryside and the rural economy.

The loyalty of the other backward classes was traditionally divided between the Congress or socialist splinter groups led by people like Choudhary Charan Singh in Uttar Pradesh or Devi Lal in Haryana, who articulated farm interests more explicitly than anyone else. The Green Revolution made it amply clear to the more prosperous segment of the community that their leaders did not have a place in the higher institutional structures of power, be it in the bureaucracy or the party political area. This was despite their numerical strength, since they constitute between 44 and 48 per cent of the population in north India. The benefits following from the Green Revolution amplified their political ambitions and prompted them to get a share of power that otherwise was restricted to a few upper castes.

They were also witness to the marginalization of OBC leaders in the Congress. Over the years no OBC leader was allowed to retain power as the chief minister either in Uttar Pradesh or in Bihar for any length of time. They had all been pulled down and in most cases the Congress party was perceived to be instrumental in ousting them.

Choudhary Charan Singh who had strongly opposed the Nehru's idea of collectivization of farms on the Soviet pattern at the Awadi session of Congress in 1956 was put on margins by Jawahar Lal Nehru and old guard had ignored his claim to the office of chief minister in March 1967. He could become chief minister only after he walked out of the Congress with 12 supporters. But he could not sustain himself for more than a year due to machinations of the Congress. In 1977 Ram Naresh Yadav government could not last so also Mulayam Singh government was brought down in 1991. Bhola Paswan Shastri a Dalit leader was thrown out within months after he had managed to be the chief minister of Bihar. The upper castes in the Congress could not tolerate a dalit as the chief minister. The Andhra Pradesh chief minister T Anjaiaya another dalit leader was insulted and humiliated in full public view at the Begum Peth airport in Hyderabad in 1982 by the then Congress general secretary Rajiv Gandhi.

The Congress leadership, lacking any effective connection with mass sentiments, due to the party's top heavy distribution of power, did not anticipate the manner in which the Green Revolution would have an adverse impact on their own political fortunes. The party made no attempt to recruit, build up and retain leaders from the newly empowered forces. Hence they had to find their own devices and structures that would enable them to wrest political power from the upper castes who had maintained the hegemony over power for the previous five decades. It was no matter of comfort for the Congress leadership that even other recognized national party Bharatiya Janata Party was stricken by the same plight. Between two of them, they were unable to stem the rise of the regional political forces that have emerged in the two major states of north India—Bihar and Uttar Pradesh. The decline of the Congress in Uttar Pradesh and Bihar led to a corresponding decline in their national power. So long as the OBCs remain outside the fold of the Congress, it prospects in these two states will remain bleak. This much is obvious to everyone else but the Congress leadership.

The possibility of rectifying this problem does exist. The Green Revolution has reached a plateau, affecting the fortunes of the dominant class in the north Indian countryside. Instead of addressing this problem through measures designed to help agriculture, the Congress continues to follow policies that have negative consequences for agriculture. The party leadership appears to have forgotten that by far the large majority of Indian's are still dependent on agriculture.

The same inertia is evident in the party's inability to stem the departure of other social groups from the party. The Dalits are a case in point. Despite Dr B R Ambedkar's stance, the Congress had the steadfast loyalty of the Dalit community in most parts of India. However, from the time Jagjivan Ram left the Congress in 1977 the party has not been able to promote and build up a single Dalit leader who can command a national following. Though Jagjivan Ram never represented himself as a Dalit spokesman, he was respected by the Dalits all over the country because he was a known name and face since he first became a minister in the central cabinet in 1937. Over the next three decades Dalits have for the most part abandoned the Congress in favour of the Bahujan Samaj Party and other parties that have advocated their cause more vigorously.

The Congress relationship with the janajatis (indigenous people) is similar. They had had no national level leader of their own but they had looked to Indira Gandhi as a leader. From Rajiv Gandhi's time the Congress has been losing them out to the BJP, who have managed to secure their support in crucial states like Jharkhand, Orissa, Madhya Pradesh, Rajasthan and Gujarat as is clear from the results of Lok Sabha seats reserved for Scheduled Tribes. But even this compelling indicator has not sounded alarm bells within the Congress. There has been no serious exercise to analyse the causes that led to such alienation and disenchantment among the traditional vote banks.

One of the biggest vote banks that the Congress lost was that of the Muslims, who had hitched their fortunes to the party since independence. No analyst or strategist of the party has been able to provide a logical and rational explanation of causes that led to disenchantment of the Muslim masses with the Congress in the most parts of the country. Indira Gandhi had sedulously cultivated the Muslim base for the Congress. In 1971, they had voted for her but not in 1977 when they voted for the Janata Party even though it had admitted the erstwhile Bharatiya Jan Sangh. This was largely to do with the atrocities against Muslims during the Emergency under the supervision of the enthusiastic coterie of political upstarts orbiting around Sanjay Gandhi. The damage was done and within five years the Muslims had abandoned the Congress in favour of OBC formations like the Samajwadi Party and the erstwhile Janata Dal in Bihar. This loss was to affect the Congress Party's fortunes irreversibly.

This was primarily due to Rajiv Gandhi's disastrous policies that alienated Muslims. On the one hand he undid the Shah Bano case judgment, requiring men to provide maintenance to their divorced wives, by amending the laws to appease the orthodox Muslim clergy. This approach assumed that Muslim life at any and every station of economic scale was dominated only by religion and no other consideration. The Muslims were painted with same brush even without a study of how many Muslims do attend the religious ceremony on Friday's noon Namaz as decreed in the Last Word- Valiullah? This assumption ignored the fact that Muslim society in India is as fragmented by caste and class considerations as the Hindu society. Even among them there is no Roti or Beti (bread-breaking or marriage relaltions) vyavahar as in the Hindu castes. Yet there is better coordination and coherence between the same castes and professions in Hindus and Muslims because their culture is same and they feel comfortable in the same milieu regardless of their religious difference. Socially they feel comfortable in their relations at same level.

Even as he pandered to orthodox sentiments that angered many Muslims, he then proceeded to alienate the majority of them by pandering to Hindu fundamentalist claims on Babri Masjid by permitting Ram Shilan Pujas organized by various hard line groups like the Vishwa Hindu Parishad. His Babri Masjid policy of the late 1980s undid whatever support he got from the orthodox clergy due to his position on the Shah Bano Case. Leaders like Arif Mohammad Khan, who as a liberal opposed Rajiv Gandhi's Shah Bano amendments were equally angered by his Babri Masjid policy and left the party to found the Jan Morcha.

This bridge was the rump that then facilitated the alliance against the Congress by bringing together the opposition parties including the undivided Janata Dal, the BJP and the Communists together on a single platform. This gave the Muslims, aggrieved by the Congress, a viable alternative in the form of OBC parties that championed their cause in UP and Bihar. These parties were quick to seize on the numerical significance of a socio-political alliance between their core constituency of 'shudra' castes and poor Muslims. This neglect of the Muslim mass was to lead to the eventual absence of a single credible Muslim leader with a mass base in the Congress.

By the time Narasimha Rao came to power there was no incentive left for him to prevent the demolition of the Babri Masjid. It was better politics to remove the symbol of hatred which provided political mileage to the BJP. While this had the effect of depriving the BJP of its main plank, it also led to the further alienation of the Muslims from the party. Since then the Congress has not had a Muslim leader of any respectable stature among the masses in its organizational power structure. The party can only muster Rajya Sabha Muslim leaders, a position significantly worse than that of the BJP. This is because the Congress still commands the reluctant support of liberal Muslims from professional and affluent backgrounds who are culturally and aesthetically uncomfortable with the more dusty and homegrown ethos of the OBC parties led by rustic, moffusil leaders who cannot speak fluent English. The demise of the Congress in UP and Bihar was completed under Narasimha Rao who, perhaps, had a vested interest in destroying the party in these states to prevent any challenge to his leadership.

This squandering of its formerly steadfast vote bank that was based on a shrewd social alliance of predominantly upper caste Hindus, Muslims and Dalits, was entirely the result of a party that had no inbuilt mechanism for organizational reproduction and survival. The exigencies of personal advancement at any cost necessarily involved the destruction of the organization, its coherence, discipline and activism. At the time of each election for the Lok Sabha or the state assembly, the leadership was given make-believe assessments of how sections of the alienated social constituencies had returned to the Congress fold but these were predictably belied by actual electoral performance.

Fritjof Capra, renowned scientists has argued in *The Hidden Connections* that the structure of social, political or economic institutions will function optimally, remain alive and reproduce itself only if it mirrors the internal biological structure of human beings.

It has to be a nonlinear structure with several loops to respond to contingent situations and demands. It has to be open to ideas. However the Congress has been reduced to a linear structure where there is no scope for upward communications of ideas. Cronyism and nepotism flourished bringing with it the attendant problems of sycophancy and the obstruction of information flows.

Rajiv Gandhi imported outsiders in preference to all those who had served the party for years and for generations, and rewarded them with offices. This trend continues to this day despite the debacles that have afflicted the party in successive elections. In the 2004 elections to the Lok Sabha, in the name of infusing new blood in the party, the high command nominated children of some leaders who had held their constituencies for several elections. Most of these young men and few women were studying or had studied abroad and had joined multinational corporations when they were asked to contest the elections in their family constituencies. They are all India born and brought up in well to do families but their roots belong to an ethos that is distant from the world of the ordinary Indian. Since they contested from family boroughs they obviously won with the support of rural Indians with whom they have no connection. These young men who will rise to leadership positions in the party organs through nomination rather than election will not be able to galvanize the party in rural India. Hence, the Congress Party's misguided hopes of a revival in Uttar Pradesh through the efforts of Rahul Gandhi will be hard to bear fruits in near future.

Thus not only structurally but also in content the party had undergone a complete transformation. The change in the quality of the content is a function of the weakness in the organization that enabled lateral entry to successful professionals from other fields who had no clue about the mass realities of Indian politics. The Nehru regime created great expectations of the government as an instrument of development and establishing an egalitarian society. It remained a distant dream. Indira Gandhi had tall promises of making two square meals a day a fundamental right of all Indians. However she failed to deliver her electoral promises that had identified the masses with the Congress and had given her the massive mandate in 1971 against the powerful forces that had controlled the polity for three decades.

Her leftist rhetoric was more a political necessity than an expression of sincere intention. It also enabled her to exercise control and regulation by manipulating the conditions under which the entrepreneurial class could survive in India. This rhetoric ran out of steam and she abandoned much of it after she returned to power in 1980. Quietly the socialist policies promising an egalitarian and equal society were discarded and market friendly policies were embraced. It was done subtly and without any level debate within the party or without a study of its economic consequence for the ordinary Indian and the political consequences of that for the Congress Party.

Rajiv Gandhi abandoned even this circumspection and openly introduce policy changes whose bitter effects the Congress is still facing without the least comprehension of why its stock has fallen so low. His finance minister Vishwanath Pratap Singh had in his first budget abolished Estate Duty as a cumbersome levy that yielded very little revenue. He could not understand that Estate Duty was a necessary political instrument to control and regulate the rich rather than a source for government revenue mobilisation. As Sita Ram Kesri, who was later to become party president observed that with that measure the Congress had lost its mass base because it would now be identified as a party of, by and for the rich. This proved to be prophetic. Since that budget in 1985 the Congress has not only never secured a majority in Lok Sabha but its performance has declined with each successive election, recovering marginally in 2004 after it had been out of power for eight years and three elections.

The Congress government under Narasimha Rao threw of all restraints and accepted the Bretton Woods formula for liberalizing the Indian economy by removing all legal, administrative and physical shackles to private investment, both domestic and foreign. As with the Green Revolution this enriched a new urban class with no firm political loyalties to anyone other than themselves. Once again the Congress was unable to anticipate the political consequences of its own economic policies.

After fifteen years of the liberal economy the visible and tangible results are mixed. No government can turn the clock back on reforms despite its known political consequences. All governments that succeeded have merely sharpened inequalities as reforms did not take into account needs and ambitions of poor as well as small and marginal farmers.

The wide difference between the two generations, both having different idioms and aspirations, has further added to the disconnect between the rulers and the ruled. The Congress managers claimed that they had brought more young faces to the party in an attempt to infuse new blood. But this blood was not of fresh young minds and hearts who had worked among people to espouse their concerns and issues but had descended on the party from safe heavens of their parents homes and had taken over their constituencies as a family fiefdom. Their parents had at least won these seats by their toil in first time.

The manifestos, resolutions and intentions declared by the Congress do not reflect any awareness of the transformation of Indian society in the last fifteen years. The Congress and its allies cling to the word secularism with great fanfare but have not found words to redefine it so that the refined meaning will appeal to the younger generation. The Congress could have easily translated it into one that provides better economic standards as secularism means peace in the society and resolution of conflicts between different cultures.

Even otherwise the Congress is not sure which way to take the economy. It is obvious that the clock cannot be turned back but the Congress mind is so used to playing populist politics that it was unable to discard it. Populist politics do not deliver any results. It only increases the administrative overheads and spreads corruption. From Indira Gandhi to Manmohan Singh, every regime has promised to eradicate unemployment and proposed new schemes for employment without making any dent on the problem of unemployment because their schemes got wrapped up in the bureaucratic rigmarole of red tape, regulations, checks and balances. Hence they failed to delivered any concrete results.

The Congress failed to bring about a transformation of the bureaucratic mindset even though it ruled for nearly five decades. During the British Raj, bureaucrats were rulers or were agents of the empire. Hence they maintained a distance from the masses to preserve their authority. But in a parliamentary democracy based on universal adult suffrage, bureaucrats are public servants answerable to the elected representatives of the people. But the legal framework continues to suffer from same malaise of being prohibitive and regulatory in nature and thereby suppress the creative urges and abilities of the people. Hence the bureaucrats continued to behave in same manner as their imperial predecessors. There was no commitment to work or ideals set by elected representatives. There were no political workers to put pressure on them to deliver what was promised in the various plans and development schemes. This disconnect between the administration and the masses due to the absence of political workers added to problems and led to failures in the delivery system.

The big plans raised hopes but when they failed at the implementation stage, they caused not only disappointment but also despair and anger where people find someone to blame for all ills and evils around them. As they had expectations from the Congress, they found it much easier to hold the Congress responsible for the failures. It also created fertile ground for the growth of radical movements like Maoists, terrorists and fundamentalists who exploited public sentiments and their anger to run a parallel administration through violent methods.

The Congress is in a dilemma. It cannot accept that it will not gain a majority on its own in the Lok Sabha in the near or distant future. It cannot accept the secondary role that in which it has been cast in several states as this will be tantamount to a public admission of its shrinking social and geographical reach. At the same time it cannot go it alone in the Lok Sabha elections except in the six states where it is pitted directly against the Bharatiya Janata Party. These six states between them account for only 102 seats. The party tried to go it alone in the 1999 elections to the Lok Sabha under the leadership of Sonia Gandhi and ended up with only 112 seats, its lowest ever tally. It partially accepted the reality and had seat adjustments with the regional forces in several states to improve its overall tally to 146 in May 2004.

With passage of time and with the changing values and aspirations of people, political parties have to outgrow their old shells. They have to adopt new ideas. What was relevant two decades earlier may not be relevant today. Old ideas and slogans will not inspire the public imagination. Great political minds discuss ideas. Others get wrapped in debating actions and lesser minds get entangled only in discussing words. Yet the Congress had capacity and capability of inspiring not only young but entire nation in those days.

2

Those Were the Days

"A leader of his people unsupported by any outward authority; a politician whose success rests not upon craft nor mastery of technical devices, but simply on the convincing power of his personality, a victorious fighter who has always scorned the use of force; a man of wisdom and humility, armed with resolve and inflexible consistency, who devoted all his strength to the uplifting of his people and betterment of their lot; a man who has confronted the brutality of Europe with the dignity of the simple human being and thus all the times risen superior.

"Generations to come, it may be, will scarcely believe that such a one as this ever existed in flesh and blood, and walked upon this earth"

-Albert Einstein about Mahatma Gandhi

Albert Einstein had summed up in his tribute the phenomenon that Mohandas Karamchand Gandhi was. He was a General without an army or arms. He was a man of indomitable courage and believer in non-violence. He was the man who taught the need for courage to say No. He was the man who took politics from the classes to the masses three years after his return from South Africa and thus converted the freedom struggle into a mass movement. He personified freedom by holding an umbrella under which people divided by religions, castes, creeds, professions, vocations, languages and geographical distances came of their volition to strive and remove the British from India so that they could establish their own hegemony in their own land.

Gandhi had learnt from his experience of four years in South Africa the modes of communications and methods of mobilization of the masses. He had the organizational capacity and had ability to touch the cords of spirituality that guides the masses. He knew only struggle and public agitations threw up persons of leadership abilities who could inspire their people, organize them and lead them in public causes. But he was an unknown quality when he arrived back from South Africa in so far as masses in India were concerned though they had heard of him.

The Indian National Congress, established in 1885 was till then merely a debating society where professionals and lawyers came to make their views heard, demand some concessions but no political action followed. Nehru had just returned from Britain after spending four years as Harrow and Cambridge and was only thirty three years old when he met Gandhi, twenty years older than him at the annual Congress Session at Lucknow in 1918. There could not have been more contrasting two figures on the stage than Gandhi' clad in a Kathiawari dress of short Cotton kurta, Dhoti and a huge turban on the head and Nehru clad in perfect European clothes. Gandhi did not say much then but he moved through the country for three years traveling to different places. The prevalent poverty and plight of poor appalled him so much that he decided to shed the symbols of feudalism from his head and come to adopt a cap that came to be known as Gandhi cap. He knew that unless he was able to identify himself with the masses, they would not look towards him nor would inspirations flow from the powerhouse was dormant within him.

The main springs of the Gandhi thoughts were essentially Hindu. In 1909 he revealed the essence of his thinking in his brochure *Hind Swaraj*. He attacked the idea of English education for India and urged the revival and study of Indian languages and religion. He wrote, "Hinduism because of its strong spiritual basis has outlived the civilizations of Greece, Babylon and Rome." He adopted the stance out of his intrinsic belief or out of the compulsive need of the time for arousing the sleeping masses of India would always remain a debatable point. But Nehru could not have been in a total contrast from him because there was nothing intrinsically Hindu in Nehru's thinking. He moved with the secular ideas all his life and had even forbidden any religious ceremony to be performed over his dead body.

Differing in their attitude to religion, Gandhi and Nehru had two qualities above all others- their sense of service and sacrifice. Gandhi's other distinctive contribution was to make non-violence and non-cooperation as his political weapons in his fight against the British Raj. He knew that he would not succeed in use of arms against the British. So he made his thought process as the weapon to confuse and defeat the alien rulers who did not know what weapons to use against the unarmed man who was leading the crowds of unarmed millions.

Gandhi had actively entered the Indian National Congress struggle in 1918 when the moderates had withdrawn and the radical leader Bal Gangadhar Tilak popularly known as Lokmanya Tilak was in Mandalay jail after having been tried for sedition. Two years later Gandhi was at the center of political events in the country. Though Swaraj and Swadeshi were words in use already, Gandhi invested a wider meaning and purpose to the words when he had first time made the demand for Purna Swaraj (Total Independence) at the Calcutta Session in 1920. He had thus intervened actively and brought new elements to join the struggle for freedom on a mass scale. A new class of leaders drawn largely from small-town lawyers, doctors and social workers, politically conscious peasants, industrial workers, students and women emerged from the Gandhian upheaval. Along with them came a small leavening of English educated middle class, and a segment of urban intellectuals drawn to the Congress mainly by Nehru's influence.

Gandhi was much less class conscious than average middle class Indian because his world was full of peasants and princes, artisans and capitalists, students and the professional middle class. His allergies for the British educated middle class were perhaps born from the fact that they were the backbone of the British administration and the armed services. Many of them were really sympathetic towards the nationalist cause.

The link between Nehru and Gandhi was rather emotional and sentimental than intellectual. Nehru could not fathom the working of mind of Gandhi because he thought that Gandhi's methods and decisions were erratic but could not say much because they had produced results. Gandhi was interested more in individuals than in institutions. He understood the mechanics of human mind and how things could be done. He picked up men and women who had emerged in different states during the struggle and moulded them into leadership. He could attract to himself more diverse personalities and individuals than Nehru could. With exception of Nehru and also Sardar Patel, Maulana Azad, C Rajagopalachari, Dr. Rajendra Prasad and some other prominent men, others had left the process of thinking entirely to Gandhi.

If Nehru is to be believed in what he said, then communication with Gandhi was a difficult process. He was autocrat and at the same time democrat. KN Munshi, the then cabinet minister in the Nehru government had described Gandhi as a benevolent dictator. Nehru also remarked, "Behind all his courteous interest, one has the impression that one is addressing a closed door." Even Gandhi wrote, "It was my habit to forget what did not appeal to me and to model my behaviour according to what did appeal me."

Gandhi looked for strength in villages of India and wanted the spread of democratic institutions from villages that could be based for the pyramid kind of a parliamentarian structure. Gandhi attached inordinate value to austerity, asceticism and poverty. For him means had to be as pure as ends. He had once launched on a philosophical exposition of the ethics, of means and ends while expressing his disappointment over an editorial in The Times of India in 1946 when Frank Moraes, after his appointment as editor of The Times of Ceylon called on him.

Nehru had one time suggested that the Congress should dissolve itself as a political party in independent India but Gandhi had argued that it should continue but not accept power. It should cease to function as political organization but dedicate itself to social service and exercise moral authority on whatever government took over the reins of power.

When independence came Mahatma reiterated his advice and had even written the resolution to be presented to the Congress Working Committee in the first week of February 1948. His hand-written draft was found under the bed on January 31 1948 when he was no more. His followers including Nehru and Patel were not willing to heed his advice of not accepting the office in the government. They argued that nobody effective enough was there to take over the administration. Gandhi feared the coarsening of the moral core of the Congress once it associated itself with the government, it would soon be converted from a party dedicated to service to a party obsessed with power and privilege that go with power.

Gandhi was basically humanist than a politician and anarchist in his thinking. Hind Swaraj, his brochure represents the quintessence of his thought. His concept of Ramrajya of which he spoke often enough was that of a society of social and economic equality, without poverty, social or economic exploitation and transparent so much so that like Lord Ram exiled Sita to deep forest to exorcise even a ghost of suspicion in public mind, the government would also function in similar manners as Ram had done, he said often enough. Gandhi has left behind a heritage of ideas and ideals more than a legacy of material achievement. Many a great figures of the past have entered men's minds only to destroy human fellowship and goodwill, but it was Gandhji's great contribution to the civilization of his time in entering men's minds he did not seek to destroy but to promote in their hearts a love for their fellow men.

His concept of development was that it should revolve around the man for the economic development was essential to bring happiness to all and should not be allowed to remain only in few hands. He was not against machinery but against the craze of machine for labour saving process. He said, 'I want to save labour but not for a fraction of mankind but for all.' He had asked his followers to look for strength of India in villages for it was the strength of India though it was in unfortunate circumstances. Gandhi's economic development concept is often regarded as elementary. But was based on his acute awareness of the basic fact of economy in poverty-ridden countries, which is that every human being must have two meals a day. His prime concern therefore was with the development of agriculture. His preference for industry was for small-scale and cottage industries with their base in rural areas. So that immediate needs of poor in rural expanse could be met promptly and they had opportunity to augment their daily earnings.

But Nehru did not agree with his ideas or with his concept and took a different route for economic development. He felt that if he had adopted the Gandhian concept for the economic development, the country would continue to travel through the bullock cart age for few more generations. For his scientific temper, labs, dams and big power projects were the new temples of India. Nehru had decided to put all emphasis on metal and machine by using capital available domestically or borrowed from abroad.

Long before India attained independence, Nehru had formulated in his own mind of India that he had envisaged when political power would pass to Indian hands. In 1927 he had begun to write and speak of his dream of socialist planning and his policy of nationalization. Among all leaders of his generation, he alone had given a clear thought to the place of independent India in the world comity. Gandhi made Indians aware of India but Nehru made them aware of the world. The image that independent India presented to the world was really the image of Nehru. Despite differences and disagreements with his views and some moves, world leaders identified India with Nehru. Only because of his personality and purposeful thrust, India enjoyed an international influence out of proportion to her economic strength and military resources.

He was thorough democrat so he could never be communist but he was attracted to the Marxist theory, more out of his attitude of anti coloniasm and anti-capitalism. That attitude became the base for formulation of his foreign policy and also the economic development process. He was naturally attracted by the giant leaps that the Soviet Union had taken in the economic development. So he had set to convert the Indian society into a prosperous through democratic means but with the Marxist economic ends.

Nehru steered away India from the path that Gandhi had indicated because he was a visionary of new India. He was a visionary but not a practical implementer of his ideas and visions. His handicap was in his colleagues who had marched a long way with him during the freedom struggle. Many of them were ignorant of what he wanted to achieve. Many did not understand the implications of his socio-economic philosophies and others did know very little of the mechanics, dynamics and purpose of modern politics. He had no great respect for majority of them and treated them like head master would treat his students. Perhaps only Maulana Azad could derive respect from him because of a rapport between the two that was established when they were in the Ahmednagar fort jail for a long duration in the freedom struggle. Nehru wrote in his book, "Discovery of India" that he had learnt of India's history from Maulana Abul Kalam Azad.

Mahatma Gandhi inspired people around him and knew how to take best out of them when he assigned them tasks. Nehru overawed and terrified his colleagues with his frequent outbursts in public and in private as well. Nehru was by temperament an impatient man and wanted things got done quickly. But he also had strong likes and dislikes for men and women around him and also at distances. He would dash out a letter pointing the lacking of others in sharp words. His ideas of social reforms were imposed on the country through legislations. Consequently many of his progressive ideas could not take deep root in the minds of the people.

He was a tall personality not only because he was but also by the fact that he was surrounded by colleagues who were physically and mentally too short in their stature. Only Sardar Patel or Rajaji could have questioned him and also challenged him. But there was no one in the party or outside who could have had ability or stature to question him on any policy matter after Patel's death and departure of Rajaji from the Congress in 1954. Nehru stood alone with all burden on his lonely shoulders.

Rajaji made feeble attempts from outside to question Nehru on his functioning. He wrote in May 1958 an article in 'Kalki' a weekly that he edited with title "Wanted Independent Thinking."

This article examined the 'present discontent about the Congress' from the perspective of one who has' spent the best part of his life-time serving the organization and who owes many honours and kindnesses to it.' He worried that "as a result of tacit submission on the part of the people of emancipated India, a few good persons at the top, enjoying prestige and power, are acting like guardians of docile children rather than as leaders in a parliamentary democracy"

"The long reign of popular favourites, without any significant opposition", wrote Rajaji, "is probably the main cause for the collapse of independent thinking" in India. But a healthy democracy required an Opposition that thinks differently and does not just want more of the same, a group of vigorously thinking citizens which aims at the general welfare, and not one that in order to get more votes from the so-called have-nots, offers more to them than the party in power has given, an opposition that appeals to reason. Such an opposition even if it did not succeed in outsting the ruling party, might yet control it and humanize it." Nehru did not take kindly to this criticism from an old colleague who was known to be the sharpest brain in the Congress.

It was said many a times that Gandhi's head was with Sardar Patel but his heart was with Nehru. He loved Nehru with a fondness that he would have shown to his son only. Gandhi had deliberately preferred Nehru to carry on though he had named Sardar as the Commandant after Patel had mobilized farmers in Bardoli in Gujarat during the freedom struggle. Even though Nehru and Sardar were two arms of Gandhi, Nehru had not included name of Sardar in the first list of cabinet ministers who were to be sworn in. Only after a prolonged persuasion by Lord Mountbatten that Nehru agreed to include his name as the home minister with designation of the deputy prime minister.

It was Sardar Patel who led the foundation of unity and integrity of India. Patel had mercilessly and ruthlessly steamrolled and integrated the princely states in to the Indian Republic without giving any time or alternative to former rulers and princely states. He redrew the map of India by redrawing the internal boundaries. Nehru had virtually come to undo what Sardar had achieved when he rushed to UNO with the Kashmir issue and internationalized the Kashmir as a headache forever. Patel had warned him that he would have a permanent problem if he went to United Nations.

After Sardar Patel's death there was no personality, tall enough who could have challenged Nehru. Sardar Patel did attempt to check Nehru through putting up his own candidate for the election of the Congress president and had also won though he was no more. Nehru refused to recognize the Congress president in Purushottam Das Tandon who was forced to quit ultimately because five meetings of the All India Congress Committee failed to break the impasse between Nehru and Tandon. That was the only challenge that Nehru had faced in the party in initial years.

Nehru never tried to combine the two posts, the party chief and the office of the Prime Minister in one person. There was no need for him to do that because of his stature. The senior leader and Gandhian Acharya Kripalani JB had raised the issue as to who would be supreme, the party president or the Prime Minister in so far as the Congress party was concerned. The issue was raised immediately after the Constitution was adopted. His suggestion was that the Prime Minister must submit to the party president as the Prime Minister was a member and owed the position to the party. However Nehru had disagreed with him and said that the Prime Minister was accountable and responsible to the Lok Sabha and thus to sovereigns- voters, the Prime Minister cannot subordinate his position to the party president. That question was to rise again in succession struggles after Nehru's departure from the scene in May 1964.

But the question was never raised during his time within the party or from outside the party. The Left divided between the Communists and the Socialists could never grow in strength because they were so enamoured in their faction fights, they continued to split over and over and unite again and again, that they could not become a challenge to Nehru in his lifetime. Rajaji had formed a new party Swatantra Party to espouse the cause of farmers and free market in 1959 but it was far from a serious challenge to Nehru who dominated all that he surveyed. Rajaji had broken away from the Congress because of sharp differences with Nehru over Nehru's proposal for collectivization of farms in India on same pattern as Soviet Union had done.

Before independence and for two decades after the Congress was formally a mass party with two categories of membership, primary and active with an elaborate and hierarchical organizational structure spanning from local to district to states and culminating in the All India Congress Committee. At the apex was the Working Committee that was the supreme decision making body of the party. Then there were the Parliamentary Boards at the Central and States levels. Its main functions were deciding political issues and nominating candidates for the party in election times. But more important was the informal structure that revolved around the Prime Minister in the independent India. Though different persons held the office of the party chief during Nehru's time, every decision on policies was taken at Nehru's behest by the party for two reasons because of the dominating personality of Nehru as the Prime Minister and also as a person. Nearly half the members of the Working Committee were elected, only those who found approval of Nehru could get pass the post in the formal election. The Congress president nominated the members of Parliamentary Boards. Nehru could indirectly reject even the elected president as had happened when his candidate Kripalani was defeated in the second most controversial election for the party post in 1951. Nehru had refused to join the Working Committee of the new president P D Tandon. When five sessions of the All India Congress Committee in five months failed to resolve the crisis that Tandon quit his office to make a way for the chosen candidate of Nehru. (First controversial presidential election was held in 1938 when Subhash Chandra Bose had defeated K Pattabhi Sitharamaiaya, a candidate sponsored by Mahatma Gandhi at the Haripura Congress.)

The informal structure was important because of the spread of factional linkages all over the country. Inherent in such linkages was the patronage system built in different regions under the command of a dominating leader. These leaders had emerged during the freedom struggle and were interwoven in the national network. They provided patronage to workers in return for their loyal support in peace times and their delivery system during the election times. They could and did mobilize voters to reach to the booth and cast their votes for the party. Thus they were the backbone of the edifice that was needed to win the elections.

At the time of independence, few were known for their clout. There was SK Patil known as the uncrowned King in Mumbai, and independent of it, Morarji Desai in Bombay state, Atulya Ghosh in Bengal, K Kamaraj in Tamil Nadu though Rajaji was the chief minister of the state, S Nijlingappa in Mysore state, Dr. Sanjeeva Reddy in new state of Andhra Pradesh, Dwarika Prasad Mishra and Ravi Shankar Shukla in erstwhile state of CP & Berar and Gobind Vallabh Pant in United Province as Uttar Pradesh was then known. Nehru allowed them their small empires because none of them had a capacity to challenge his political supremacy. Some of them were even accommodated in important political offices. Because of their positions, they had also worked up contacts with each other.

In fact Nehru strived to sort out differences among various factions so that the centre space within the party remained intact. He was sharp in expressing his disapprovals but these were only in written forms, a letter or a note dashed out to different factional leaders in states. He was quick in responding because of the net work that had emerged during the freedom struggle. The struggle had thrown up men and women of capabilities to lead people of their areas of influence. They were not managers picked up from the top but had emerged from the ground to take command by inspiring people.

Nehru allowed more independence in electing chief ministers in states though he did put his foot down when the most unwanted man was being hoisted on the state. He had to bow to the pressure of Morarji Desai in 1962 in changing the chief minister Dr. Jivraj Mehta in the newly formed state of Gujarat though Nehru was not in favour of the change. In fact it was the first indication of the weakened position of Nehru within the political edifice known as the Indian National Congress over which Nehru had ruled as a supreme leader for thirty years.

The final blow that weakened his position was not delivered from within the country but it came from outside the country. It was delivered by none other than China with whom Nehru had established closer bilateral ties for establishing the third block outside the two Super Powers, United States of America and the Union of Soviet Socialist Republics. The Panch Sheel (five principles) was made basis of friendship between India and China. Nehru had even ignored the Chinese occupation of Tibet for the sake of good neighbourly relations

China under Mao tse Tung suddenly decided to redraw the borders between the two neighbours, in October 1962 through a posse of Chinese troops. The armed conflict of a week had shaken India completely because the Indian troops were driven back deep into Indian territories in Himalayan ranges. The skirmish became a Himalayan blunder. The Prime Minister Nehru was shaken beyond belief. More because he was forced to sack the defence minister V K Krishna Menon under an ultimatum from the Congress Parliamentary Party. No one had ever dared to look up at him was suddenly brought down to ground reality that he was on a weak wicket now.

He could sense the pressure building up in time to come. He was advised to carry out a purge in his government for two reasons. One was to divert the attention and second was to weaken the strong leaders who could be potential threat to his position in case they began to mobilize. Hence six leaders were chosen, in reality only three potential dangers, for depriving them of the office. Morarji Desai, then finance minister was one and Jagjivan Ram, a strong harijan leader from Bihar with wider base and rail minister, and Chandra Bhan Gupta, a strong man from Uttar Pradesh. Lal Bahadur Shastri was who was then home minister was also asked to move to the party work under the Kamaraj Plan, devised by the strong man from Tamilnadu who was to be the next Congress president. Kamaraj Plan was essentially a game to weed out the potential dangers from the proximity to the seat of power. None of them was assigned the party post though they were removed for ostensible purpose of strengthening the party organization. In fact within few weeks, Shastri, a Nehru loyalist was back into the cabinet as a minister without portfolio but almost a second in command in the Nehru government.

Kamaraj Plan and purge carried out under it had exposed the fact that the towering personality that had dominated for eighteen years was disintegrating with a one rude shock. It was a signal to the regional bosses who were tolerated by Nehru since he feared none began to consolidate their positions in their regions and increased contact to almost become a caucus of veterans who had participated in the freedom struggle but only in secondary roles. Mahatma Gandhi and few men whom he trusted despite their ideological dissimilarities had built the political edifice for the country that went under the signboard of Indian National Congress. Mahatma was responsible for shaping the social content and Nehru had undertaken the responsibility of its economic wing while Sardar Patel was responsible for the political unity and integrity of the party. After Gandhi was gone, the Congress did not remain a mass movement that could transform India through socio- economic and political reforms. Sardar Patel's departure weakened the party organization because Nehru never made any attempt during the eighteen years of stewardship to reinvent the party with necessary organizational reforms so that new generations could rise in the party and receive the training at his hands. Because of lack on his part, the men smaller in stature and without a proper understanding of dynamics of socio political life continued to hold offices and did not allow the second generation of leadership to grow within the party

Nehru could never recover from the political jolt he had received on the borders with China nor could be again assert his position. The trauma had affected his health severely. He brooded for days and could not get proper sleep. Those close to him were worried but the end came mercifully after a short spell of illness on May 27 1964. A great visionary disappeared into oblivion leaving behind a shocked nation and orphaned party men.

His chinks were exposed only ten days earlier at the Congress session in Mumbai where the regional bosses had played an assertive role in managing the session and party men. It was in this session that the Congress chief ministers had established closer links to prepare themselves for the future.

Kamaraj had virtually become the second strongest man in the party and was calling the shots. They had come to a conclusion that the inevitable was not far off and they would have to find the answer to the question that was in speculation for the past few years- After Nehru Who?

As expected by the most, Morarji Desai, senior in stature and years in the party threw his hat in the ring for succession. The caucus under the then Congress president K Kamaraj set to work immediately to thwart the attempts of the man whose astringent nature had not won many friends in the party. It was obvious from his performance as the finance minister that he would be a hard nut to crack for the caucus in the party and would not share power with them. Hence their obvious choice became Lal Bahadur Shastri, a Kayastha from Allahabad district who had never attended the English medium school. The mild by nature and diminutive in physical structure Shastri had come from a poor family and with Victorian concepts. He was most loyal to Nehru though his concepts were closer to Gandhi. The caucus thought that they would be able to run this soft-spoken and suave man as the Prime Minister.

But he was to prove them all wrong when he faced a war with Pakistan in two installments. His stature might have given ideas to Pakistan that it could make a bid to gobble up Kashmir. In a diversionary tactic, they marched in Kutch in April 1965 and then in Kashmir region in September 1965 and had virtually cut off the Indians entry into Kashmir. Shastri gambled with a diversionary tactic by sending the Indian troops onto Lahore. His bold decision had received the national welcome and his stature went up overnight. He received the national ovation.

It would have helped him to carry out and implement other agenda where he had already initiated action for administrative and economic reforms to end the prohibitive structure for industry and finances that Nehru had erected with his socialistic policy framework. Shastri knew that it had led to stagnation of the growth potential of the country. An able man LK Jha who also worked as his principle secretary was assigned task of economic reforms.

But the three-week war did not allow him sufficient time. He did not even have time to go through the Jha report.

Pakistan had entered into the Indian borders and had captured territory and two strategic positions but India had nothing in hand though it succeeded in halting Pakistan from further aggressive moves. On invitation from Soviet Union leaders, he went to Tashkent to settle with Pakistan. Since he gained nothing though got Pakistan to vacate the Indian Territory, he felt that the settlement would not satisfy Indians. The shock of realization was cause of his death same night on January 11 1966 that he signed the agreement. It was tragedy that the man who won a decisive war died in peace efforts. But the Congress was faced with yet similar question. Now who should lead the nation? The generation that had grown with Gandhi and Nehru had faded out leaving behind the memories of the glorious days that the party had seen. Now the second phase was to begin.

3
An Uneasy Transition

People with high ideals don't necessarily make good politicians. If clean politics is so important, we should leave the job to scientists and the clergy.

Michio Watanbe, Japanese politician

The first twenty years since Independence meant an opportunity to define the broad parameters of the national enterprise. The two decades simplified the earlier struggle for national movement as a period in which experiments to widen the social base for a new type of governance could be attempted. Jawaharlal Nehru, as Mahatma Gandhi's chosen one to give a broad direction to the Indian state, manfully struggled to make his vision of a new, modern, democratic and secular India understandable to the people. Purely in terms of the logic of what he tried, Nehru was a qualified success. He was successful in exemplifying the need to evolve a scientific temper; an understanding of history and an ability to comprehend the links between internal and external compulsions. The deft manner in which he steered the country's foreign policy showed how a very articulate and brilliant mind was trying to establish an Indian presence in a deeply divided world.

Unfortunately for Nehru, his thinking needed to be supplemented by certain hard and categorical steps to orient socio-economic policies to meet the expectations of a newly emergent nation. The fact that Nehru chose to be influenced by external models and his inability to convert the Congress into a thinking, ideological battleship meant that whosoever succeeded him would automatically inherit an element of prestige without economic power.

The first three five year plans were all excellent documents in themselves; in fact, the second plan was a masterly exercise in delineating the wider contours of an economy in transition. Unlike the rest of the leaders who had emerged during and after the freedom struggle, Nehru was perhaps the only one who understood historical and conceptual frameworks, and what they should be converted into for the nation to emerge as a separate identity distinct from contending power blocs. The distinction was not contrived; it was consciously forged, and as time went by, the entire Third World save the communist bloc knew and understood that Nehru spoke a language that they should also try and incorporate into their policy framework. The Non-Aligned Movement became the target of vicious calumny and worse. But from Josef Tito of Yugoslavia to Abdul Gamal Nasser of Egypt to even Sukarno of Indonesia, most of the newly emergent leaders of an anti-colonial upsurge readily recognized the need to join Nehru's brilliant endeavour.

All this brilliance was however not accompanied by internal advance. Nehru's socialist blueprint may have had tremendous seductive potential, but it had neither the infrastructure nor the people to carry it through. Nehru imposed on the nation his pathological dislike for commercial class as the British aristrocacy had done a century earlier because the emergence the commercial class in Europe had made the feudal lords irrelevant. Nehru believed that all trading class was dishonest and would not help in nation building processes. He adopted the most restrictive industrial policy, which did not allow the entrepreunal temper any space for growth in the country. Consequently the economic growth stagnated in his lifetime. Nehru's dreams died young.

Lal Bahadur Shastri had realized the need for reforms and had taken initial steps also. Unfortunately he did not get enough time to carry out what he had set to do. The Congress party was once again faced with the task of selecting the leader who would be able to carry on. This time also Morarji Desai was to challenge the kingmakers in the party was apparent. But they had not expected that he would even force an election through ballot to decide the leadership issue. He stood like a rock with his claim even though it was apparent from the start that the kingmakers- five regional bosses with the backing of nine chief ministers were arrayed against him because of his astringent nature and also because of their fears of a strong-headed person like Morarji Desai. His image was that of an adamant old man.

K. Kamaraj had played a vital role in selection of Shastri as successor to Nehru. He was again the main center of the brisk political activities within the party at Delhi. The Madhya Pradesh chief minister Dwarika Prasad Mishtra, (an ardent follower of Sardar Patel and had abused Nehru from the floor of the state assembly at Nagpur in 1952 after Nehru had forced the then Congress president PD Tandon to step down unceremoniously and was expelled from the party for few years) became the chief mobiliser of support of other chief ministers against Morarji Desai. Indira Gandhi became a natural choice for Morarji baiters because she was the daughter of Nehru. Hence she was the "least unacceptable" candidate in the race that Morarji Desai had made difficult one. Mishra was able to mobilize eight more Congress chief ministers to stand by Indira Gandhi and also influence Members of Parliament from their states. Till then Congress chief ministers had their own standing and strength within the state. Most MPs would not dare defy their word. Only chief minister who stood by Morarji Desai was Hitendra Desai of Gujarat. He could not have done otherwise even if he had desired. Another strong leader who remained in the Morarji camp was Chandra Bhan Gupta with his loyal band of MPs of the party. Morarji polled a third of votes in this election. It was surprising because almost all factions were arrayed against him out of their personal dislike and suspicion of him.

For the first time a ballot was held for electing the leader of the Congress Party in Parliament with much excitement caused by the controversial race for the post. Scenes in the Central hall of Parliament were hectic with Morarji Desai sitting with a group of MPs from other states as well. It was a contest between an organization and an individual. Morarji had forced the party to hold a secrete ballot so that views of MPs could be ascertained without fear or favour. His stature grew in the country. Though caucus had succeeded in defeating him with their collective efforts, they had not earned much respect because their conspiracy was obvious. Morarji had established his democratic bona fides by accepting the defeat even though he was aware of the circumstance in which it was caused.

Even though Indira Gandhi had been once a Congress president, she had not held any administrative post nor did she display any brilliance on any issue between her relinquishing the party post and her ascendancy as the prime minister. In twelve months that were at her disposal before the fourth general election in February 1967 only major decision her government had taken was that of devaluation of the Indian Rupee in June 1966 on advice of the kitchen cabinet around her. She never forgave the men who had advised her to go in for the devaluation because that decision had left a tremendous political impact on the prospects of the Congress Party when it faced the general election. It was also the first election in absence of Nehru- the tall leader who was respected, loved and trusted by Indians despite his several failings, especially on the economic field. The electorate of India had given him unquestioned support through three general elections and had not allowed any opposition to grow to an extent that it could have become a challenge to his authority as the leader of the nation. Shastri was also trusted and respected especially after the decisive war he fought with Pakistan and proved his mettle to the masses and to the world at large.

The results of the fourth general elections came as a disaster for the Congress party though it did retain its hold over the power corridors in Delhi but its majority was reduced to a razor thin level. It had won 283 seats in the Lok Sabha with the total strength of 516 seats. But more shocking was the defeat of the Congress party in Tamilnadu, Orissa, Punjab, Bengal, Bihar and Haryana. It lost the hold over Uttar Pradesh and Madhya Pradesh due to defections from the Congress party in the state within few days after the election over the leadership disputes.

Once again Morarji Desai made his claim for the leadership for he believed that he was best suited to lead the country. However others were not willing to countenance with him as their leader. Young members who had seen the demolition of heavy weights in this election also became active. The younger generation made it clear that they would split the party in case Indira Gandhi was not accepted as the leader. Kamaraj conveyed the fears of split in the party to Morarji Desai and his supporters. Whether the threat was real or used merely to cow down Morarji Desai would always remain a debatable because no one had made public the threat. However Morarji accepted the fact and also climbed down to accepting the post of deputy prime minister with finance portfolio that he desired to preside over. The old guard, though defeated and dispirited, had ultimately won the battle against Morarji Desai and imposed the least unacceptable Indira Gandhi as the prime minister. After Nehru no one has become the most acceptable leader in the Congress party.

One major development in this election was the emergence of a defined Right wing party clamouring for free enterprise: the Swatantra Party. It even captured power in Orissa, and it had come close to winning a mandate in Gujarat and Rajasthan. In the Lok Sabha, it had a significant 44 members. Ostensibly because of the Avadi resolution of the Congress seeking drastic reorientation of the land-ownership structure in the countryside at the All India Congress Session in 1956 at Avadi in Maharashtra, the 'C.R.' (Chakravorty Rajgopalachari who was popularly known as CR) parted ways with the party and established the Swatantra Party as a vehicle to project the ideas of an existing think-tank called Forum for Free Enterprise. Disgruntled big landlords, top industrialists and peeved erstwhile princes were drawn to the Swatantra Party like a magnet.

The Swatantra came within a whiff of enjoying power in Rajasthan when Gayatri Devi, former ruler of Jaipur managed to woo a significant section through personal appeal and because the Congress was organizationally not up to the occasion to match the resources of the big-business lobby working to project the Swatantra Party. Gayatri Devi brought her retinue of MLAs to Rashtrapati Bhawan when she was not invited to form the government in the state . The inimitable S. Radhakrishnan, then the President of India simply said: "The real place for a headcount is the state assembly, not Rashtrapati Bhawan." The emergence of an incongruous Right wing signaled a new set of politics taking root in the comfortable confines of the bourgeoisie and feudal lords.

The Congress ultimately did enough to muster support for Mohanlal Sukhadia, but the fact that the Swatantra Party had to be staved-off by a combination of manipulation and populism brought no credit to the Congress. In fact, it showed that the party's socialist and democratic instincts were becoming hazy and timeworn.

In that uncertain ambience, Congress Working Committee held its very first two-day session in May 1967 in Delhi to analyze the causes and consequences of the electoral results that had gone against the Congress for the first time. By all accounts, the May CWC meeting proved to be a stormy affair. Ashok Mehta, then union petroleum minister was also invited; he was to play a major role in helping an uncertain Indira Gandhi for political management and governmental cohesion.

The Delhi establishment challenged by the brilliant spark of the Left from tiny Naxalbari in West Bengal and the consolidation of disgruntled feudal lords who found refuge in the Rightist Swatantra needed fresh blood supply and ideological oxygen. The CWC devised a ten-point programme to shift the focus of the economy; this was not easy. Sharp differences over several key issues had to be ironed out. The most breathtaking one, the nationalization of major banks, became particularly difficult to steer in the face of stonewalling by Morarji Desai. The latter had a vague, social control of banks, as an alternative to offer. The onset of the Swatantra, with its pronounced support-base among ex-princes and the feudal lords, necessitated a clear move: this became the precursor to a process culminating in the abolition of privy purses.

By this time, Indira Gandhi had realized how a radical, vaguely left-of-centre platform would suit her better. She activated think-tanks designed to produce the blueprint for a new socio-economic shift. Thus, various forums came into being (for more detailed elucidation of these forums, please refer to the relevant portions of the book).The so-called Young Turks, comprising Chandra Shekhar, Mohan Dharia, Krishna Kant and Ramdhan came into their own, and their presence came handy to a beleagured but determined Indira Gandhi to snuff out internal dissidence and opposition from outside the party fold.

The AICC Session that took place in third week of June 1967 in the post-1967 polls phase was an ideological battlefield of sorts. It was the first large scale political meeting within the party after the disastrous general elections and loss of nine states. Indira Gandhi was surrounded on the dais by a whole set of an earlier generation of leaders who commanded majority in the Parliamentary Board and the Congress Working Committee. There were not even handful few on the dais who could be called her real supporters; Indira Gandhi relied on the rank and file to help her out in this battle for organizational hegemony. Men like Fakhruddin Ali Ahmed, Jagjivan Ram and YB Chavan chose to hitch their wagon with Indira Gandhi. This was not because they agreed with her; it was largely their own insecurity vis-à-vis the regional bosses that made them to accept Indira Gandhi as their leader.

Another shock awaited the old guard when the Young Turks forced two amendments to the Economic Resolution. The proposal to nationalize major banks and the abolition of privy purses followed. The AICC ratified the proposals, and a chagrined old guard had to accept the inevitable. The preceding reverses in elections and the uncertainty that faced the Congress in view of strong ideological bulwarks emerging both on the Right and the Left of the political divide provided the flavour for a renewed and vigorous Congress.

A proactive rank and file now challenged the party's top-heavy structure. This had a profound bearing on Indira Gandhi's eventual consolidation as the undisputed expression of the new mood. The old guard was hopelessly unable to understand the meaning and content of the new idiom that was taking shape. The resultant schism was mirrored in the selection of the new party president since the incumbent, K.Kamaraj had already completed the two customary terms. Morarji wanted a change for obvious reasons, because the veteran from Tamilnadu had botched up Desai's hopes to capture the party leadership.

It was at the Hyderabad Session in 1968 that S. Nijlingappa, then the chief minister of Karnataka (then called Mysore), was brought in to replace Kamaraj as the party president. The choice was not to the liking of Indira Gandhi; nevertheless she had to agree to the selection since she did not enjoy a majority either in the Congress Working Committee or in the AICC. Morarji's wails of dissent went unheard.

Meanwhile a battle was raging within the party to seek implementation of the ten points programme that had been earlier cleared by the AICC. This was an era of hectic Parliamentary debates as well. The decision to appoint the Hazari Commission to examine the role of monopoly houses was a result of one such debate. It had taken the Indian state more than two decades to equip itself with the legislative power to clip the wings of monopoly houses. The Congress as a party benefited immensely from these radical measures. The challenge posed by the entrenched traditionalists and the Right represented by the Swatantra and the Bharatiya Jan Sangh had been accepted and won. The socialists and the communists had to acknowledge the shifting paradigm, even though they had themselves played a negligible role in the radicalization of state policies.

The exhilaration of these victories was somewhat dimmed by the decision taken by the then Union of Soviet Socialist Republics to send its troops to muzzle dissent in Czechoslovakia. This was in 1968, the year of great ferment throughout Europe and also at home, where the Naxalites were becoming increasingly active in several parts of the North East India. Geo-politically, the Indira government faced a tough problematic. It could neither support the Soviet action nor openly oppose it.

Within the Congress, the regional bosses found it increasingly impossible to control a rampant Indira Gandhi. She was proving far too clever for them; in private, she would assure them that their sensitivities will not be hurt. In actual fact, she did exactly the opposite. The humiliating defeat of arch fund-raiser

Sadoba.K. Patil (named as uncrowned king of Bombay) at the hands of 'giant killer' George Fernandes, then a fiery trade union leader, in South Bombay constituency shattered the myths which the old guard loved to believe in. Kamaraj had the mortification of seeing massive inroads being made into his base by the rising tide of Periyar-inspired Dravida Munnetra Kazhagam that ended the road for the Congress to come back to power in the state forever. Another party factotum, Atulya Ghosh was humbled by a left-leaning United Front led by Ajay Mukherjee. Though in an organizational minority, Indira Gandhi had won a major political victory.

More good news for her was to follow soon. The Congress plenary session at Faridabad close to Delhi in April 1969 saw a recharged Indira Gandhi. The party was compelled to initiate steps that meant greater involvement of the rank and file in decision-making. The AICC became the sounding board for new strategies and ideas. It was at Faridabad that the hitherto ambivalent Yashwantrao Chavan made bold to suggest that the party needed to have support from like-minded parties to unsettle the Right-wing consolidation against the Congress. For inexplicable reasons, the usually sharp Jagjivan Ram ruled out such strategy. Kamaraj was opposed to have any truck with any other party. To him, that would have meant that the Congress would need to shift its ideological stance.

Before the various sectional leaders could formulate their assessment at the end of two days of stormy debate, an open session was convened with Nijlingappa delivering the keynote address. The conservative line he took drew immediate criticism from the restive Young Turks and the AICC as a whole. As it happened, the even while the speech was on, a part of the 'pandal' (podium) caught fire and the session had to be abandoned mid way. The Banaskantha by-election in Gujarat in May 19969 was chosen by the humbled S.K. Patil to author his political comeback. He won the election, but that by no means meant that he had come in a position to challenge the writ of Indira Gandhi, who proceeded to refashion state governments and party units to her own liking.

Her first victim was Mohanlal Sukhadia who had till then enjoyed the run of 18 years as chief minister. She drafted Barakatullah Khan as the chief minister, even though he did not have support of even three legislators in the state assembly party. With this change, she indicated that she meant business and would brook no dissent to her ways. K Bramhanand Reddy was the second victim when she replaced him as the chief minister of Andhra Pradesh.

Indira Gandhi had to combine both the great vision of her father and the need to bolster internal cohesion—something, which Nehru neglected. Certainly not by design, but simply because he thought on a grand scale, which was unintelligible to the people and untranslatable in not one but several lifetimes put together. Indira Gandhi had to work under another handicap; she was Jawaharlal Nehru's daughter. That implied that she would have at least some of the great man's vision, and that was not possible because neither in intellectual nor in practical terms was she prepared to carry on a legacy which during its course left as many questions unanswered as it resolved. Nehru's deep commitment to secularism, nurtured through an unprecedented freedom struggle that saw the coming together of people from every section of India, was a requirement that was both humane and practical. Nehru's socialism, on the contrary, was a brilliant man's experiments with various variables, which could have been more successful if he had oriented the entire national mood towards a workable, attractive and cost-friendly ethos. Nehru was always a step ahead of even the best brains of the Congress and the country. His earnestness was transparent, even infectious; his ability to give it concrete shape was never so categorical.

When Nehru died, he left behind an excellent blueprint for the future; but during his own lifetime, his success towards meetings his basic postulates was rather limited. Indira Gandhi, perforce, had to become a "doer," a rather vulgarly constructed contrast this to describe the difference between what the so-called Nehruvian perspective meant and its essential weaknesses in terms of practical realization.

Indira Gandhi did not have either the unparalleled control over the party, which her father enjoyed nor did she have a hunky-dory transition to power. It was very difficult to become the sole leader of a party that had till then only seen one, principal centre of power. Indira Gandhi's elevation to the top was effected at the mercy and desire of a set of regional and central bosses who had been dwarfed into nothingness by Nehru's aura. The 1962 debacle in the China war that weakened and broke Nehru in spirit and in his resolve, had given these busybodies an opportunity to control at least the organization that ruled the country. None was individually in a position to challenge Indira Gandhi's credentials for the top job. That, in retrospect, became the greatest tragedy of both the Congress and Indira Gandhi.

She may not have had any challengers; but she herself was far from ready or equipped to handle the job which was now her's. For all his genuine democratic credentials, even Nehru had not left behind a party structure that could automatically find a replacement to him. As a person who had inherited the legacy of the national movement because Gandhi found him to be the best-equipped person to articulate differing aspirations with informed coherence, Nehru found the phase after Gandhi's departure easier to handle. He trusted people enough to give them top positions both in the party and the government; this trust was however not met with an equal level of either commitment or intellect. Nehru was a great man; in the context of the Congress, he was perhaps a shade too great, too grand, to be real.

Indira Gandhi's early years, as we shall see through this narrative, were governed more by the need to assert her own prima donna status rather than get on with the nitty-gritty of governance. Nehru's voluminous writings, especially his correspondence with chief ministers, showed a brilliant mind at work—at once insightful and aware of what was needed in macro-terms. But in terms of day-to-day governance, even well meaning chief ministers and state administrations needed not just perspective but timely guidance to get things done. Vladimir Lenin combined a theoretical vision with a ruthlessly practical perspective. But the Bolshevik Party had grown in the aftermath of a spontaneous upsurge from change occasioned by the 1861 Tsarist Act, which, while signing the death warrant of serfdom, unconsciously created the fertile ground for several brilliant thoughts and movements to emerge. The Congress had the legacy of the national movement to fall back on. But what to do with freedom when it did finally come along through a transition of power left the post-Independence party leadership quite flummoxed.

Twenty years after freedom, Indira Gandhi became Prime Minister of a nation still grappling to find answers to the basic problems of transition that the end of the British rule left in its wake. She could not have brushed aside either the satraps who surrounded her; nor could she forget the ideological imperatives so painstakingly charted out by a tradition that began with the national movement and reached their logical shape in the mind of Nehru.

This backdrop is to be kept in mind when one tries to locate Indira Gandhi's strengths and weaknesses in the years immediately subsequent to her becoming the country's Prime Minister. The two years of her personal consolidation: 1966 and 1967—were also the years in which the Congress was caught in internal wrangling and political uncertainty outside the confines of the party. This came to the fore in more concrete terms when the uniformity that determined the political structure at the Centre and in the states came under challenge for the first time. She had to do something dramatics to consolidate her position so that she could be in a true sense the leader of the nation. She was waiting for the opportunity to take on the defeated and dispirited old guard so that she could turn tables on the leaders who had emerged out of shadows of the giant leader Nehru only after his death.

The real clincher for her kind of politics arrived with the death of President Zakir Husain on May 3 1969. That tragedy provided her an opportunity to assert her might in the party by determining who should fill in the breach caused by the great educationist's death. The period since Nehru's exit and Dr Zakir Husain's demise had been a topsy-turvy one. Indira Gandhi was under siege. She badly needed a new script. During these five years, she had managed to assert herself bit by bit. Now the stage was set for a frontal go. The conjuncture that she was looking for had arrived.

4

The Great Divide

"Successful democratic politicians are insecure and intimidated men. They advance politically only as they placate, appease, bribe, bamboozle, or otherwise manage to manipulate the demanding and threatening elements in their constituencies"

Walter Lippmann, US journalist

The inner-party struggle within the Congress was in full throttle when Dr Zakir Husain died in harness. May 3, 1969 thus incidentally became a factor in the fight for hegemony between Indira Gandhi and her detractors. The search for control now assumed a different dimension. The preceding three years had made it clear enough to the old guard that Indira Gandhi will not easily relent on what she had so haltingly achieved during this period.

From day one that she had taken over as the Prime Minister, she was under the threat of being made a puppet with the old guard controlling her. The then Congress president Kamaraj had not minced his words when he had remarked that no single leader could fill the vacuum left behind by Nehru. He said, "The party would, therefore, have to function on the basis of collective leadership, collective responsibility and collective approach." The intent was far too obvious for even a greenhorn was unlikely to miss.

In practical terms, Kamaraj 's message was clear. Indira Gandhi was merely the façade, the face. The real power rested with the "collective leadership," nothing but a euphemism for the old guard and the regional bosses. As such, this would not have spelt any delegation of authority but just fragmentation at the top, and the old guard thought that Indira Gandhi was in no position to challenge this game plan. In contrast to her father whose legitimacy did not just derive from Mahatma Gandhi's categorical projection, Indira Gandhi had to fight every inch to increase her individual political space. This inevitably meant that in the unfolding scenario, she would be forced to either completely submerge her own individual identity or take the old guard head on.

Jawaharlal Nehru was a product of the freedom struggle and a mass leader in his own right. In terms popular appeal and powers of articulation, no one could approach him or threaten him. Acharya J.B. Kripalani had, immediately after Independence, asked: "Which of the two would be supreme: the Party or the Prime Minister? Nehru responded with characteristic aplomb. He said that since the prime minister derived his legitimacy from the people at large, he obviously had to be supreme. The objective circumstances helped sustain Nehru's reasoning further.

In contrast, Indira Gandhi, during her first three years in power, was in no position to claim either popular support or organizational backup in her favour. As socialist leader Madhu Limaye said, Indira Gandhi was chosen because she was the " least unacceptable" leader. Being Nehru's daughter was an added factor in her favour. The role of the regional satraps could not be minimized, however; it was they who ensured Indira Gandhi's choice over Morarji Desai not once but twice. Indira Gandhi was acutely aware of their clout, since she knew that those who could make her could also unmake her. This obvious reality bred a sense of permanent insecurity in her mind, which was to find a reflection several times as the events unfolded.

Thus, it was imperative for Indira Gandhi that she freed herself from the constraints of the old guard as early as she could. She had to independently establish her control over the party so that she the old guard was kept at bay. This dilemma played heavily on her mind, which was evident from several of her utterances. The preceding phase had provided the opening she needed. And the impending Presidential election was to be her litmus test.

Parliament had already enacted a law providing for succession temporarily by the Chief Justice of India in the eventuality of such a need. It was a part of the strategy being evolved by Indira Gandhi. When the Congress president S Nijlingappa and K Kamaraj suggested to Indira Gandhi on May 10 1969, within a week after the death of Dr. Zakir Husain, a need for a strong party man as the candidate, she remarked, "the choice of a candidate was not merely a party matter. I do keep in touch with other parties and the chief ministers."

Indira Gandhi had to play her cards close to her chest. That much was patently obvious. Several names were doing the rounds as the possible Congress candidate for the election of the President of India, but Indira Gandhi was determined that it will be her choice that will finally prevail. The fact that in the Congress Parliamentary Board of eleven members, Indira Gandhi was in a minority was not something she was too worried about. That she was working on a different plank altogether was not clear to those who opposed her—after all, she initially seemed to have no objection to supporting the candidature by Dr. Neelam Sanjiv Reddy, the then Speaker of the Lok Sabha.

But this support for Reddy was only a façade. The fact that the latter was the favoured choice of the old guard, out to stymie her at every possible opportunity, made Indira Gandhi look for more acceptable replacements. She consulted some of her advisers and friends (Chandra Shekhar, with whom she at best enjoyed a love-hate equation, was also consulted) to resolve her dilemma.

On the face of it, or so went Indira Gandhi's reasoning, two names had emerged as principal aspirants for the Presidential slot; Sanjiva Reddy and defence minister Jagjivan Ram. (The third name that made rounds earlier was that of Jay Prakash Narayan, the Sarvodaya leader.) The problem with the latter was not his stature, which was not in doubt. It was known to Indira Gandhi that Morarji Desai was holding on to the files pertaining to Jagjivan Ram's income tax returns. On the other hand, oblivious to her at the time, Sanjiva Reddy had already begun holding meetings at his place to muster support. The essential focus of all these meetings was to use the Presidential election as a tool to subjugate Indira Gandhi into a more submissive mode vis-à-vis the recalcitrant old guard. She obviously agreed with the old dictum that a comparatively compatible person was always more preferable to a confirmed manipulator.

All this while, Indira Gandhi was bracing up for a strategy that she will unfold after the Parliamentary Board meeting was over. Her sights were trained towards the forthcoming AICC session at Bangalore, which began in the third week of June 1969. By then, the Jagjivan Ram option had been considered and found unfeasible. As a mass leader, she knew that the AICC session could provide a bigger platform to win over the support of a larger number of Congressmen. She had to provide her followers with a game plan, and the fence sitters with an option. The AICC session was thus to be converted into a test case of how far Indira Gandhi could lean on the party at the grassroots to consolidate herself better.

Indira Gandhi desperately needed a political facelift. She needed to emerge as a clear-headed, egalitarian, concerned and sensitive leader. She needed to project the image of a person not imprisoned by hard-nosed apparatchiks. She had to assume the avatar of a new leader who detested committee room huddles and intrigues and took issues that affected people to them rather than dictate with the aid of impersonal resolutions and promises. This, in turn, indicated the need for her to evolve a politics based on popular perceptions and felt-needs. The new-look Indira Gandhi was to be presented as the solution to the stagnation creeping into the Congress. The main problem with the old guard was the latter's inability to comprehend the need for an organizational revamp. The idiom had to be changed a new ideological veneer too, and the décor demanded a smarter, leaner look.

But the issue of the moment was choosing a new President of India. When she proposed the name of Jagjivan Ram as the Congress candidate for the Presidential election due in August that year, she was confronted with the name of Dr. Neelam Sanjiva Reddy. The old guard had also come prepared. For the first time in the history of the Indian National Congress, the final outcome was decided by votes. Never before had a division of this nature in the Parliamentary Board been seen. Given her numerical support within the CPB, Indira Gandhi was defeated as expected. Her proposal was rejected by a majority of one. She was livid, but that was not enough. That she was also unsure of her next move made things worse. Her immediate reaction was to sound those with whom she had been in touch during the run up to the CPB meet. C. Subramaniam had by then disclosed those waiting for the outcome that the Prime Minister was out to submit her resignation*.

The battle-lines were now sharply drawn. Indira Gandhi's politics had not lost. She needed to convert her defeat at the CPB into a victory outside the Board. Her candidate was defeated, but in the CPB, she was in a minority in any case.

In a bid to hit back at the entrenched regional bosses, she unfolded her political strategy when she addressed the AICC while participating in the debate over the Economic Resolution and

---

* (The 'news' infuriated those, like Chandra Shekhar, who had interpreted the result differently. He managed to reach Indira Gandhi, to tell her in unmistakable terms: " This is no time for you to resign. You should instead fight the old guard." One reason which was chiefly instrumental in forcing Chandra Shekhar to join the Congress and leave the Praja Socialist Party was the latter's decision to debar Ashok Mehta from accepting the post of the deputy Chairman of the Planning Commission Nehru had offered Mehta. When Chandra Shekhar met Indira Gandhi for the first time after he had joined the Congress party, she had asked: "Why did you join the Congress"? He told her that the PSP was a small party that had stagnated. Nothing could grow in it and nothing could be done through it. Hence he decided to join the larger party that the Congress was. Indira Gandhi asked him, ' But do you think that the Congress is a socialist party?' He promptly said that he did not think so though the people said so. "Then why did you join it," she asked. The candid reply was: "To convert it (the Congress) into a socialist party. If I do not succeed then I would attempt to break it. It is a banyan tree under which nothing grows. Unless the Congress changes or breaks, no revolution would be possible." This candid conversation did shock Indira Gandhi but it also showed a different kind of personality of Chandra Shekhar. Thus a new equation was established between the two that was to last till the death of Indira Gandhi. V.S.)

revealed her "Stray Thoughts." Copies of her stray thoughts were distributed to the AICC members when she began speaking. It was an indication how prepared she had come to Bangalore to meet the challenge of the old guard expecting her defeat in selection of the Congress candidate for the Presidential election. They wanted status quo to continue on the economic front. Her stray thoughts suggested an immediate shift and changed emphasis to the left orientation. It remains a mystery even today as to who wrote her stray thoughts. Some credit Chandra Shekhar and his team of academicians for the stray thoughts. Others believe that her Principal Secretary PN Haksar a brilliant academic and left oriented person had penned down her thoughts for he also knew what to expect at the Bangalore session. He had joined her Secretariat in October 1967 and had given the concrete shape to the shift in the economic approach.

She received a standing ovation at the AICC when she concluded her address. The veterans who were on the dais impassively watched the tumultuous reaction. In their schema, the CPB setback should have had a humbling effect on Indira Gandhi; instead, the manner in which she chose to take the battle to an entirely different plane upset the old guard comprehensively. Far from a being mellowed version of her earlier self, Indira Gandhi had if anything become even more combative and sharp. Her address, and the overwhelming response it received, was an indication that the old guard had lost control of the party. It was an indication that she had gained a firm grip over the Indian National Congress. The failure of the old guard to see the writing on the wall was not just a case of bad political timing. They were not quick and alert enough to read the message she had conveyed while unfolding her strategy. By authoring a left-of-centre political script for the Congress, the "dumb doll" had silenced her skeptics into utter disbelief.

Armed with the resounding support of the AICC for her new thinking, Indira Gandhi decided to keep fighting. A change of strategy was necessitated for the stage was set for a major confrontation in the Indian polity. At Indira Gandhi's instance, V.V. Giri Vice President of India resigned, left the papers on the office table of the President. For a few unprecedented hours, the offices of two of the highest functionaries were vacant in the wake of Giri's move. Later only Justice M. Hidayatullah, the Chief Justice of India, was sworn in as the acting president of India for the Constitution was amended soon after the death of the President to provide for such contingency.

Abiding by the formality of the CPB decision, Indira Gandhi, filed the nomination papers of the official candidate of the Indian National Congress: Neelam Sanjiva Reddy. But the air was thick with an impending showdown. The battle to actualize Indira Gandhi's plans pitted her in a direct confrontation with those who had made her Prime Minister. The ensuing division was interesting; for instance, a pro-changer like Ashok Mehta, who was with Indira Gandhi from 1963, also decided to hitch his fortunes with the old guard. Neither side was certain as to who would command a majority support within the Congress parliamentary party since it was the determinant of the final outcome. The Indira camp was certain that it would be able to have majority support in most legislature parties in the states.

As soon as the battle began, missives started to fly from both directions with allegations, counter allegations, mutual trading of charges in public and the like. Some of the letters that went from the Indira camp accused the party chief of having "ulterior motives," knowing well that there was no such case. Jagjivan Ram and Fakhruddin Ali Ahmed were used as the main signatories to send such missives from the Indira Gandhi since she could not trust Yashwantrao Chavan who had voted against her candidate in the parliamentary Board. Some worried leaders within the party made feeble attempts to bring about a rapprochement between two camps but efforts proved to no avail. Her political design was for a different cause.

To demonstrate their respective clout, either side held meetings of party MPs in their camp. The media was fed exaggerated figures and deliberate misinformation in this battle of attrition. The game went on till the actual voting took place: in

August 1969. The war of words and missives continued till November 1969 when the final great divide became a formal fact.

In the midst of this fierce campaign Piloo Mody, the Swatantra party member, gave the call for a conscience- vote, and ironically, a suggestion emanating from a political adversary became Indira Gandhi's best bet. The Congress was faced with its moment of truth. By design, Indira Gandhi had enlarged the battle raging within the confines of Congress to a much wider constituency. Unconventional tools were required to further the battle, and Indira Gandhi did not forget to heed the advice of Dwarika Prasad Mishra who asked her to restrain herself from taking out her vent against Chavan who ad earlier ditched her at the CPB vote. In a snide remark aimed at Chavan, she had said 'people should stick to what they say in private. Otherwise how can one trust anyone?' D.P. Mishra told her point blank that if she sacked Chavan from the cabinet, Morarji would trigger off a crisis by handing over his resignation. But if she decided to strike against Morarji Desai, the latter would have no backers. Ultimately, to the surprise of some Congressmen who had wagered against Indira Gandhi removing Desai, she did precisely that. On July 19 1969 Indira Gandhi divested Morarji Desai of his finance portfolio to take it over to herself and make Morarji Desai the Deputy Prime Minister without a portfolio. In palpable anger Morarji Desai sent in his resignation in protest against the cavalier manner in which he was treated. His angularities ensured that he did not have too many sympathizers.

While forwarding the resignation to the Rashtrapati Bhavan for acceptance, Indira Gandhi convened the meeting of the cabinet to adopt the resolution to nationalize the 20 major private banks of the country. It was only to justify the resignation of Morarji Desai, who was portrayed as a stumbling block in the way towards radical transformation. By enlisting the support of Yashwantrao Chavan, the tactical need to have an old guard by her side was ensured. He issued a statement welcoming the bold step initiated by the Prime Minister Indira Gandhi as the need of the economic decision. The Congress was placed on the road to achieve socialism that Nehru had dreamt but had never achieved due to the inherent pressures within the all-composite Indian National Congress.

The unceremonious dismissal of Morarji Desai, with the old guard watching helplessly, set the tone and tenor to the final outcome of the most crucial and controversial Presidential election that the country had ever seen. The left parties and the Socialists had decided to align with the independent candidate VV Giri against the official Congress candidate as they predictably saw the divide of the great Indian National Congress. Their objective was to ensure the ouster of the Indian National Congress from the corridors of power. The scenes in side the Central Hall during the fierce political activities were clear indication that the battle for the Presidential post would be a close fight between the Right and the Left. It turned out to be so with fortunes swaying as results from each state were beamed on the scoreboard. Party managers in the Congress held their breath at the party office in the Parliament House as results from different states poured in. Ultimately the final result came to indicate that the official Congress candidate had lost by a narrow margin by less than 14650 votes in the electoral college of more than 2 million votes. This was the first victory of Indira Gandhi over the old guard of the party. The Syndicate did not know what had hit them. All its plans had come unstuck. The old guard could not understand how the party, that was so much under their control, could go out of its grasp? Indira Gandhi held all the aces now. Her reorientation to a more radical Congress concretized her hold. The Congress took a left-turn to suit her new clothes.

The Monsoon Session of Parliament was not a cakewalk for her, but she had pigeonholed the old guard into a no-win zone. The Presidential polls were a precursor to the final decimation of the old guard. The first surprise was released when a story was let out on October 31 that the Congress president Nijlingappa had planned to expel Indira Gandhi, the Prime MInister from the Party for her defiance of the Parliamentary Board decision on the candidate for the Presidential election. Nijlingappa had gone to sleep when the story was released by a news agency. Nijlingappa was woken up and asked what had transpired. He immediately denied the story as hogwash, a mischievous 'plant.' Nevertheless most newspapers had carried the agency story that the old guard had planned to expel Indira Gandhi from the party.

The meeting of the Congress Working Committee on November 1 1969 was a stormy affair with supporters of Indira Gandhi shouting slogans outside Jantar Mantar office of the Congress headquarters. Only 11 of 21 members attended the meeting with Indira Gandhi staring away and leave the old guard to decide and vote over her fate and future in the party. The House was equally divided on the next plan of action against Indira Gandhi who had willfully and deliberately defied the Congress High command in sponsoring and ensuring the victory of the independent candidate in the Presidential election and thus embarrassing the party high command. Indira Gandhi was unconcerned about the marathon deliberations in the Working Committee for she was already thinking of her next move. One clever ploy was to make fighting elections an exorbitant affair; with the opposition deprived of the resources that were needed to fight a successful election. That too against the incumbent party having the state apparatus under its thumb.

Indira Gandhi knew that the high command would ultimately decide to expel her from the party. So she had to mobilize the maximum support within the Parliamentary party to remain politically afloat. Members of her kitchen cabinet were sent out on a mission to convince fence sitters that their future lay with the popularly acceptable Indira Gandhi and not with organizational chieftains. This helped in snapping the link between regional bosses and the old guard. The structure of the Congress party was thus being metamorphosed. The old guard was being slowly reduced into irrelevance. Instead of they holding the strings of power, it was the other way round from hereon; the old guard could exist at the behest and the pleasure of Indira Gandhi.

Events had been manipulated to such a nicety that the lady was the one who mattered. She commanded the party's core support. The message that made its way down to the ordinary worker was very significant: Indira Gandhi was all set to assume political stewardship at the expense of the old guard which was reduced to debating whether her expulsion would be of help. There was just the hint that the old guard was nursing doubts about carrying the party along as they confronted the now resurgent and confident Indira Gandhi. Although outwardly, they still held the reins of control in the party, the challenge posed to them was of a qualitatively different dimension altogether.

As it happens, the CWC found itself, in sporting parlance, "tied." The two rival camps had ten supporters each, while only A.M. Abraham taking a neutral position. Abraham even at this sage tried for a compromise, but the respected leader from Kerala was fighting a lost cause. His formula to avoid a direct confrontation was this: Let Indira Gandhi tender an apology, which, in turn, the old guard would immediately accept. Both sides would thus let bygones be bygones. Such a formula could be a face-saving device for the old guard. For Indira Gandhi, it was considered to be a minor concession necessary for ensuring inner-party cohesion. However, since tempers still ran high, Indira Gandhi showed no enthusiasm to sue for peace with those who had been sidelined in the run of play. Abraham soon gave up, and reconciled to join the Indira Gandhi camp when the Congress Working Committee decided to expel Indira Gandhi from the Congress. Incidentally, the great divide had come in the 75th year of the party's existence.

It is very important to emphasize at this stage that it was from this moment onwards that the party had become an appendage to Indira Gandhi the individual. Her new politics rendered the party ineffectual and effete. In both political as well as ideological terms, it was the individual who assumed a decisive role. The Congress as a party was now irrevocably wedded to the politics of a personality cult. She was ruthless and amoral person and did not fight shy when she was accused of possessing these qualities in her nature.

It was in this tumultuous backdrop that the egalitarian foundations of a new Congress took root. Even before Indira Gandhi was sacked from the primary membership of the party for the act of gross indiscipline, she had already set up the office for her new party and had decided to hold a separate AICC at Delhi instead of holding it in Gujarat as was earlier decided. The venue was suitably modest: the lawns of the constitution club. C. Subramaniam was named as the new president of the Indian

National Congress, with the majority of the AICC members attending the meeting. The old guard was caught off-guard. Acumen scored over logistics. Indira Gandhi had generated new enthusiasm in the party by her deft and skillful but swift moves.

The old guard had underestimated Indira Gandhi. Not just that; it had reckoned without the political skills of DP Mishra and Chandra Shekhar. The great divide had become a fait accompli. By pitch forking Indira Gandhi, the old guard had made an investment which, or so they reckoned, would ultimately be neutralized whenever they wanted. It was a gross miscalculation. For the record, only 54 members had gone along with the old guards in the parliamentary party while the clear majority had preferred to remain with Indira Gandhi. The Left bloc and the Socialists had decided to allow the minority government headed by Indira Gandhi to remain in power for the time being; little did they know that their wisdom of the moment would prove so disastrously at variance with the popular mood.

In line with her move to clip the wings of those who may still consider investing their faith in her adversaries, Indira Gandhi imposed a total ban on company donations to political parties. That in the long run, Indira Gandhi was creating a situation, which would encourage generation of black money proved to be of no avail in face of Indira Gandhi's determination. Since industrial houses and individual companies were allowed to include political donations while filing their returns, it was easier for parties to raise funds. However Indira Gandhi had other ideas. She foreclosed the option, and wittingly or otherwise, this was the beginning of moneybags and jute barons becoming arbiters of the new political culture. Indira Gandhi was clearly not in the mood to reflect on the consequences of her expediency. The distortions that have since plagued the electoral process can in part be traced to this deliberate myopia. Those who were behind-the-scene manipulators now came to occupy a centrality, which over time has only succeeded in progressively eroding the credibility of the system. Dr Ram Manohar Lohia, the veteran socialist leader had pithily stated way back in 1956: "The bania-brahmin alliance is one of the prime-movers of Indian history. The Bania lords the nation's belly, the Brahmin lords the nation's mind."

In the new political environ generated by Indira Gandhi, the status quo as represented by entrenched lobbies and the bania-brahmin alliance had no locus standi. The box-wallahs and fund-raisers had all the resources to manipulate the course and direction of both politics and policies. Politics was subservient to money-power, and not just during elections. The unchecked access of those who could materially manipulate politics signified an invitation to the entry of criminals in the political arena that many lament thirty years later, without understanding who had opened the floodgates for the criminalisation of the polity in the first place.

As far as Indira Gandhi was concerned, she hardly cared for such distortions and their legitimization. She had defined her target constituents. She wanted to win over the poor and the lower middle classes who always looked to the future and not the upper class and the middle class who forever lament over their yesterdays and to days. The succession of steps to drive the Indian economy towards the left was to ensure that the poor and the lower middle class believed that their future was interlinked with what Indira Gandhi was doing. She peddled the message through a cleverly devised campaign. The direction of policies appeared to have changed overnight.

Seasoned veterans and political pundits were simply unable to comprehend or keep abreast with the fast-moving scenario. Steps such as nationalization of banks could not have been visualized to become a reality so soon. The astounding speed with which the populist package was pushed through resulted in strengthening Indira Gandhi's vote-banks. A climate had been assiduously created to woo the underclass to start believing that its time had come. Indira Gandhi was playing a highly clever but emotionally counter-productive game. The revolution of rising expectations soon went beyond her control. The message that the upper segments could be checked by state policies while the poor could now dream of a change in their favour was what Indira Gandhi meant to convey.

The populist onslaught stumped the Opposition. Clueless, they tried to picture the new ethos as a gimmick. Maybe, they were right in certain respects. But their slavish attitude towards the model handed down by the westernized elite rendered them completely incapable of responding to her politics in a popular idiom. If they derailed the process unleashed by Indira Gandhi through judicial caveats, their political platform became weaker still. They simply played into Indira Gandhi's hands. Any which way they tried, the net result was the same: Indira Gandhi had come to symbolize the yearnings and aspirations of the masses.

After she had established her identification with the poor, she went ahead to enhance her political gains by depriving erstwhile princes of privy purses- a thundering symbolic slap on the feudal order. In material terms, the exchequer saved only ten crore or so. But in symbolic terms, Indira Gandhi had shown the uppity princes their place. When a Planning Commission member asked Indira Gandhi why was she making so much song and dance about such a paltry gain? With a laconic smile, Indira Gandhi explained that what the state gained in material terms was secondary to the political gains that would accrue from the abolition of privy purses. The underprivileged were delighted. Indira Gandhi was about to politically convert their glee into votes.

She pushed this egalitarian line until the 1970 winter session of Parliament was through, Morarji Desai had been divested of his ministerial portfolio and she herself had taken over the country's financial management into her hands. The first, and as it turned out, last budget she had moved reflected her future economic drives. Minor hiccups, like her forgetting to formally move the Finance Bill after her speech got over was only an aside. Even this was invested with high drama: the Lok Sabha members had to be hurriedly assembled before midnight to enable her to introduce the Finance Bill on Feb 28 1970. All such actions were oriented towards making her identification as the unchallenged boss of both the party and the country complete.

The Rightist camp in the form of the Swatantra Party and the Jan Sangh, tried to use the discontented princes as a political counterweight. This cut no ice with the popular mood, which was decisively with Indira Gandhi. The Left had been silenced by the sheer glitter of the new economic package, and its criticism fell on deaf ears. Even some of her detractors had to admit that this was the best government baulked by numbers could do in the circumstances. Indira Gandhi's quicksilver sense of timing had come to the fore once again.

Purely in terms of changing the mood within the party in her favour, Indira Gandhi could not have done better.

At this juncture, DP Mishra had virtually assumed the role of a Commandant General in the battle that Indira Gandhi had waged against the old guards of the party since the presidential elections. He remained perched firmly in the house of Niti Raj Singh Choudhary on Rakabganj Road in Delhi and all foot soldiers and campaign managers were told to visit him for taking instructions for their duties from him. Indira Gandhi remained in touch with the old man over the phone or she communicated through her ministers. DP Mishra could be seen sitting in the lawns of the bungalow with a Chess Board spread out before him. He would not even look up when the ministers of state came to see him. No one sat down before him and always addressed him as "Dada". Lalit Narayan Mishra, then minister of state for commerce was assigned duties of keeping the members happy by catering to their needs. Inder Gujral was assigned the task of handling the media persons and keeping them abreast with the developments of the day. Inder Gujral used his skills to the fullest extent and had even won over the critics of Indira Gandhi. He had with characteristic mastery upturned the criticism of Indira Gandhi in the main national dailies to build a different character for Indira Gandhi. The media was clearly divided with the main papers joining the camp of the Opposition.

Chandra Shekhar took up the task to spread awareness on the shift in the economy that had followed the party split. With some friends in tow, he moved from state to state to win over more supporters for Indira Gandhi. Chandra Shekhar reveled in this new role, as he always wanted to project socialism as the new mantra informing the Congress. He was close to achieving what he had promised Indira Gandhi in his first meeting with her on her invitation of not only converting the Congress into a socialist party but also splitting it.

While Indira Gandhi camp was a unified command with only one person issuing instructions, the old veterans were a divided and dispirited lot where there was no coordination or united strategy to deal with the war that was thrust on them. Their views and objective were drastically different. Kamaraj and Yashwantrao Chavan were in favour of bank nationalization but they would not openly say so till the last minute. Chavan issued a statement only after the cabinet had approved it. Morarji Desai was dead set against it. Even on the issue whether or not a compromise should be worked out with Indira Gandhi, they were divided. Morarji Desai did not want even an attempt be made to sue for peace with Indira Gandhi. They had not come together by design and same objective. They had to come together because they were all pushed to the wall by the political circumstances that were engineered by Indira Gandhi and her campaign.

Nijlingappa had two meetings with Indira Gandhi between November 2 and November 9 1969, (though the third planned dinner meeting was cancelled by Indira Gandhi as she found not use in meeting the party chief who had closed his mind on action against her) to find a solution to the problems caused by the indirect support lent by Indira Gandhi to the independent candidate in the Presidential poll that caused defeat of the official candidate. It was an issue of indiscipline by the person who held high office. The Indian National Congress could not live down such an insult and gross indiscipline. To worsen the situation, the Presidential poll was challenged in the Supreme Court because several pamphlets were circulated prior to the voting in the election. These were scurrilous documents aimed at tarnishing image of the Congress candidate Dr. Neelam Sanjiv Reddy. It was alleged that these were issued and circulated with the tacit approval of Indira Gandhi though she had flatly denied that she had a hand behind such a scurrilous propaganda against the official candidate. She was not ready even to express regrets for what she had done while the old guard could not live without her apology in the same party with her. But they had no idea what to do and how to fight her. Thus the split became inevitable event because old guard had no options but to take disciplinary action against her. She had no option of apologizing to the party and yet continuing to hold the office of the Prime Minister. Thus their differences were irresoluble. The great divide of the party was thus destined by the outcome of the Presidential poll though it was engineered long before. Indira Gandhi had driven the party towards the great divide, as she wanted to be beyond reach of anyone to threaten her position. Her security was the main objective of her battle.

Indira Gandhi had taken on the old guard, and worsted them at its game to trivialize her into a rubber stamp. She had unequivocally won the battle for political survival. She had always felt threatened by their close proximity for she felt that they would conspire against her if she were to refuse to carry out their instructions. She was not greatly interested in keeping her electoral promises. As she told Fritztof Capra years later, she conceded that she would have liked to start afresh looking at the conditions that prevailed but she could not throw away all that was built over the years. It was a comment on the achievements of her father for she believed that all that her father had started was not in right direction. She could not change other things but she did get rid of old colleagues of her father who had participated in the freedom struggle along with Nehru and had contributed their might. But as it is generally said, there were no foe or friends in war. She had waged the war for survival and had succeeded in it. She was now set to emerge as the strong leader who was loved by the masses as she prepared for another battle: the battle of votes.

5

Triumph and Decline

Power is of two kinds. One is obtained by the fear of punishment, and other by the art of love. Power based on love is thousand times more effective and permanent than one derived from fear of punishment.

M. K. Gandhi

No one with absolute power can be trusted to give it up even in part.

Louis D. Brandeis

Indira Gandhi had unwittingly breached the psyche of the ordinary Indian. By reordering the politics and economics of the Congress, she had won a new set of adherents. She had broken the spell of fatalism under which Indians have lived for centuries. They accepted a meal if they got one as a pleasure of the Almighty. If they did not get one, they believed it to be the Almighty' wish. People died of hunger and starvation by the side of the British trucks that were laden with rice in Bengal in 1943 but none thought of even touching the grain since the Almighty had not given it to them. For the first time in their life, they had heard a leader who said that the poor had a right to two square meals a day and she would provide it to them by removing their poverty. That was the promise of Indira Gandhi during the entire election campaign of the Lok Sabha Polls in 1971.

She had electrified the political atmosphere to an extent that her persona became an ideological reassurance. Practically the entire mainstream media failed to understand this, and carried on a campaign underscoring her by now confirmed distance from regional bosses. What the media was obviously unable to understand that this distance, which was a consciously effected one, was Indira Gandhi's way of saying that she had emerge as an unchallenged, independent centre of power in her own right. Helped by the fact that some of the country's leading liberals and left-leaning intellectuals were more than ordinarily eager to encourage her bold moves to signify a departure from the old guard helped in offsetting the media's focus on her weaknesses. It is hard to imagine how such substantial sections of the media had so badly misread the political mood of the moment. To say that this was only a reflection of the mindset of newspaper magnates will be tantamount to oversimplifying the issue, because even they could not have taken a stand that was at such variance with popular perception.

The Grand Alliance that came to be nicknamed as the Syndicate by Indira Gandhi followers was the brainchild of Dr. Ram Manohar Lohia of the Socialist party. He had united various opposition parties before and after the fourth general election and had succeeded in getting the United Opposition Front governments in Uttar Pradesh, Bihar and Haryana. Dr. Lohia was a brilliant intellectual but he could never overcome his pathological hatred for the Indian National Congress, the techno-managerial elite and most specifically, for the Nehru family. He personally hated Nehru for different reasons that had nothing to do with politics. That had made him an obsessive Congress-baiter, always too eager to try any method to trounce the Congress. He succeeded in bringing the Old Congress, the Swatantra party, the Bharatiya Jan Sangh and the Socialist party together to take on the new juggernaut led by Indira Gandhi.

After bargaining and haggling over seat shares, this motley crowd finally arrived at some tendentious adjustments to Indira Gandhi. The abiding principle was to ensure one-to-one contests so that a splintered Opposition vote did not help the Congress. But what eluded them was a common joint programme to counter the radical leftist platform projected by Indira Gandhi. So they decided to fight the elections on the basis of their own symbols, their own party flags and on their own respective manifestos. With some fiery orators in their arsenal and with the media by and large playing their game, they were confident that they would halt the Congress march to power in its tracks.

They were confident that the Supreme Court would adjudicate against both bank nationalization and the abolition of privy purses. The Opposition tried hard to draw attention to Indira Gandhi's lackluster past in the Prime Ministerial chair. But what they had sorely missed was the fact that a 'new' incarnation of Indira Gandhi had emerged to capture public imagination. They perceived themselves to belong to a generation that had made sacrifices during the freedom struggle, and deserved to see the fruition of the past then and there. Through a caveat, they had also deprived the Indira Gandhi Congress of the traditional party symbol: a pair of bullocks carrying a yoke. The Indian National Congress had successfully contested four general elections with that symbol. So they were confident that in absence of the traditional symbol, the Indira Gandhi faction would not be able to identify herself with the great party that had fought for and won the independence. For two thirds of the electorate, freedom struggle was a matter of living memory and not merely a page of history as it was for the one third of the electorate that had joined the electorate as the first post independence generation. Much was to depend on this one third of the electorate that had come into the electoral arena for the first time. But the Syndicate leaders were confident that the two thirds would lead them to victory.

Indira Gandhi carefully chose the cow-and-calf symbol after she failed to get the old Congress symbol from the Election Commission. Many in the old Congress tried to ridicule it with the jeering remarks that it represented Indira Gandhi and her son Sanjay Gandhi. This ridiculous sense of humour was hardly likely to amuse people. Conscious that her "economics first" political gamble was her best bet, Indira Gandhi pushed on. Contradictory pulls and pressures were at work. But Indira Gandhi decided to stay clear of them, focusing her attention on her main task. Those keen on winning her to their contending points of view however converged on one central point: the Grand Alliance had to be humbled. The old guard had already bungled in underestimating the emotive potential of the Indira Gandhi script.

The script had all the necessary ingredients. A radical shift in terms of economic concerns; a conscious dilution of the monopoly houses; a sustained attempt to ensure two square meals to every family and an identification with the power structure which ruled the country. She had by then already nationalized the oil and coal sectors. Insurance was also brought under governmental ambit.

The final results left everyone bewildered. Friends and foes were equally stunned when the results began pouring in indicating the decimation of the opposition. The electorate that had given a massive mandate to Indira Gandhi threw many stalwarts in the Opposition by the wayside. The extent of confusion and bewilderment in opposition ranks can be highlighted by one representative instance. The wily Jagjivan Ram knew that Indira Gandhi did not trust him as was obvious from the fact that she asked Uma Shankar Dikshit to "shadow" him at every media briefing. On the eve of the election results, Jagjivan Ram told the media, "I am not a sleeping president of the party." His quip had come in reply to a question whether the Congress would have an alliance with other parties in case the Indira Congress failed to obtain a majority on its own.

Many senior leaders in the Indira establishment were not confident that they would have a clear majority. They were not so sure that Opposition stalwarts and bigwigs will provide them with such a cakewalk. The essential truth was that the mutual chemistry between the bold Indira Gandhi and her new constituents was enough to alter all existing paradigms and equations. It was for the first time that forces to both the 'right' and the 'left' of the political spectrum had come together. But one Indira Gandhi was enough to blur these ideological distinctions by the sheer sheen of her populism. The shadow of the 1967 disaster lingered in many a mind in the Indira camp. The doubts had occasioned tentative parleys of a possible post-electoral realignment with other like-minded parties at the time of the Faridabad session of the All India Congress Committee. Though the rank and file was confident of the eventual outcome, men like Jagjivan Ram were not so sure, and his uncertainty and doubts about the future course of developments forced him to keep doors open for a contingency plan. Such private expressions of doubt did not worry Indira Gandhi who was by now convinced of the efficacy of the path she had chosen for herself.

The final tally that was larger than what was notched by her father in the first general election. Indira Gandhi had arrived as the new, charismatic, supreme leader. Of the party as well as the Indian people. This facilitated follow-ups like easing out Jagjivan Ram from his party pedestal. As a stopgap arrangement, D. Sanjivaiya a Dalit leader from Andhra was brought in as replacement. While Shankar Dayal Sharma became the titular chief, Indira Gandhi held all the reins of power in her own hands. Nehru always avoided giving out the impression that he was an autocrat or a tyrant, out to stymie everyone else. Indira Gandhi in contrast was always insecure and feared that her position could be challenged if she shared power with anyone else.

The Syndicate was stunned by the outcome of the elections, more so those who had fought on the Jan Sangh symbol. They could not fathom their decimation. Several senior stalwarts were defeated. The Swatantra Party that had won 44 seats in the previous House was reduced to three in numbers including indomitable Piloo Modi. The Jan Sangh and the left parties had also suffered heavy casualties. Bal Raj Madhok, senior leader of the BJS had come up with a theory of Invisible Russian Ink being used to alter ballot papers the cause of decimation of the opposition in the elections. Nobody took him seriously though. If she were so efficient that she could use the Invisible Russian Ink to influence the final outcome of the elections without any one having even an inkling of it, then she deserved her victory!

The Opposition had to pay a heavy price for their own inefficiency in face of Indira Gandhi's superior tactics. The Opposition tried to invent one excuse after another for its debacle, without publicly acknowledging that a master-tactician had outwitted them completely and had made people's support more important than considerations like caste, community and interest groups. Indira Gandhi had understood the psyche of the ordinary Indian better than perhaps any other leader—her late father included. Narrow, sectarian considerations have a field day only when personalities do not get identified with ideology and issues. By becoming the personification of the Great Indian Dream, Indira Gandhi had become larger-than-life. In actual fact, it was at this pinnacle of power that the seeds of her decline were first sown.

Indira Gandhi said she wanted to remove poverty; her opponents only wanted to remove her. The people knew which side to choose when it came to the crunch. Populism is a concomitant of cavalier rhetoric. Indira Gandhi avoided that trap wonderfully. She was never a verbose leader who promised people the moon. She believed in talking about elementary bread and butter issues. She talked of housing; she talked of dignity; she talked of giving self-respect to the poor. The underclass had never heard a popular leader say all this and more. They loved her. Adored her. Treated her as an idol to be worshipped.

The myth of invincibility was given fresh impetus by events in India's neighbourhood. The Pakistani military junta unleashed a reign of terror in the eastern part of that country. This followed an election that saw the western part overwhelmingly root for the mercurial Zulfiqar Ali Bhutto while East Pakistan chose Sheikh Mujibur Rehman, already spearheading a movement against army atrocities. The fractured verdict led to a constitutional impasse. Numerically, the eastern part was clearly the winner. But the landed aristocracy of west Punjab did not accept this defeat, and it was this refusal to abide by democratic norms that led to a crackdown in eastern Pakistan. India became a 'victim' of an unprecedented influx of refugees and Indira Gandhi was pushed into playing a role that called upon the best of political and diplomatic acumen.

In a matter of few months, a huge humanitarian, political and diplomatic crisis had gripped India. The failure of the Pak elite to resolve its own contradictions forced India's meager resources further. Though Indira Gandhi was able to rally the entire country in her favour as she sided in favour of the forces of change in eastern Pakistan, her aplomb had to be matched by action. The tide was inevitably assuming a form where a desperate Pak junta needed an excuse to bolster itself at the expense of a reasoned solution to the Pak political crisis.

India needed a strong and dependable ally who could help both on the diplomatic and military fronts. It was in this backdrop that the historic Indo-Soviet Friendship Treaty was signed on August 9 1971. It provided an insurance of total Soviet support to India. Indira Gandhi had shown her leadership skills when she had visited the US and told the US President Richard Nixon that his politics had created an explosive situation in the Asian subcontinent. The climax was the decisive victory of India in the 14 days war with Pakistan and creation of Bangladesh on the eastern borders of India. Indira Gandhi did not intend the bifurcation of Pakistan but the force of the political circumstances that emerged during the 1971 from March to December only this was the unavoidable result. She was felicitated by the Joint Session of parliament held in the Central Hall where paeans of praise for her were sung by one and all.

The decisive victory in the war with Pakistan silenced her critics completely and she had easy victory in the state elections that were held in 1972. She had reached the pinnacle of power and was supreme leader whom no one could question. Perhaps her position of supreme leader also contributed to sowing of seeds of decline of the party. She did not trust any one not even her senior colleagues like Jagjivan Ram, Yashwantrao Chavan nor Fakhruddin Ali Ahmed. She had missed no opportunity to show them their place in her scheme of things. She also wanted to ensure that the chief ministers were of her choice and did not enjoy a majority support on their own in the state legislature party so that they would remain dependent on her pleasures and her whims. The majority support within the state legislature parties had become a thing of a distant past She imposed the chief ministers on various states. Nandini Satpathy who had played a role as a minister of state in the PMO was sent to Orissa. Sidhartha Shankar Ray was dispatched to Bengal and Ghanshyam Oza to Gujarat. She did not allow a change in Maharashtra because Vasantrao Naik did not belong to the Maratha community that was the single largest and well-organized community standing behind Yashwant Rao Chavan. She did not want Chavan to gain a position of strength in his own state. In Andhra, she would have neither a Khamma nor Reddy as chief minister. Jagjivan Ram had once described her rule as an era of drafted chief ministers because she had imposed them on the state legislature parties and not allowed them any elbowroom of their own. She was perhaps not an autocrat or an arrogant politician but she was a ruthless person who had seen and perceived the moral and amoral positions that he father had taken as occasions demanded. She did not want to make distinction between the moral and amoral position and situations, as she wanted to protect her position at any cost. This was confirmed opinion of Piloo Mody and had even told her on her face in a private chat once. She had converted the federal structure of the country and the party into the unitary structure where she decided every thing. She did not take kindly when Chimanbhai Patel, aspirant for the office of the chief minister in Gujarat took a definitive stand that was opposed to her ideas of how the chief minister be chosen.

Nav Nirman Movement

The crisis erupted when Chimanbhai Patel rebelled against the imposed chief minister Ghanshyam Oza who was earlier a minister of state for industries at the Centre in 1972. Even though he could not identify six legislators of the party by name on seeing them, he was sent to take over as the chief minister of the state though Patel had a majority support within the state Congress legislature party and was a rightful claimant. His claim was ignored because he belonged to the well-organized single community of the state that had all resources at its command and also for a reason that he was loyal and ardent supporter of Morarji Desai before the split. Patel could go out of her hands if such a situation arose was the fear for the selection of the candidate for the post of chief minister of the state. She chose a Brahmin Ghanshyam Oza who did not enjoy the support in the state legislature party.

Chimanbhai Patel and his supporters tolerated Oza for fifteen months between March 1972 and June 1973 and then he went to confront Indira Gandhi after she had unceremoniously removed him and election for a new leader became inevitable. The confrontation took place at the Raj Bhavan in Mumbai where Indira Gandhi was visiting. After twenty minutes talks that was nothing more than the heated exchange of words, Chimanbhai told her that the leader of the state legislature party would be chosen by the party and not by her. These were strong words to be hurled at Indira Gandhi who was the supreme leader of the party. She asked him to see Swaran Singh, the then foreign minister in Delhi who was appointed as the observer for the party affairs in Gujarat after Ghanshyam Oza was forced to hand over his papers when things had become too hot for him in June 1973.

Chimanbhai met Swaran Singh in Delhi same night and worked out the arrangements for the election of the leader of the state legislature party. The election was held in Gandhinagar but the counting of ballots took place in Swaran Singh's office in New Delhi. Never before such a practice was adopted because the state legislature parties were supposed to elect the man who was chosen by Indira Gandhi. Chimanbhai won the election by seven votes though some suspect even today that he had not won the election against Kantilal Ghia the other contestant but Swaran Singh declared the result in favour of Chimanbhai Patel at the bidding of Indira Gandhi, as she was eager to teach Patel a lesson that he would never forget in his political life. Chimanbhai Patel never did forget the lesson.*

The method she chose to clip Chimanbhai's wings was novel. She cut down the allocation of wheat quantum to Gujarat from one-lakh five thousand tonnes to merely fifty five thousand tones. There was a wheat zone prevalent then that banned inter-state movement of wheat. The issue price of wheat through the Public Distribution System was seventy paise per kg. while the open market price in Gujarat was Rs. 5 per kg. Union food minister Fakhruddin Ali Ahmed issued the formal orders to that effect in September 1973. The quantum cut was applied only to Gujarat. The inevitable consequence was that Chimanbhai Patel had to remove the students' hostels from those receiving subsidized wheat.

---

*(On July 17, 1973, after being sworn in at Gandhi Nagar, Chimanbhai Patel came to Delhi, ostensibly to make a courtesy-call on Indira Gandhi. The meeting went off cordially with Indira Gandhi coming out to see him off. I was standing at the porch by his car. As soon as he came, I asked him: 'How was her mood?' Chimanbhai said that it was all right. He said she had come to the door to see him off. I could not resist myself from saying: "She had not come to see you off the main door. She had come to see where you would land when she delivers a kick on your bottoms." The late Gujarat finance minister Amul Desai was within earshot of this conversation... VS).

The food bill of every resident student rose fivefold. The central order spelt student unrest, which erupted with full force in October 1973.

Indira Gandhi had known that it would be an unpopular move. She gave clear instructions to Jaswant Mehta, former finance minister of Gujarat in the Oza ministry that he had to bear the brunt of the anti Patel campaign. The instigation was provided so also the resources to start the Nav Nirman movement. Jaswant Mehta had come for lunch to the residence of Krishna Kant, then one of the famous 'young Turks.' Chandra Shekhar was also present at the lunch. Jaswant Mehta began pouring venom against Chimanbhai Patel. Chandra Shekhar who had also attended the inauguration of the Phulpur Plant of the IFFCO, immediately remarked, "So Jaswant, you have been briefed fully to start an agitation against Chimanbhai? But go back and tell your leader, event she was creating with her intention to remove Chimanbhai would go out of her hands since the event also has its own logic." Jaswant Mehta did not reply but carried the resources and literature that was provided by Uma Shankar Dikshit to Gujarat via Vadodara.

Chimanbhai accompanied by his finance minister Dr. Amul Desai who had once defeated Morarji Desai, the then chief minister of Bombay state, met the food minister Fakhruddin Ali Ahmed to press him to increase the issue quantum of wheat to Gujarat. But he expressed his inability to do so. When Chimanbhai and Dr. Desai came out from the meting, I was standing outside along with the PTI correspondent Dinubhai. We both suggested that he should throw his resignation on the face of Fakhruddin and the people of Gujarat would not allow any one to take him off their shoulders. Chimanbhai replied, "Yes. That would make the individual but destroy the party." Yet he paid a heavy price for defying Indira Gandhi who did not like any challenge to her authority from any one. Chimanbhai had challenged her authority to impose chief minister on any state by insisting that the state legislature party would decide its own leader. He paid the price for it. He was branded as the corrupt man only because he had defied the ruthless Indira Gandhi. Through Nav Nirman Movement but Indira Gandhi also paid the price in the long run. She had to face a similar movement in Bihar in few months. This time the initiator was Laloo Prasad Yadav, a postgraduate in political science from a Bihar University.

Though Indira Gandhi succeeded in forcing Chimanbhai Patel out in February 1974, she did not dissolve the state assembly. She had hoped that she would be able to install the chief minister of her choice. But Morarji Desai stepped in and started a fast unto death in support of his demand for dissolution of the state assembly and fresh polls in Gujarat. Chimanbhai Patel accompanied with Chhabildas Mehta came to New Delhi and met Indira Gandhi. He pleaded for dissolution of the state assembly and also told her that lot of young blood would flow on streets of Gujarat if the demand was not met. Indira Gandhi remarked with total disdain. "But that would not be my blood." Patel and Mehta were stunned by her coldblooded remarks for they had never expected such a reaction from Indira Gandhi. Ultimately she was forced to dissolve the assembly and bring the state under the central rule, as Morarji Desai remained adamant on his demand.

There is no doubt that the Nav Nirman movement was instigated and promoted only to get rid of Chimanbhai Patel who had dared challenge the authority of Indira Gandhi. When Jay Prakash Narayan, popularly known as JP visited Gujarat and wanted to join the movement, the movement leaders refused to allow him to be associated with the movement because they did not want the movement to go out of their hands and become a popular upsurge against the Indian National Congress. The clear indication of the source of inspiration for the Nav Nirman movement was available in the fact that most leading members of the movement later joined the Congress party. Only Indukumar Jani remained outside and was later to edit a journal "Khet Mazdoor" that was started by a senior Congress leader Zinabhai Daraji.

Indira Gandhi had prompted an event like Nav Nirman movement in Gujarat with the intention to effect an organizational overhaul. However, instead of streamlining the party in her favour, Indira Gandhi indirectly fuelled a veritable campaign against her. In Bihar, Laloo Prasad Yadav started the anti-corruption campaign in which a person with proven probity like Abdul Gafoor got caught in the crossfire. The latent discontent within the masses found an outlet. The disenchantment with Indira Gandhi was a rejection of her newfound disdain for the very agenda she had pushed for so hard. The promised expansion of employment avenues remained stillborn. Relief operations to counter natural calamities were used as a political weapon in the three years that followed the elections. Those affected by natural calamities were handed out doles and not jobs. Since the allowance was used selectively, Opposition-run states were given step motherly treatment.

Indira Gandhi's cynical manipulation bred political unrest. Among those who became key protagonists of the anti-establishment upsurge was Jai Prakash Narayan. Once a committed Marxist, J.P. subsequently became a votary of party less democracy. He once declined an invite from Nehru to become a part of the union cabinet. While several commentators have criticized J.P. for giving undeserved legitimacy to right-wing parties like the Bharatiya Jan Sangh, this was not the intended direction of the JP movement, which, was primarily a platform for all non-Congress tendencies.

The country was in the throes of a severe economic crisis. The substantial cost of the Bangladesh war was followed by the imposition of sanctions against the country by the western bloc led by the United States and the United Kingdom. The fourfold hike in oil prices in 1973 was an unprecedented burden running into billions of dollars. The disaffection in the working class was apparent when the railway strike in May 1974, which lasted twenty days and caused the exchequer heavily and the politics of Indira Gandhi more particularly. It derailed whatever impetus there was in the economy. Indira Gandhi did not know how to tackle the situation that was going out of her hand each day. In the backdrop were stormy debates that she had to face in the two houses of parliament. One related to what had by then come to be known as the Pondichery Licenses scandal. Other related to the allotment of land to Sanjay Gandhi for his small car-manufacturing unit in collaboration with a Japanese firm. A part of the land piece allotted to him was that of the Indian Air Force base at the Palam Airport. The Pondichery scandal came to light only after the commerce minister Lalit Narayan Mishra was shifted to the railway ministry. Tulmohan Ram, a dalit Member of Parliament from Bihar had helped some firms to obtain import licenses for firms that had paid him in advance by forging signatures of other colleagues. When the opposition mounted the attack Indira Gandhi had to defend Mishra, his minister who was considered to be the main fund-raiser and resources mobiliser for Indira Gandhi and her party. He had known also too much so she could not sacrifice him immediately. But it turned out to be the fiercest parliamentary battle between the ruling party and the opposition. Inquiry was ordered and Tulmohan Ram was expelled from the Lok Sabha for the contempt and also breach of privileges.

The intriguing circumstances surrounding the death of Lalit Narayan Mishra in a mysterious train mishap near Patna have not been cleared to the day. The death came soon after the exposure of the Pondicherry licenses scandal. There were several aspects connected with the accident suggested that it was not an accident on its own but it was an engineered event to silence Mishra forever. So many believed but no inquiry was ever conducted. Another intriguing death was that of Jimmy Nagarwala who had withdrawn Rs. 60 lakhs from the State Bank of India, parliament street branch by imitating the voice of Indira Gandhi. It was a special account maintained for the emergency operation abroad. Nagarwala was soon apprehended but cash he had collected was never found. The Teller at the bank who had handed over the cash without the cheque later resigned and joined the Maruti Car Unit as its Chief Accounts Officer.

Another contentious issue was the land given for Sanjay Gandhi's Maruti project in a notified defence zone. Jagjivan Ram, the union defence minister at the time, was hard put to explain the transaction. The issue kept recurring whenever the Opposition ran out of ammunition against Indira Gandhi. Finally, the project was shifted out of the defence-sensitive confines. Jagjivan Ram tried hard to justify the original allotment, but that was purely a formal disclaimer on his part. This was the first time that the Nehru family was directly accused of nepotism through use of the political power.

At this juncture, the quality of Indira Gandhi's advisers was hardly inspiring. Men of experience and seniority had been replaced by an insincere bunch of power-seekers and carpet beggars. Trusted seniors like Jagjivan Ram and Yashwant Rao Chavan had been sidelined. In fact she had used them only to attack her political enemies but never trusted them with her political moves. So they were also not willing to give her correct advice. She had become lonely at the top of the pyramid.

As for those of the 'left' who had joined her in order to keep the radical momentum going, the consolidation of the Sanjay brigade signaled an early exit. Mohan Kumaramangalam, once a communist cardholder, died in a plane crash in May 1973. Nandini Satpathy, another left-leaning leader, was handling affairs in Orissa. Differences of opinion began to inform the Indira Gandhi- P.N. Haksar interaction as well. The once all powerful and highly trusted principal secretary was replaced by a well-known economist, Prof. P.N.Dhar. Haksar was instrumental in giving a definite shape to many of the bold moves made by Indira Gandhi; but he had enough self-respect to quit when the schism between him and Indira Gandhi came to the fore. Loyalists rather than men of proven ability comprised the new network around Indira Gandhi. Thus, Bansi Lal was inducted as union defence minister and Dev Kant Barooah became the party chief. The ubiquitous man for all seasons, the maverick Rajani Patel, was there, in any case.

In 1974, the Provincial Armed Constabulary in Uttar Pradesh revolted; chief minister Kamlapati Tripathi was replaced by the more dynamic Hemvati Nandan Bahuguna, but to no avail. In fact, Bahuguna's penchant for building his own independent centre of power brought him into direct confrontation with the mother-son duo. Bahuguna used his clout to get party nominee and big time industrialist K.K. Birla defeated in the ensuing Rajya Sabha polls. Indira Gandhi never forgave him for that direct affront.

Meanwhile the Bihar movement was getting intensified by the day. While JP insisted that his struggle was for cleansing the system rather than capturing political power, Indira Gandhi took it as a direct onslaught against her. She tried to discredit JP in public by accusing him of being on the payroll of industrial houses. Not many were convinced by this facile charge against someone who had consistently defied the lure of office for a given set of values. JPs call to the armed forces and the state apparatus not to carry out anti-people measures of the government was seen as open rebellion by Indira Gandhi and her advisers.

The issue was discussed at a brainstorming session in Narora. Winter was fast approaching the northern plains. Another kind of chill awaited Indira and her brand of politics. Amid a cacophony of praise for the great leader, AK Anthony from Kerala stood up to quietly suggest:"The situation is very bleak for the party because the trail of corruption had reached the doorsteps of even the Prime Minister's office." Anthony's statement was resented but he was unrepentant. He rejected suggestions that he should apologise. He felt that he was only performing his duty by telling the leadership about the perceptions of the people at the ground level. The disquiet within a section of the Congress created additional pressure on an already embattled leader. In desperation to correct the political situation and win back her popularity, Indira Gandhi had even carried out nuclear tests at Pokharan in May 1974. The operation Buddha was described as a nuclear fusion and experiment for the peaceful use of the nuclear energy. If she had hoped that when Buddha smiled (Code to describe the success of the tests) people also would smile, she was in for disappointment for it did not impress people though her party men were elated at the display of the strength of the government Only three years earlier, the masses had placed her at the pinnacle of power and made her into a charismatic leader. But her failure or reluctance to deliver the electoral promises had disappointed her own vote banks. She had created a situation due to her strong desire to secure her position. She was left without any honest and sincere people around her. Her isolation from reality was complete. She stood out as some kind of a heavily depreciated product. By removing anyone with substance from her proximity, Indira Gandhi was unwittingly hastening her own downfall. She resorted to cheap tactics to regain popularity, even when she was sitting on a powder keg herself. The final blow was delivered in six months. But it came from the most unexpected quarters. She was never to forget June 12 1975.

6

Turning Point

"Mourn not the dead...
but rather mourn the apathetic throng the cowed and meek
who see the world's great anguish and its wrong
and dare not speak..."

Indira Gandhi's favorite lines, which she often recalled, in moments of rare reflection

June 12, 1975. That Thursday would remain a day enshrined in collective memory. A day that dawned as a nightmare for Indira Gandhi and the Congress. Three different events of contrasting velocity had shaken the phlegmatism out of the iron lady. Two of them were to become the precursors to the stifling of democracy. First, Indira Gandhi was unseated, as the Allahabad High Court found her election to the Lok Sabha from Raebareli constituency null and void on several counts. The second blow was delivered by the failure of the Indian National Congress to defeat the Jan Morcha and win a clear mandate in its favour in the Gujarat assembly polls. The third event, in distant Moscow, was the death of Union minister D.P. Dhar, a close associate of Indira Gandhi, that very morning.

The world had suddenly come tumbling apart for Indira Gandhi. Morally she was bound to resign and go in appeal to the Supreme Court against the single judge verdict which unseated her from the Lok Sabha. The Congress as a party was stunned as it awaited the reaction from Indira Gandhi. There was just one lone voice, which counselled that she should resign on moral grounds. That voice was of Chandra Shekhar. No one echoed his sentiments. Other sentiments. Other leaders and workers waited for her to react first before they gave their own views. No senior leader was willing to comment nor was willing to go to her residence. Only the closest of the close advisers rushed to evolve strategies so that she could remain in her office and face the situation.

What transpired during these huddled confabulations resulted in one central response: Come what may, Indira Gandhi had decided to cling to her office even after the high court verdict. That she should continue irrespective of whatever compunctions saw her adherents and supporters begin mobilizing around their besieged leader. A new kind of politics was introduced from that day onwards. The street became the battlefield for Indira Gandhi to wriggle out of the tight moral and political pigeonhole. Vox Populi was used as a weapon to consolidate support for her. This ploy was the best available option in the circumstances.

The other stunning event were the drastic results of the Gujarat assembly polls completed the previous day and the final count had shown that the Congress was in no position to form a government in the state. The Jan Morcha, a combination of the various parties, had also failed to get a clear mandate. The man who held the key to the immediate permutations and combinations was former chief minister Chimanbhai Patel, who by then had formed his own party after being expelled from the Indian National Congress in March 1974. His outfit fought the assembly elections on its own steam. He won a crucial 13 seats in the state assembly of 182 members, which could prove decisive. Indira Gandhi had campaigned intensely and fiercely as never before. At least not for any state assembly election had she laboured so hard .She, after all, had a point to prove to Chimanbhai who had shown nerve to challenge her authority in the party. It was important for her to win a clear mandate for the party in the state.

She had to accomplish several political points in one go. For one, she had to establish her authority as the Prime Minister, not in doubt as such but certainly being threatened by a thin cloud, by showing the world that she was still in total command of the political situation. But the fact of a popular setback in Gujarat was disastrous for her. The timing was particularly so. She was now looking at the consequences of actions that spelt out a personal and moral dilemma besides terminating her membership of the Lok Sabha. The fact that there was growing popular resentment as implied in the electoral verdict came as a severe body blow. It was all the more significant because Gujarat had a fourteen per cent tribal population and another seven per cent comprised the Dalit vote. The Dalits were considered to form one of the traditional strongholds of Indira Gandhi and her party.

Events were moving fast. For the first time her younger son Sanjay Gandhi who till then had been perceived as the overzealous accelerator to manufacture a "people's car", a type of "Volkswagen." appeared on the political lawns of Indira Gandhi to provide her protection against the onslaught that was launched against her political career. Who could have visualized that this rather abrasive and unsmiling man was to play such a crucial role in coming years? He made it abundantly clear that he was against his mother resigning and going in appeal. She would remain in office and seek a fresh verdict from the apex court. Indira Gandhi considered a judicial bailout as the other option- the first of course being popular support for her, which she had taken for granted.

It was obvious that any one who replaced her while she was engaged in the legal battle would not be willing to quit and make a way for her to take over if she won a reprieve; basic logic dictated that the replacement would strive to consolidate in the interregnum. The family, as a kind of a congenital problem, could not bring itself round to trusting any one in the party to keep her seat warm and hand it over when she demanded. Soon enough, considerations of morality lost to the expediency of politics.

The coterie around Indira Gandhi began to assess the attitude of other senior party leaders to find out who among them could stake a claim to replace Indira Gandhi. The other need was to mobilise public support for her continuation in office. Third, it needed to be assessed how much damage the opposition could and would inflict and what strategy the opposition would adopt to use the morality factor to make her quit office. It was a difficult proposition. Answers had to be found immediately, lest others joined the chorus for her resignation.

At this stage, everyone was closely following the moves and body language of Jagjivan Ram for not only was he the senior-most; he was, at the same time, an astute politician, cunning to the core and hugely ambitious by nature. The expectation was that he would engineer a process, which would build pressure for the resignation of Indira Gandhi. The court verdict came as a godsend. Further, he was the only possible political adversary within who could challenge her and also succeed in his game. Two days later, an agency reported that Jagjivan Ram was preparing to challenge Indira Gandhi.

As soon as the report began doing the rounds, Indira Gandhi dispatched Swaran Singh to persuade Jagjivan Ram to desist from any such move. After an hour when no message came from Swaran Singh, she sent her closer confidante Uma Shankar Dikshit to see what was cooking. She had come to a stage where she could not trust anyone and suspect all. An hour later, she herself drove down to the residence of Jagjivan Ram to strike a deal with him in case she was compelled to resign. A deal was indeed struck, but its details were, predictably, kept a closely guarded secret.

That it was a deal became apparent when Jagjivan Ram attended a meeting of Congress Members of Parliament at the AICC office and urged them to remain united in the hour of the party's worst political crisis. He had scrupulously avoided making a direct statement, which said that Indira Gandhi should continue and would continue in office, despite the moral obligation to resign after the court verdict. An unprecedented crisis need not require a predictable response. Adroitly, Jagjivan Ram continued to talk about the party and its future. Other senior leaders were also made to address the meeting and express solidarity with the leader, but they were hardly as subtle or clever.

On June 20, along the lush Boat Club lawns of Rajpath, Indira Gandhi and other senior leaders were to address people who had been ferried in trucks and buses not just from Delhi but also from the neighboring states of Haryana, Uttar Pradesh, Rajasthan and Madhya Pradesh. Messages were flashed even to other states to send maximum crowds to display the extent of mass support that existed for the flummoxed but determined leader.

Sanjay Gandhi who had undertaken the organizational and logistic responsibilities to leave no stone unturned also wanted that her public address must be relayed live on All India Radio and also on the government owned television Door Darshan. However information minister Inder Gujral put his foot down and refused to allow the government own media to be used for a rally that was essentially a party affair. It would have been blatant misuse of the government media, Gujral told Sanjay Gandhi in so many words. This show of principled autonomy cost Inder Gujral heavily.

For the record, it was the first time that such a huge crowd had been assembled on the lawns of the Boat Club, which from hereon became an akhara for many to show their political and organizational muscle.

On June 24, Congress members were asked to assemble in the Central Hall of Parliament. Even media persons were allowed free entry because the Congress managers wanted the media to see for themselves how unfazed and confident of her continued popularity was Mrs. Gandhi. It was here that the then Congress president Dev Kant Barooah made his now (in) famous statement: "Indira is India and India is Indira." The entire nation was equated with one person. It was quite simply the height of sycophancy. Not to be left behind, even the seasoned Yashwantrao Chavan chipped in with his pearls of wisdom. Paraphrasing Barooah, he added to the cacophony of endorsement thus: "What happens to India happens to Indira, and what happens to Indira happens to India." The senior leaders had swallowed all their self-respect in order to save themselves from a probable, perhaps inevitable, chopping block that would otherwise have awaited them. Jagjivan Ram also addressed the meeting but mercifully and to his credit, did not indulge in such fancy statements. He was relatively somber and reflective in his tone as he asked party men to stand united with Indira Gandhi and face the crisis that had been thrust upon the party and the leader.

The scenario had a diametrically different hue elsewhere. The Opposition parties were united in their demand for resignation of Indira Gandhi on moral grounds. They had a dharna outside the outer iron gate of the Rashtrapati Bhavan. This demonstration could be seen from the rear window of the Prime Minister's office in South Block. After three days dharna, they assembled in force at the Young Men's' Christian Association Hall to chalk out their strategy to force Indira Gandhi to step down. 139 men of all parties barring the Marxists and the Communists had attended the meeting where fiery speeches were delivered but no strategy was evolved. But their determination to confront the Congress with the moral and ethical issues was evident. The battle lines had been sharply drawn.

In a famous judgment Justice VK Krishna Iyer of the Supreme Court had given a conditional stay to Indira Gandhi on the Allahabad High Court judgment in the noon of June 25 and thus had cleared her path to stay in office. Later in the night SS Ray, DK Barooah and Rajani Patel were huddled together at the residence of Indira Gandhi when the law enforcement machinery swung into action. The dreaded "midnight knocks" at the residences and offices of the opposition leaders in Delhi and outside as well commenced. It was a well-planned and meticulously executed operation. Jai Prakash Narayan was taken to the Parliament street police station from the Gandhi Pratishthan. Chandra Shekhar also rushed to the police station after he had received the information to ensure that JP was comfortable. When he was turning to go away after JP was taken away in the police jeep, the SHO told him that there was warrant of his arrest as well*.

---

* ("In the evening of June 25, I went to Gujarat Bhawan to meet Chimanbhai Patel who had come to Delhi on his way to Varanasi. It was impossible not to notice the unusually high movement of police jeeps. Intuitively, it struck me a precursor to that Indira Gandhi had planned some move to stifle the opposition. I requested the phone operator to inform me if there was anything happening, as Charan Singh was staying at the UP Niwas that was close to the Gujarat Bhavan. After midnight, he rang up to say that the police had come to the U.P. Niwas in three jeeps. I immediately rushed to UP Niwas to see Charan Singh being taken away in the police jeep. The officer in charge casually asked me since he knew me well: "What are you doing here? You better go to the Parliament Street police station. I rushed and saw J P sitting in the police jeep and Chandra Shekhar standing by. After J P was removed, Chandra Shekhar

Indira Gandhi had summoned her Cabinet before midnight and obtained its endorsement for declaring an Internal Emergency. In her opinion, the Opposition had created such conditions that it was impossible to run the government without recourse to extraordinary measures. JP's call to the armed forces and the police were cited among the reasons for the creation of chaotic conditions in the country. She also pointed out that the Gujarat and the Bihar movements had led to political confusion and discontent in the country. Hence she wanted drastic actions to control the situation before it slipped out of her hands. The Cabinet but had to endorse her proposal. No one had protested, or asked her what she had in mind while she imposed the Emergency.

The Emergency was in fact the sum of her desperate response to the moral and constitutional crisis that she herself had created. It was a traumatic moment, but also, for us journalists who had cared, a special, political wild night in pursuit of The Great Story.

(Footnote contd.)

began to walk towards his car when the station house officer stopped him and said: "Sir, there is a warrant for your arrest also but you better speak to the PMO first. Chandra Shekhar rang up the PMO and after listening to what was said over the phone, he virtually banged down put down the receiver and asked the SHO whether he would be taken directly from there or via his residence?

I rushed to inform Piloo Mody. It was around 2.45 am. By then, he was also ready, baggage and all, to move to the police jeep. He told me that Morarji had also been arrested. By then I had alerted my office in Ahmedabad and told the Editor as to what was happening in Delhi. He could not believe me but got the staff assembled to bring out the 'Extra' immediately. I had also established contact with Arun Kumar of UNI relaying to him the story of what was happening. He had got his Editor VP Ramachandran awakened and got him to rush to the office. By four o clock I had got 39 names of the persons who were arrested from various locations in the capital and fed to my office over the phone. I phoned home, where my wife Meeta was there to convey the message to my Ahmedabad office. By seven in the morning, our 'Extra' was out—". V.S.)

At 8.15 am on June 26, Indira Gandhi addressed the nation on All India Radio to rationalize her action. She cryptically informed that Emergency had just been declared. But she had launched the operation for suppressing the democracy eight hours before her radio talk. The operation was completed in five hours with most opposition leaders in Delhi and outside already in police hands and lodged in various jails across the country. The police slipped on only one person: George Fernandes, who flew to Bhubaneshwar that morning being unaware himself what, had happened during the night. She also imposed media censorship at the same time making it necessary for all media reports to be vetted by the censor officers. More enthusiastic officers put up proposals for arrest of media persons whom they thought were, or could potentially be troublemakers and engage in mischief against the government.

The imposition of Emergency had, to be polite, shocked the nation out of its wits. It created a fear psychosis, which inversely propelled a modicum of ordinary efficiency in a bureaucracy hitherto completely ill-equipped to handle routine functions as routine. Much was made of crisper timings in offices; lesser man-hours whiled away in the alleys and lawns during interminable break periods. But that was only out of fear rather than for any considerations of efficiency or some newly found commitment to work. The ordinary and much reviled 'babus' could scarcely dream of having adverse remarks in their Confidential Reports.

Countrywide, the response to the Emergency varied from region to region. It was utilised in the southern states and also in upwardly inclined Gujarat and Maharashtra to improve day-to-day administration. But in the north, the Emergency provided an opportunity to settle old scores. The improvements in the administration, and in the newly gained discipline lasted only six months. Then reports began pouring in of excesses in many fields. The Emergency period also proved beyond doubt the efficacy of verbal communication in contrast to cold print. Any untoward incident happening anywhere managed to reach the people, without the powerful Fourth Estate, now reduced to a mere cipher, could even go through the motions of telling facts as they were. Censorship had not completely succeeded in keeping people in the dark about the real story behind the façade. The presence of clipped but still active foreign media was of help: Everybody relied on the word of the BBC, leaders in detention and outside, included.

Those who have generally rightly credited Indira Gandhi with possessing extraordinary political acumen are even to the day wondering why did she respond the way she did. Why did she resort to state terrorism to face the self-imposed moral, political and constitutional crisis? Acres of precious newsprint have been spent on answering this yet unanswered question. Why was it that a seemingly buoyant and upbeat democratic superstructure was so hollow at its base?

There were several straws in the wind and ideas too were floating at large. Shashi Bhushan, then an active, intellectually-inclined politician, was at the same time a proponent of "guided" democracy. Vasant Sathe even to this day misses no opportunity to project the Presidential form of the government as a solution to all the problems that face the country. The Emergency provided an opportunity to most Congressmen to rethink over the Constitution of India. But even this was a half-baked, sterile exercise of servile minds. A committee was formed with union minister Swaran Singh (a highly respected individual, but more often than not, one who was too diplomatic in times of crises) as its head to rework the Indian Constitution to suit the Congress needs. Rajani Patel was the leading light who insisted on reviewing the Constitution so that the Congress could remain in power forever. Seventeen Congress leaders burnt midnight oil to rework the statute books.

The main person who wanted the change to enable Indira Gandhi become President of India for life was the then defence minister Bansi Lal. With the approval of Sanjay Gandhi he got three state assemblies to adopt resolutions seeking the review of the constitution. Indira Gandhi was annoyed at the move that was initiated without her prior approval. She was keeping Bansi Lal at an arms length; simply, he had begun to irritate her. She had even confirmed her dislike for Bansi Lal to her Principal Secretary Prof P.N. Dhar, who was working hard on her to go in for elections that she had put off second time in December 1976 by extending the term of the Lok Sabha till February 1978.

When finally the document purported to be the new constitution was ready, Bansi Lal who had by now become the close crony of Sanjay Gandhi was assigned the task of obtaining the clearance from Indira Gandhi for formalizing the document. All excited, on a day she was about to move out of her house in a car to attend a function; a breathless Bansi Lal approached her and told her that new document was ready. When can the Constitution Assembly be convened, he asked. Indira Gandhi did not even turn in his direction, and said: " What is wrong with the existing constitution?" She then drove-off, leaving Bansi Lal dumbfounded. All the effort of the servile set to ensure the Nehru-Gandhi family Raj in the country forever had come to nothing. Such contradictory indications from her responses to different questions made it difficult to discern why did she have to impose the Emergency in the first place?

She knew for a long time that her unwillingness to deliver on the promises she had made in 1971 had disenchanted the masses. She had been presenting all conceivable excuses for non-delivery. First she blamed the old guards in the party who were opposed to change and insisted on maintaining the status quo. The masses gave her a clean sweep and massive mandate by getting rid of the old guard. She subsequently blamed the judiciary. People accepted that too—even when she superseded three senior judges in the Supreme Court to appoint A.N. Ray as the Chief Justice of India. She then blamed the bureaucracy and the masses accepted whatever changes she had affected. When no further excuses were at hand, she blamed the Central Intelligence Agency (CIA) for the myriad problems troubles and ills afflicting her 'socialist' India. The people were willing to even bite that bit, but they could not fathom why she failed to deliver even after the masses had accepted every alibi of hers for inaction.

At the level of the Congress, the Emergency saw the marginalisation of seniors like Jagjivan Ram and Yashwantrao Chavan. If they had any conscience, they cleverly kept it hidden from sight. Mrs. Gandhi had put up Jagjivan Ram as a front to legitimize the Emergency proclamation for approval. He faced the Lok Sabha, while Chavan was made to defend it in the Rajya Sabha. Dev Kant Barooah apparently remained a trusted lieutenant, but there was an element of speculation about the longevity of this trust. Sure enough, he suddenly went out of the immediate picture-frame. Indira Gandhi decided to replace him also and install PV Narasimha Rao as the party chief at the Chandigarh Session that was held in December 1975. It was the first Session of the Congress during the Emergency. Every thing was decided before hand and Narasimha Rao had even prepared his presidential address that was printed and kept in readiness by the AICC for distribution. However at the last minute she changed her mind and got Barooah re-elected as the Party chief at Chandigarh. The election was completed in a matter of two minutes. Narasimha Rao was made to propose the name and Yashwantrao Chavan was made to second the proposal.

The assembly waited for a minute if any one wanted to propose any other name. When no one got up, and no one could have dared to get up to propose another name, Barooah was declared elected. Sanjay Gandhi who appeared for the first time on the stage of the Congress Party at Chandigarh had played a vital role in forcing the change and in retaining Barooah as the party chief. Obviously Bansi Lal, who had become a close friend of Barooah, had influenced the mind of Sanjay Gandhi.

Sanjay Gandhi had for all purposes become the heir apparent to Indira Gandhi and had a free run not only of the party but also of the government. But he became the undisputed leader of the Youth Congress at the Guwahati session of the Congress in December 1976. In fact he was now donning the clothes of the Congress president who had virtually become a marginalised office holder. He had announced his five-point programme which the party and the state governments were expected to implement vigorously. While adult literacy and environment protection were important vital issues that he had covered in his five point programme, the programme received a bad name only because of the overzealous officials who wanted to earn his favours by implementing the family planning part of the programme.

There were reports of forcible sterilizations in different parts of Uttar Pradesh and Haryana by the local administration. There were few cases of forcible sterilisations in Delhi also but largely fears were imaginary and whispered campaign those to malign the programme. The family planning programme received such a setback largely due to the whispering campaign launched during the Emergency. It had to be hastily abandoned completely by successive governments, with the nomenclature "family-welfare" becoming more acceptable.

In swift moves directed inwards, Indira Gandhi ensured the installation of the state government in Gujarat with Madhavsinh Solanki heading the state government. The Babubhai Patel government was earlier dismissed on the pretext of irregularities in the Panchayat elections that the Congress had lost. But she had also set the stage for the elections when she announced the conference of the agriculture ministers of states to discuss the land reforms in January 1977. It was a first indication that she had planned a major political move though most of her colleagues could not read her mind or the fact that even though she had extended the term of the Lok Sabha till February 1978, she still had powers to dissolve the Lok Sabha on any given day.

The agriculture ministers' conference was held on January 18 1977. The same day, she dissolved the Lok Sabha and set the election schedule for March 1977 even while retaining the emergency but relaxing the Censorship rigours that had affected the media coverage. But before she set the election schedule, she made overtures to win over Chandra Shekhar to her side. Emissaries were sent to Chandra Shekhar to rejoin the Indira Gandhi camp even while keeping him under detention in the Rouse Avenue House with Mohan Dharia in the next bungalow but with a partition between the two bungalows so that they could not converse freely. Morarji Desai who was also kept in a solitary confinement for 17 months or so was released only after she had announced elections. His detention was the longest among all leaders because he refused to entertain any talk of appeal.

By January 25, she had begun receiving reports that H.N. Bahuguna was feeling restive and uneasy after he had been removed as Uttar Pradesh chief minister, and replaced by a more pliant substitute in Narayan Dutt Tiwari. She invited Bahuguna to New Delhi but kept him waiting for six days. It did cost her heavily because a fuming and frustrated Bahuguna contacted Jagjivan Ram and the two of them planned a coup against Indira Gandhi and her party. But their plans remained a closely guarded secret, even though Jagjivan Ram was under constant watch during the entire period of the Emergency. The waiting constables from the Crime Branch accosted many visiting media persons at his residence to know what was happening inside. Jagjivan Ram quipped once when he was told that there was a close watch on his residence, "If constables were to provide inputs of political analysis to the Prime Minister, then she deserves to be doomed."

As soon as the election schedule was announced, the Opposition parties put their heads together and decided to oppose the Congress on one to one basis in each constituency in the elections. The Socialists were dead-set against participating in the elections. But they were persuaded once the four parties decided to merge to form a new party, Janata Party. The new party came into being on January 30 1977. Two days later Jagjivan Ram and Bahuguna announced formation of the Congress For Democracy. The surprise of the day was the presence of Nandini Satpathy on the lawns of the residence of Jagjivan Ram when he announced the formation of his new party. Nandini Satpathy, a communist fellow traveller, was a close associate of Indira Gandhi and was known to be an ardent supporter. Yet she had decided to rebel against Indira Gandhi.

In the formation of the CFD, Indira Gandhi's internal calculations went all awry. It signaled the possibility of crystallized internal rebellion within the confines of the party organization. Indira Gandhi understood the meaning of this, even as her myopic supporters spewed venom against Jagjivan Ram and associates as being betrayers of the Indian National Congress. But the shindig was to no real avail. Concrete steps to repair the political damage caused were not forthcoming. The CFD and the Janata party had arrived at an electoral arrangement, even though it was not easy for Charan Singh to accept the fact given his antipathy to Jagjivan Ram which was to assume more serious dimensions later. But that is another story.

(For the record, Charan Singh's logic was that the CFD members had enjoyed power during the emergency while others languished in prison. Hence, the reasoning went, the CFD could not be given the same benefits as the others).

> After a period of deceptive lull in the Congress but buoyancy in the rest of the political class, things were moving towards a befitting climax. A public rally was organized on February 6 1977 at the Ramlila Grounds to be addressed by JP and Morarji Desai. Jagjivan Ram also came to attend the rally. The massive turn out was one indication of the anger felt by the people at the Emergency period and the Congress. The Congress managers had spared no efforts to frustrate the rally. Police stopped trucks and buses that were coming from the neighbouring states. To prevent the people from reaching the venue, a special telecast of the blockbuster 'Bobby' was organized to keep people glued to television inside their homes. In other words, all attempts were made to thwart people from attending the rally, which however turned out be an overwhelming success. Spontaneous liberal donations followed once it was made clear that the new party had no funds to fight elections. The fervour for change was there for all to see*.

Once the election run-up began, the media went out of its way to mirror popular perceptions. This was so even when the Emergency was still formally in force. Surendra Mohan, a socialist who was not fighting the Lok Sabha election became the spokesperson for the Janata party; the hall was always packed with newsmen who hung on to each word spoken. In contrast, for

---

* ("As I was standing behind the stage at the rally venue, a person approached me and handed over a packet wrapped in a newspaper. I did not know him but he apparently knew me as the media person. He requested me to hand over the packet to Morarji Desai. The wrapper contained Rs. 20,000. An unknown person had donated such a large sum and yet was reluctant to give his name. Morarjibhai was amazed when I handed him over the sum and told how it had come to me."—V.S.)

A.R. Antulay and Poorbi Mukherji, the two general secretaries who handled the Congress briefings, a tepid response that greeted them. All the snacks and assortments meant for the media at the AICC briefings did not seduce media-persons, now prepared to settle down for not even a cup of tea because the politics of the moment had made everything else secondary.

There was a belated realization in the Congress camp that they were up against it. " Why do people tell me lies?" Indira Gandhi asked a senior media person who had accompanied her on the Bihar campaign trail. Both were on their return flight to Delhi after a strenuous campaign had ended. She added, " Sitaram Kesri told me just now that we will win 48 seats out of 54 seats of Bihar. I know that we will be lucky to win even four seats in Bihar. One look at the audience tells me something else. I can read their body language while I am addressing them." These words clearly indicated that she had sensed the defeat. But did she expect the total rout that awaited the party from the entire North? Not even in her worst nightmare could she have visualized her own personal defeat in a constituency that had been nursed and nurtured with such elaborate care.

In terms of populist steps, Indira Gandhi announced a twenty-point programme in July 1975 to help the poor and downtrodden; credit was vastly liberalized. The programme was vigorously pursued for 25 months and provided benefits to thousands across the country. Her economic programme in 1970 had helped her reach the pinnacle of power. Yet a similarly radical economic programme was inimical to the same set of constituents. Had she over-reached her conclusions? Had she misread the political situation prevailing in the country when she decided to go in for the polls? Was she let down by her intelligence agencies over the possible outcome of the elections? Questions, which soon were emphatically answered.

Sushila Adivarekar, the then Rajya Sabha member who had met Indira Gandhi on Republic Day to inform her of the moves afoot among some Congressmen to defect to the other camp had found her in a disturbed mind set. The intelligence inputs added to the general discomfiture. She even summoned Om Mehta, then minister of state for home affairs to seek an elaborate explanation about the intelligence feedback.

Many Congressmen also reckoned, but conveniently only after the election results, that defections by the senior minister like Jagjivan Ram made all the difference. Even though many Indira spin-doctors termed the Jagjivan Ram's Congress For Democracy as the Congress For Defections, it was treated as a sick joke emanating from frustrated minds. The CFD had played its role as a catalyst almost to perfection.

On reflection, why did the southern States react differently to the Emergency? After all, Indira Gandhi had won just one seat in the entire north, India but bagged 150 out of 204 seats from the non-Hindi belt. Orissa, Bengal and Assam also had gone the Hindi heartland way. What had caused such a heavy erosion of the Congress vote base in the Hindi belt? Was it due to the manner in which Emergency provisions were handled in the non-Hindi belt and in the Hindi belt? Or was it due to the perceived cultural difference? Such imponderables abound in politics.

7

Lonely at the Top

"The gift of loneliness is sometimes a radical vision of society or one's own people that has previously been not taken into account."
—Alice Walker, American author and critic

After the electoral debacle, Indira Gandhi was not only a dejected and dispirited person but also a lonely one. Most leaders who were in close proximity deserted her for the fear that they might invite action by the new government. Others who were annoyed by the ham-handed functioning of Sanjay Gandhi left her in isolation to nurse her political wounds. The perplexed rank and file was still too bewildered to decipher what made her go for elections, even after the second extension of the term of Lok Sabha? Even those who had functioned as cronies of Sanjay Gandhi and had virtually driven the party for the new constitution so as to perpetuate the Gandhi Raj in the country were surprised by her sudden decision to dissolve Lok Sabha on January 18 1977 and declare elections.

They came to know only later that her Principal Secretary PN Dhar was working on her conscience for months so that she should go in for elections. He had told her that the first extension of the term of Lok Sabha could be, and indeed was, justified on the grounds that the government needed sufficient time to implement the programme that she had announced in July 1975. But the second extension could not be justified in any way. In fact it would also remove the justification for imposing Emergency. Probably Indira Gandhi was convinced that her move of extending the term of the Lok Sabha for the second time would send wrong signals, particularly to her interlocutors abroad.

Maybe, she also wanted to go back to the people and establish her popularity and magic once again as she had done in 1971. Vijay Lakshmi Pandit, her aunt and sister of Jawahar Lal Nehru once described her as the only man in her cabinet. She was no ordinary person. She was a great leader who possessed abundant common sense and natural ability to quickly assess individuals and circumstances. She was courageous and determined person. Yet she failed to properly assess the consequence of her action, her response to the moral and constitutional crisis that she was confronted with by the Court verdict that had unseated her.

Along with those who had a bitter experience of the emergency period also asked why did she impose emergency in first place by allowing herself to be dragged by Sanjay Gandhi and his cronies on that disastrous course of action? It has been argued again and again by the ardent supporters of Indira Gandhi that the Emergency was incorrectly viewed from the wrong end of the telescope. The emergency was evaluated on the basis of its consequences rather than why it was imposed in the first place.

In a nutshell, the country was passing through an economic ordeal due to various factors. The 1971 war had cost heavily so also the drought of two years when the food production had come down by 8 per cent creating difficulties in maintaining supplies through the fair price shops. The USA and UK had imposed sanctions on economic aid in the wake of war with Pakistan. The fourfold hike in oil prices had imposed an additional burden of a billion dollars.

The twenty-day Rail strike had disrupted the supply lines. Even though the government successfully broke the strike, its impact and ill effects had spilled over the next year. Instead of understanding her difficulties, the Opposition was bent upon destabilizing her government through various agitations that had plagued the political scene in the country. In that came the electoral disaster in Gujarat and the Court verdict that had encouraged the

Opposition to go for her jugular vein. She was like a tigress cornered from all sides. Inevitably, she would have sparred at the first opportunity to repay her opponents in kind. It was also understood that the administration would misuse the draconian powers that were given it through the emergency laws. But that was inevitable consequence of the political response.

The blame for the electoral disaster was being ascribed to her alone. Not only her party colleagues, but even son Rajiv Gandhi felt that the Sanjay-Dhawan machinations had been responsible for undoing her. The fact that trusted cronies of yesterday like Dev Kant Barooah deserted her. She had dispatched Hari Kishen Shastri, young secretary of the Congress party to bring Barooah directly to her residence from the airport when he landed at the airport coming from Guwahati on March 22. Shastri conveyed the message that she wanted to see Barooah immediately. Instead of driving to the residence of Indira Gandhi, Barooah asked driver to take the car to Rashtrapati Bhavan. He was immediately given the audience by the then Vice President BD Jatti who was acting as the President since the untimely and sudden death of the President Fakhruddin Ali Ahmed on February 11 1977. In the presence of Hari Kishen Shastri, Barooah told Jatti categorically: "If Indira Gandhi were to ask you to negate the verdict or revoke the elections, you should refuse to act on it." Barooah knew Indira Gandhi and her nature thoroughly since he had worked in close association with her for more than four years.

Only after the meeting with the Vice President did Barooah go to the residence of Indira Gandhi and told her what he had done. Indira Gandhi was furious but she also knew that she had finally lost the game and the election because even her party would not support any such move. Whether she would have made such a move or not would always remain debatable since she had not made any formal move in that direction. But she was desperate to wriggle out of the tight corner was evident from the delay in revoking the emergency proclamation for two days after the verdict was crystal clear leaving no scope or space for any doubt. Many had wondered why she had delayed the cabinet meeting for revoking the proclamation by two days. In the circumstances, it was expected of the loser to immediately concede the defeat and take necessary steps for the transfer of power.

Rumours were floating in the capital that the Janata government would move against her and set up inquiries in the excesses committed by her government. She expected that to happen for she had known the personal hatred some of the Janata party men had for her. She was more afraid of some thing worse happening to her son Sanjay Gandhi to who had earned enough notoriety by his cruel and hot-tempered actions for implementing some of his pet ideas during the emergency period.

Her immediate concern was saving the huge election fund that had remained unspent. VB Raju, then general secretary had summoned the manager of the Andhra Bank, New Delhi Branch requesting him to keep the cash with the bank but without entering into the bank records. The manager expressed his inability to do so. Ultimately the huge cash was deposited at the residence of the MP from Andhra who was also a Minister of State in the Indira Gandhi Council of Ministers. He was told to join the Janata Party same evening. It was to protect cash that she had rushed her junior to join the Janata Party. His rush to immediately defect even before the Morarji Desai government was in saddle had surprised many because the member was considered to be very loyal to Indira Gandhi. Or there was no mystery for Morarji Desai and his advisers. For they demonetized the thousand rupee notes without attributing the convincing reason for the step. What was the loss of the Congress party in terms of funds due to the demonetized currency would remain shrouded in the clouds of mystery. Obviously no one can expect those who were in charge of keeping funds to come forward to lament on their loss.

The next worry concerned residential shift. The Shipping Magnate of Mumbai Sumati Morarji had rented a five bed room accommodation for her in Vasant Vihar, just in case, the government refused to provide her with an alternative residence as former Prime Minister. Morarji Desai was reluctant to provide the accommodation, as it did not come under the existing rules. Finally Morarji relented under the pressure from Chandra Shekhar who had met Indira Gandhi after the elections on her invitation. She wanted to call on him but he said that he would visit her at her residence and went. When she pointed out her difficulties, Chandra Shekhar immediately assured her that he would take responsibility of providing her the alternative government accommodation and 12 Willington Crescent, was allotted to her.

In the first week after she had handed over the charge, there were only a smattering of visitors, who were at a loss to find the words to console her. Her isolation was clearly reflected in the fact that Dev Kant Barooah had not sent her an invitation to attend the first Working Committee meeting that was convened on April 2 1977 to assess the political situation in the wake of the electoral debacle and drubbing that the party had received. Most leaders were furious that no invitation was extended to the former Prime Minister by the AICC. Yashwantrao Chavan and K Brahmananda Reddy were sent to her residence to escort her with due respect to the AICC office to attend the Working Committee meeting. The rest of the crowd sat glum faced and silent awaiting her arrival for nearly an hour while media persons waited impatiently outside. No slogans were raised when she arrived. Barooah announced his resignation and Swaran Singh took over and presided over the meeting. Indira Gandhi did not utter a word while others dwelt in brief on causes of defeat and finally resolution was adopted accepting the verdict without apportioning blame to anyone or any cause. She had remained a passive but stoic observer to the proceedings with a grim face. Two leaders had escorted her with honour to the meeting venue at the AICC headquarters but she went back alone in a car that was driven by a family friend. Some leaders occasionally visited her but normally most avoided.

There was no immediate indication that she would activate herself in the political arena. There were few public appearances. She knew that she would have to face a lot of trouble, as there were few vindictive individuals in the Janata Party who commanded positions of influence. After the Janata party government dismissed, immediately after its take over, Congress governments in nine states on the plea that they had lost the mandate to continue in the office, her difficulties increased manifold. The Morarji Desai government decided to appoint the Shah Inquiry Commission to go into several instances of irregularities that were committed. Her sources of information had also dried up though few media persons who had known her before her rise as the supreme leader in 1971 kept visiting her and spend some time to comfort her that all was not lost. At one such meeting, a question was put to her: "Why did you decide to go in for polls at this time when the term of the Lok Sabha had been extended till March 1978? Why did you not use the year to consolidate your position?"

With a smile she answered: "Do you think I am less democratic only because I resorted to the Emergency?" This answer was in contrast to what Hari Shastri had narrated a few years later about the encounter between Barooah and her on March 22 1977. But there are other indicators that firmed up the belief that the Emergency was a regrettable aberration in her book. Her essential impulses were broadly democratic. It will remain a moot point battles she had to fight with Sanjay Gandhi once she decided to go in for the polls. It would never be known since both the main characters have now faded into oblivion but there was no doubt that there would have been several confrontations between the mother and the son on this score before and after the 1977 elections, particularly because of the drubbing that the Congress party and Indira Gandhi had personally received.

She did not venture to campaign for the Congress party in the state assembly elections for the fear that her presence might arouse animosities and affect the prospects of the Congress candidates. Actually no Pradesh Congress had asked her to come to the state for campaign for the party. It must have been a killing realization, as she must have tossed in her bed every night that the person who had led the party from victory to victory was not wanted by the party men now that she had the first rout in the election. The state election results went on predictable lines. The Congress was humbled in most states and had to depend on other parties for retaining its government in Maharashtra.

Destiny provided an opportunity to resume her activist profile. A large number of Dalits were burnt alive in Belchhi village of Bihar on May 29 1977. She toyed with the idea of launching herself in the active politics with a visit to Belchhi but was unsure. She was also told that the Monsoon would not allow a free movement to reach the village as roads become inaccessible during rains. Sitaram Kesri suggested that he would arrange for elephants for her to ride to the village as Mahatma Gandhi had done to reach villages in Champaran district of Bihar decades earlier.

She promptly prepared to re-launch herself on the comeback trail to the corridors of power. It was the most important impulsive decision of her life. There was no looking back then onwards on her dramatic return journey to the corridors of power. She had accepted the challenge of the political struggle that lay ahead of her though she did not know how many years she would have to fight her political battle. It would depend only on whether or not the anti Congress movement would transit into formation of the Janata party as a political apparatus. She was not sure how long the Janata party government would last. But she was mentally prepared for a long drawn fight after she visited Belachi and drew applause all over the country.

Sanat Mehta, a senior party leader from Gujarat who had come in September 1977 to organize her visit to Gujarat in the first week of October narrated one incident to her that cheered her up immensely. He told her that the incident took place in a bus journey between Surat and Vyara in southern Gujarat. A Bania-trader needled an Adivasi youth from a tribal village in Vyara Taluka, occupying the seat next to him with a comment, "Tari Maa to hari gayee, have shu karish tu? (Your mother is defeated. What would you do now?) When he repeated the comment third time, the Adivasi soundly slapped the trader and told him, "Maari maa bhale hari gayee pan mane hath aapi gayi chhe." (My mother may have been defeated but she has given me power of hands) This was a clear indication that her vote bank among the downtrodden was not completely lost.

She repeatedly asked him, "Sanatbhai, is it true or you are making up only to cheer me up?" Mehta assured her that he was reporting a real incident. Encouraged, she readily agreed to visit Gujarat via Mumbai on October 5. This was to be her first visit on invitation of a state leader who had come specially for extending it. She saw it as a happy sign for a comeback route.

But before this happened, several other things had happened as well. There was her first visit to Parliament's Central Hall in end-July during the course of the Monsoon Session. It was a royal entry into the Central Hall at noon. The entire parliament staff had lined up and crowded the corridors. Several media persons were also present in a group in the middle of the Central Hall. She was the cynosure of all eyes. It was a majestic walk up to the seat where Kamala Pati Tripathi, leader of Opposition in Rajya Sabha was waiting for her. She spent few minutes with him and then walked up to the group of journalists. (She asked me: "Chai nahi pilayoge kya?" It was an electrifying move. Several media persons ran to get tea, coffee and sweats for serving to every one who was present in the Central Hall. She spent half an hour with the group of media persons and then walked away. But she did ask me to accompany her up to the main gate. On the way she asked why did you insist on my coming to the group. I frankly told her that these journalists were middle class. They would never cease to tell their grand children how they had tea with Indira Gandhi in the Central Hall and paid for it. "It did not matter whether you are the Prime Minister or not but you are Indira Gandhi. They will remember this fact," I told her. V.S.) The confidence of old was returning.

Earlier the Congress leaders had held the AICC Session at the Mavalankar hall where she was not invited. K Brahmnand Reddy was installed as the Party president. Her ardent supporters were disappointed but could do nothing in her absence, as there was no one to guide them with a strategy. However another event was to cement her determination for a political fight with the Janata Party and its government. In an overzealous action, Charan Singh, the then home minister had ordered her arrest on October 3 1977 from her residence. As soon as the CBI officials reached her residence at 12Willingdon Crescent, many leaders were informed who rushed to her residence. Media persons also rushed to see the drama. Only slogan that caught the fancy of all was "Dapha Charan Singh Nahi Chalega" (Article Charan Singh would not run). After considerable time and wait, she agreed to allow herself to be arrested and was taken to the jail.

As the home minister Charan Singh was addressing the media persons next morning, a message came that the District Magistrate had let her off without any conditions as he found no substance in charges pressed against her for her arrest. The crestfallen Charan Singh could not explain the gaffe either to media persons then or to the cabinet colleagues later in the day. The cabinet discussed the gaffe in details and then the Prime Minister Morarji Desai asked the law minister Shanti Bushan to sort out the problem. During their discussions over the issue, Charan Singh told Shanti Bushan that he had thought that there was a foolproof case against Indira Gandhi. To that, the law minister remarked, "Choudhary sahib, this was not a court in Chhaprauli (home town of Charan Singh). It was in New Delhi."

But she was elated by her arrest and immediate release by the District Magistrate next morning even before the Public Prosecutor could say even a word. She came back home along with a large crowd. Her elation was visible and perceptible on her face and also in her gait. She was restlessly moving all over the house. The crowd had begun to swell on her lawns as a word spread that the Court had released her unconditionally. She wanted to climb on the roof so that she could see the swelling crowd fully and address it. Few media persons had also quickly reached her residence. She was reminded that she had to go to Mumbai next day for her visit to Gujarat and she should keep her date with her visit to Gujarat as there was a big welcome awaiting her. She looked dazed for a few moments and then said, "Yes. I would keep my date with Gujarat. Do not worry. Tell your friends to wait for me." Dhiren Brahmachari brought a wooden ladder so that she could climb up. He wanted to follow her on to the roof but she prevented any one from coming up behind her. She stood on the rooftop for half an hour and savoured the crowd of supporters shouting slogans in her praise and condemning the home minister Charan Singh for his temerity to arrest her in this fashion.

After her successful visit to Belchhi and the applause she received that leaders began to flock her house with their visits and with suggestions what should be done next. It was then the suggestions came up that she should have her own party because the old leaders would not allow her to have a place among them. After her visit to Gujarat, she asked the Karnataka chief minister Devraj Urs to organize an AICC meet in Delhi, The Sapru House became the venue in the third week of October that was to lay the foundations for yet another split in the Indian National Congress at the behest of Indira Gandhi. She was determined to have her own band of loyal soldiers. Devraj Urs was allowed to be the president of the group because the Brahmanand party had refused to attend the session. She allowed Devraj Urs an upper hand because she had planned yet another coup. She was to fight the bye-election from Karnataka to come to the Lok Sabha and make her presence felt. She needed the support and full assistance of the chief minister to win the seat.

She fought the bye-election in November 1978 amidst speculative reports that she would be defeated. But she won with a handsome margin of 65000 votes. She accepted her position as an ordinary member without disturbing the arrangements that were already in place. Her presence in the House was reassuring to her ardent supporters while other leaders squirmed in displeasure that she had come to occupy a seat among them. Even the Janata party was not too happy by her presence. Hence it decided to proceed against her on the contempt of the House and expel her from the House. It was carried out in December 1978 barely a month after she had taken a seat in the House. Morarji and Chandra Shekhar were against it. Even Madhu Limaye opposed any such move. But Charan Singh and George Fernandes remained adamant on her expulsion.

The drama that followed her expulsion from the House as a member was recorded by the media in full detail, and Indira Gandhi utilized on it to the hilt. She was sentenced to seven days' imprisonment for her contempt and privilege breach. Her arrest and consequent deportation was meant to signal her supporters that that she was a persecuted politician only because she was struggling to return to her place in politics. In her mind, the breach had already taken place. The electorate of the country once punished her for whatever excesses had taken place during the emergency period. But now the Janata Party was inflicting a second punishment to her through the Inquiry Commissions and depriving her of her seat in the Lok Sabha even though she had won by fair means. She had sat through two hours in the chamber awaiting her escorts to her place of detention with broad and beaming smiles while many of her supporters had broken down and were publicly weeping for the punishment meted out to her on the basis of the contempt of the House motion. She was happy for she thought that the Janata Party had fallen in her trap. There were leaders within the Janata Party also who had thought that her expulsion would only add to her political strength but men with narrow visions were unwilling to hear the voice of sanity within the party. They prevailed to ensure that she was punished.

While the media and others were engaged in watching her dramatic exit from the Lok Sabha chamber two hours after the House was adjourned, she was keenly watching the reactions of her party men. She could clearly see that only a handful were her true followers but a majority had walked out on her while she sat through in the Chamber awaiting the warrant to be issued by the Speaker KS Hegde. It was in these two dramatic hours of December 1978 that she decided on her next moves.

She was already in command of her party since she has caused a split on January 1 1978. There was a last minute hitch because Kamala Pati Tripathi insisted that he be named as the chief of the new party. This time, she was not willing to allow anyone else holding the office but herself. She had seen what Barooah had done to her in her hour of need. She could trust no one, not even titular head of the party. She conveyed to Tripathi that she intended to be the head of the party. After some persuasion, Tripathi agreed to attend the session on the lawns of the Mavalankar hall where the first great divide of the Congress was carried out on November 22, 1969. Thus Indira Congress was born with 54 Lok Sabha members joining her new party while the rest remained with the Brahmanand Congress in the Lok Sabha with Yashwantrao Chavan as its leader and CM Stephen, an ardent follower of Indira Gandhi as the leader of the group of MPs of the Indira Congress.

The second split had virtually removed all senior leaders from the proximity to Indira Gandhi for they had preferred to remain in the other part of the party. Only those who had a full faith in the leadership of Indira Gandhi as a leader but had no base of their own remained with her. They knew that they had no separate or independent existence in the political arena. They could swim or sink only with her politics. They were willing to accept her displeasure, her kicks but were also ready to remain standing before her with the folded hands seeking favours and her blessings. They had seen her struggle against the Janata party regime and popularity she had won back after she was punished for the second time.

Indira Gandhi had also perceived the uneasy calm that had prevailed within the Janata party and the government. Three old men of the Janata Party had not been able to reconcile their differences and nor contain their ambitions. They were engaged in shadow boxing while Chandra Shekhar was playing the role of a wet nurse to keep their ambitions and their politics within tolerable limits. Raj Narayan, health minister who was closely associated with the home minister Charan Singh was the cause of trouble within the Morarji Desai government. Ultimately Morarji Desai was forced to act and he sought authority from his cabinet colleagues to sack the home minister Charan Singh. The letter seeking his resignation was dispatched to Sohna Rest House in Haryana where Charan Singh had decided to set up his camp. It was June 1978 when the crisis had erupted in the Janata Party. But the differences were patched up a month later when Charan Singh returned to the Morarji Cabinet as the Deputy Prime Minister with the finance portfolio. Jagjivan Ram was also elevated as the Deputy Prime Minister with defence department. But it was obvious to every observer that it was a temporary and uneasy patch up. Their differences and basic contradictions were not resolved because Charan Singh had not reconciled himself to the idea that he would not be able to be the Prime Minister of the Janata Party as long as Jagjivan Ram was there as the third claimant.

She evolved her strategy of causing a rift between Morarji Desai and Charan Singh because Charan Singh had more supporters in the party than Jagjivan Ram had. Only a rift between the two old men could cause a split in the party. The masterstroke was in moving resolutions in the two Houses demanding a probe into the allegation against Kanti Desai, son of Morarji Desai and against the relations of Charan Singh, especially his daughter. NKP salve moved the resolution in the Rajya Sabha and Vasant Sathe gave a notice to move similar resolution in the Lok Sabha. The parliamentary affairs minister Ravindra Verma who was considered to be close to the Prime Minister made a political blunder when he sought the debate and voting in the Rajya Sabha first where the Congress had a majority and it was inevitable that the Upper House would adopt the resolution. Verma had thought that the effect of the passage in the Rajya Sabha would be nullified once the Lok Sabha refused and rejected the resolution seeking a probe. After a great debate in the Rajya Sabha, the resolution was adopted. It was to be taken up next day in the Lower House but Vasant Sathe refused to move the resolution. The Janata party managers were bewildered at this for they had expected that he would move the resolution and the House would reject it. They had not envisaged such a refusal since it was against the political and parliamentary morality. But the Congress leadership was at the moment concerned more with causing a rift within the Janata party than in observing norms of political or parliamentary morality. The Desai government was thus compelled to appoint the Rangnath Commission.

Indira Gandhi set to work. Sanjay Gandhi had taken to street politics and had caused many side-shows including riots inside the Courts when he was arrested and produced in the courts. He was adept at such methods because earlier also he was engaged in many fracas and also many casual affairs. When Indira Gandhi had taken up the matter with him after two union ministers complained to her because their daughters had got enmeshed in his affairs, he is believed to have slapped her and walked out to live with Padmaja Naidu, daughter of the freedom fighter and close colleague of Jawahar Lal Nehru Sarojini Naidu. Even though she knew his capacities, but there was always a tension in her relationship with her younger son because he was hot tempered.

But the imposition of Emergency had changed Sanjay a bit and he had worked hard in protecting his mother and also further her political interests. He was able to establish contact with Raj Narayan who was not taken back to the Morarji cabinet when Charan Singh was re-inducted. They met at the residence of the liquo baron of India Capt V. Mohan. They worked out a deal. The Indira Congress would support Charan Singh if he were able to split the Janata party. The Congress did not care what should be the basis of the split as long as Charan Singh was able to muster an adequate number of MPs from the Janata party fold. The main purpose for Indira Gandhi was to break the Morarji Desai government.

The Dual membership of the erstwhile Jan Sangh members, who had merged into the Janata Party, was converted into an emotive issue for Charan Singh to break away from the Janata Party. Indira Gandhi asked her party leader to move a no confidence motion against the Morarji Desai government. Madhu Limaye, a brilliant academician became the major domo of Charan Singh to lure members from the Janata party to the Charan Singh fold. His major achievement was to lure George Fernandes who had made a brilliant speech in defence of the Morarji Desai government in the Lok Sabha on Friday July 19 but he was lured into handing over his resignation on Sunday so that he could join the Charan Singh camp. HN Bahuguna had also announced his resignation along with his supporters. Desai government had lost the majority support when it was facing the no confidence motion. When such characters as Fernandes and Bahuguna left the Morarji government, there was a suggestion within the Indira Congress that they should now withdraw the no-confidence motion and let Morarji government survive so others would become irrelevant and thus leave the space for the Congress. But Indira Gandhi cautioned them that if Morarji Desai survived in office he would become invincible and the Congress would be in trouble.

The Marxist party sought a deal with Morarji Desai on its 12 demands in return for support of the party. Not only that but also gave a promise of bringing back Bahuguna and Fernandes. Morarji Desai thundered that he would not allow the office of the Prime Minister to become a counter for political blackmail. Jagjivan Ram who was also present at the meeting tried to intervene by suggesting that they should at least talk. Morarji snapped at him, "You can when you are Prime Minister and turn the office into a bargaining counter for blackmailers. But not now when I am the Prime Minister."

On the fateful Sunday that week in July 1979, Jagjivan Ram had also decided to quit and had told Chandra Shekhar, then the Janata Party president. He had striven hard but in vain to ward off the crisis of his intention to resign. Jagjivan Ram did not know that the Prime Minister had convened a meeting of the parliamentary party executive to announce his stepping down rather than face the vote in the Lok Sabha and get defeated. But he refused to step down as the leader of the Janata party in Parliament. His resignation as the leader would have given an opportunity to Jagjivan Ram to make efforts to stake claims. Morarji Desai was adamant on not resigning because he did not want Jagjivan Ram to become the Prime Minister. It was neither a caste bias nor the race bias. He personally disliked Jagjivan Ram as an individual. As the finance minister at the Centre and as the chief minister in Bombay state, he had known very many escapades of Jagjivan Ram that no one else knew.

But for Indira Gandhi, the choice was between supporting Charan Singh or Jagjivan Ram when a group of the Janata party men succeeded in getting a letter from JP in support of Jagjivan Ram. Whether JP was alive to the moment or even conscious or not when he signed the letter of support remains a debatable point The erstwhile BJS had played the trick for they wanted to support Jagjivan Ram, as the Prime Minister in place of Morarji Desai and not Chandra Shekhar, yet another bull of the Indian politics who could not be controlled even by his supporters for Chandra Shekhar had let it be known that he was also in the race. Indira Gandhi sent Vidhya Charan Shukla to Chandra Shekhar with a message that she was willing to support Jagjivan Ram provided he and Morarji Desai took guarantees that he would not make any moves against Indira Gandhi. Neither Chandra Shekhar nor Morarji were willing to give any such undertaking. Yashwantrao Chavan was invited to form the government as the single largest party after the Janata Party but he was diffident and did not want to form the government. He refused to accept the invitation. So Indira Gandhi carried Charan Singh to Rashtrapati Bhavan to get an invitation from the President Neelam Sanjiva Reddy to form the government. The President had ignored the claim of Jagjivan Ram on a pretext that some members whose signatures were appended on his claim letter had denied that they had signed such a memorandum of support to Jagjivan Ram. The grateful Charan Singh reached back his residence via the residence of Indira Gandhi on a courtesy call after his swearing in as the Prime Minister.

As soon as Charan Singh was sworn in and was to appear in the Lok Sabha to seek a vote of confidence as prescribed by the President in his letter of invitation, Indira Gandhi conveyed to him that she would not be supporting him any longer. Instead of appearing in the Lok Sabha, he reached Rashtrapati Bhavan with a resolution of his cabinet seeking dissolution of the Lok Sabha and fresh elections. Even though he had not established that his government enjoyed confidence of the Lok Sabha, the President agreed to dissolve the Lok Sabha. Thus the Indira Gandhi Congress had succeeded in playing the politics of conspiracy to dethrone a legitimately elected government and thrust a mid term polls to the Lok Sabha. She had received the political aid from the most unexpected corner. The man whom she had opposed and defeated in the Presidential elections in 1969 had conspired with her to ease out Morarji Desai government and prevent installation of Jagjivan Ram on flimsy grounds and accepted the cabinet decision to dissolve the Lok Sabha even before the government had established that it was legitimate and enjoyed the confidence of the Lok Sabha. The stage was set for her dramatic return.

Charan Singh had presented a very impractical budget as the finance minister. His main idea was to punish the urban middle class that consumed most goods while rural middle class that suffered for want of resources. This was his general belief and basic political philosophy. His proposals in his first and the last budget were born out of this belief. His budget was tuned to encourage the forces of inflation and price rise. The drought that year also had affected the agriculture in the year. Consequently onion prices had reached new scale when the elections were around. There was also spurt in the gold prices in the international markets. The increased prices of two commodities came handy for the Indira Gandhi Congress. She exploited them fully to her political advantage. However she had won the election only because the masses perceived that the three old men with high ambitions would not allow stability and might affect the national integrity and unity.

She made an attempt to win over Jagjivan Ram to her side. A dinner meeting was held at the guesthouse of the Calcutta industrialist RP Goenka's that was located at Golf Links. But the deal did not work out. But she did succeed in roping in Bahuguna to her side. He was made the Secretary General of the Indira Congress. But she made no attempt to win over the other Congress that had aligned and joined with Charan Singh in the government. She had no need for men and women who had deserted her. She had found new people who were eager to join her.

It was also a time for introduction of new methods in politics for wooing different social blocks. She introduced the use of Iftar parties. Dr. Najma Heptulla came to her aid by organizing the parties that attracted the diplomats from Arab countries towards Indira Gandhi. It was to ensure that the Muslims voted enbloc for the Indira Congress in the coming elections. She had set herself with a divided political force. She had the full party at her command only 27 months earlier. But the large number of the regional leaders had parted company with her in these 27 months because they could not agree with her politics or rise of Sanjay Gandhi in her fold. They thought that they would be able to stand on their own feet. Devraj Urs who had supported her till Chikmagalur election had also parted company with her due to differences over the role of Sanjay Gandhi in the new dispensation. Sanjay Gandhi was brusque and autocratic, and did not tolerate any opposition to his commands. He was in habit of questioning not only opinions of others but also their wisdom. He was blunt enough to tell them on their face that he did not believe their argument or their reasons for he had a different set of reasons. He had annoyed more people than anyone who worked around Indira Gandhi. His tongue-lashing in public were bitter, humiliating and unpalatable but he cared the least for he was an extra constitutional authority. These minor hiccups did not bother Indira Gandhi for she knew that she was on her way to the corridors of power. The adivasi of Vyara taluka had given her the confidence that she would win back her vote bank and also her place in history of India. She was both right, and wrong.

8

Destiny and Doom

An error does not become truth by reason of multiplied propagation, nor does truth become error because no body will see it.

M.K.Gandhi

The symbolic view of things is the consequence of long absorption in images. Is sign language the real language of paradise?

Hugo Ball

Was it a chastened Indira Gandhi who came back to power in January 1980? The electorate that authored her comeback definitely hoped so. The Janata dispensation had flattered to deceive the voter for whom liberty and self-respect were not mere abstractions but implied at least the semblance of a decent living. 'Decent' in terms of getting not only two square meals a day, but the voter also wanted those who ruled should take the voter seriously and not be governed by ego hassles and considerations of office. The meaning of 1977 was a rejection of Indira Gandhi's arrogance and her authoritarianism. The defeat of the Janata Party was a rebuff to its squabbling leaders who refused to cohere and forgot all about the promises they made at the onset of "second freedom".

The intervening phase of hibernation had seen Indira Gandhi distancing herself, or in some cases, even discarding, several of the so-called senior leaders who had chosen to remain at a distance with her immediately after the 1977 defeat. In a way, Indira Gandhi's comeback route had to perforce traverse a totally different road. The party organization had not recovered from the huge inroads made into it by the Janata wave and was in no state to fight a tough political battle. Once again, it was an individual, that is Indira Gandhi, who had to become the sole rallying point. The 1980 elections thus became a kind of referendum to resolve one issue: Should Indira Gandhi be given another chance?

The key variable was going to be the way the north would react to her. The fact that many of those who had made all sorts of compromises to succeed Morarji Desai were from the north helped her on the comeback trail. The electorate in the southern states had stood by her even in 1977; and it did so in 1980 also. The result was a comprehensive tally of 353 seats in the Lok Sabha for the Indira Congress.

As if to rub salt into the wounds, opportunists like Brahmanand Reddy, who had dared to float what he claimed was the "real" Congress, were thrown by the wayside. At this stage, the Reddy rump was keener on getting the original Congress symbol rather than politically resist the return of Indira Gandhi. The treasury bench in the aftermath of the 1980 elections wore a totally new look, with several first-time entrants getting a chance. The Indira Congress, now slimmer and wiser after the earlier electoral disaster, was fortunate that it was confronted by a badly splintered and divided Opposition. Such a fairy-tale comeback had its drawbacks too. The style and content of Indira Gandhi's politics underwent a total transformation. This was because no sooner had the differences within the Janata reached a flashpoint, the whole edifice of the hydra-headed combine crumbled. In that disintegrated state, individual variables that had come together for the Janata experiment were in no position to take on a milder, less volatile version of Indira Gandhi.

Although there was a radical shift in the outward appearance of the Congress, it was purely skin deep. The electorate had re-invested their trust in Indira Gandhi. The latter had not done anything tangible to reorganize the party. Her easy victory in the elections postponed that necessity still further. There was no one who could put a pressure on her to go in for immediate actions to revitalize the party or politics. Jagjivan Ram, the acting Speaker in the new House, observed that the face of the Lok Sabha had completely changed. Both in terms of background, ideology and even in sartorial terms, the old order had virtually disappeared. The men and women who had come to the Lok Sabha could not be recognized as Congressmen or women. There was no compulsion to be attired in the traditional Khadi dress.

Indira Gandhi was a changed person too. She knew that the new circumstances did not warrant her to spell out concrete tasks that faced her. She also knew that her return was largely a product of her individual struggle and the squabbling within the Janata Party. She had won because the electorate was not only prepared to reinvest their faith in her, but also because the ordinary voter had become completely disillusioned with the kind of governance provided by the Janata Party and the ego-hassles that had engaged its top leaders. Indira Gandhi did not have to refashion a new political agenda. And, to the detriment of the party, she was not required to undertake the kind of revamp that it needed. The preceding years had seen Indira Gandhi embattled with the old guard on some ideological issues; but essentially, the split was nothing but a power struggle through which Indira Gandhi sought to establish her complete control and hegemony over the Congress. In the event, the fact that the Congress under her had now become a career-driven party, where peripheral issues took precedence over matters of policy, was hardly surprising.

Her return signified two important aspects. For one, the electorate was prepared to consider the Emergency and its excesses an aberration. Secondly, the incoherence that marked the Janata phase provided Indira Gandhi with a readymade opportunity to structure her comeback. Her opponents had underestimated her capacity to make a comeback and they had also taken the electorate for granted. The 1980 elections thus became a referendum on Indira Gandhi. The personality-factor was again at work. The price of essentials like onions became an electoral issue; the fact that the electorate had become divided between the primarily Hindi speaking north and the south also became a factor. But issues were secondary; the elections represented a categorical rebuff to the Jànata type of governance.

Indira Gandhi decided to make the party an adjunct rather than a vibrant entity on its own. The top-heavy, entirely nominated structure, which was controlled by one single leader her, got further reinforced. In the absence of organizational polls, party functionaries were reduced to being nominees of the all-powerful leader. After 1972, the Congress under Indira Gandhi never had organizational polls. The office-bearers at every level were bereft of any popular legitimacy. The internal democracy within the party was completely absent.

State-level leaders wanting to see or seek favours from Indira Gandhi were first directed to be "cleared" by gentlemen like M.L. Fotedar and R.K. Dhawan before they had an audience with her. A smokescreen of immediate loyalists prevented access between party workers and their leader. 'Loyalty above all' became the presiding norm in the Congress. This weakened rather than strengthened Indira Gandhi's hands, because she depended almost entirely on the feedback and feelers she received from a set of badly chosen individuals to take decisions affecting both the party and the government. The quality of cronies surrounding her determined the nature of the party's politics. Inputs from the grass root level were just not readily available to the leader while taking decisions. Even selection of ministers even in the states became centralized in a coterie at the top. A rootless set of busybodies became important in the party. And this "importance" was largely illusory because all of them were Indira 'Madam's creatures of comfort. With Jagjivan Ram, Y.B. Chavan, H.N. Bahuguna and seniors of their level having parted ways with Indira Gandhi, there was little in common between the Congress of the pre-Emergency phase and now.

From 1978 onwards, Indira Gandhi combined the twin functions of being the sole party boss and the leader of the Congress parliamentary party that is prime minister. The bitterness of the immediate past still rankled in her mind; the ideological sparkle of the pre-Emergency phase was now completely gone. Instead of using consultations as a tool for organizational reform,

Indira Gandhi preferred to use the broom to sweep all dissent under the carpet. Till he was alive, Sanjay Gandhi continued to have a major say in the day-to-day running of both the party and the government. His extra-constitutional writ still ran large. But his untimely death in June 1980 removed even that pretence. Indira Gandhi, by her own choice, had decided to take decisions as they came to her. The quality of governance and the atrophy in the party did not mean anything in this scheme of things.

The PMO also wore a totally changed look. Unlike in the past when senior and often brilliant bureaucrats like P.N. Haksar, T.N. Kaul and P.N. Dhar were there for advice and consultations even regarding party affairs, there was nobody of comparable stature in the new dispensation. There was no representation or intermediary between Indira Gandhi and the world around her. Taking a leaf out of the Janata stylebook, Indira Gandhi dismissed those state governments where the Janata Party was in power. In Punjab, the Badal government was hacked and after fresh elections, the Congress came back to power in the state.

Events oblivious of these cynical and vindictive changes were taking place simultaneously. In Assam, the Congress faced direct confrontation from outfits such as the All Assam Students' Union (AASU), which later assumed the shape of the Assam Gana Parishad. This subsequently took the shape of a violent anti-foreigner struggle that was more virulent than any sons' of the soil movements of the sixties. The Congress became a dead entity as disgruntled and largely unemployed Assamese youth took out their wrath on Bengalis and other 'outsiders,' even when the latter had been part of the state for generations. The state unit of the Congress was now perceived as an oppressor, especially after the Nellie massacre.

In Punjab, discontent took a separatist tinge when sections of the rich-peasantry that were never enamoured of the Congress, were remote-controlled from abroad to launch a movement for Khalistan. Indira Gandhi did not respond to either the Assam or the Punjab crisis politically; instead, she used the state machinery to suppress the growing discontent in these two states. This further accentuated the rift between the Centre, controlled by the Congress, and sub-national and ethnic aspirations. The party was left in no position to challenge such tendencies.

In her quest for total control, Indira Gandhi had succeeded in creating several mine fields for herself. She had been trapped by the illusion of her invincibility. Complete cynicism and dangerous dithering led to the erosion of central authority. There was nobody in the party whom she trusted enough to take them into her confidence. The nominated chieftains were all servile and spineless appointees. They depended entirely on her wish her whims and her fancies to continue hold their offices. Any variation from her directions invited only her wrath and loss of the office that was given them.

After the elections, Sanjay Gandhi naturally assumed the responsibility of selecting the chief ministers in different states. Madhavsinh Solanki was obvious choice for Gujarat for he was the chief minister for 100 days before the Congress government was dismissed in May 1977. The difficulty was in selection of the chief ministers for Uttar Pradesh and Maharashtra. Abdul Rehman Antulay was also one of the serious claimants but the question was whether the Congress High command should select a person who had unsavoury past in the state politics. Sanjay preferred Antulay to the majority community Patil candidate for the state. He also chose Viswanath Pratap Singh for Uttar Pradesh. Both choices turned out to be hotly controversial, as we shall see.

Sanjay Gandhi was never to know that he had made the wrong choice, because he was killed in a plane crash on 23 June 1980. That brought to an end one of the most controversial careers in Indian and Congress history. Sanjay was nasty, brutish, boorish, arrogant, restless and worse; but he had one single quality. He was personally honest. His mother was disconsolate beyond belief. Rarely in public had Indira Gandhi allowed this aspect of her personality be reflected lest her myriad opponents took advantage of her one fatal weakness. Sanjay had become her saviour and nemesis turned into one. Indira Gandhi's friends were caustic even in her moment of tragedy. All that her old friend Bhupesh Gupta had to say after Sanjay died was: "Nobody should die so young."

In terms of the party, Sanjay Gandhi's exit was a mixed blessing. While he represented some of the most notorious aspects of the Emergency and he had also by then shown little time for either reflection or considered action to be one of his qualities, Sanjay Gandhi had at the same time a loyal band of servitors who reported directly to him. People like V.P. Singh, N.D. Tiwari, Gundu Rao and Antulay were all Sanjay men. They had little or no interaction with Indira Gandhi per se. Indira Gandhi's biggest problem was that among these Sanjay men and an entirely new set of bureaucrats, she had nobody of consequence who had the guts to question anything, which she did or even planned to do. They were too servile to formulate any independent agendas or policies, which they could provide the leader to work upon.

The party was now completely bankrupt both in terms of ideological content or a new set of leadership ready to take over if the need arose. Indira Gandhi, grappling as she was with the crises of Punjab and Assam, needed counsel. She however had little faith in those who may have had ideas on the matter. Since both in Punjab and in Assam, the state units were now completely lacking in representative or popular character, it was very difficult for creatures of the high command to make any contribution to the leader. Indira Gandhi's frustrations kept mounting as the immediate fallout of all this was the reappearance of a hostile press. But there were no left wing or liberal intellectuals left with her anymore who could help in staving off the challenge. Popularity in terms of individual credibility was all that Indira Gandhi had to offer to the people in her post-1980 reincarnation. But even that possibility was completely eroded by her own lack of definite policies or responses. In Punjab, after pitting Union home minister Zail Singh against Darbara Singh, she settled in favour of the former because he was more servile. Darbara Singh was at least trying to offer a semblance of a fight against the militant conglomeration around Jarnail Singh Bhindranwale. Indira Gandhi, on Zail Singh's advice, thought she could use Bhindranwale as a counterweight to the mainstream Akali leadership when she was struggling to come back to the corridors of power during the Janata Party regime.

Matters came to a head in 1983, when in spite of specific orders for Bhindranwale's arrest after he had been involved in getting a Nirankari sect leader killed, the extremist leader was allowed to move around in an open truck in the streets of Delhi, mocking at the central authority and daring it to arrest him if it could. Once earlier, in 1981, Bhindranwale had been arrested but let-off. These stupid errors were a result of the late Sanjay Gandhi's style of pitting one individual or group against the other so that both would feel insecure at the same time. Indira Gandhi was not clever enough to understand this—or was she deliberately allowing this cynicism to convert it into a political weapon later? In actual fact, that is what she did.

The argument was that separatist and ethnic unrest need "hard" solutions. What she essentially meant was that the state apparatus and the law and order machinery, and not the Congress as a political party could meet the challenges around her. A more categorical vote of no confidence in the calibre of her own party could not have been made clearer. Every decision depended upon her whether it was a candidate for the chief minister or for the district congress committee. Her endorsement to every appointment even to the smallest functionary in the state unit or the district units of the party was necessary. Unfortunately these men and women were not chosen by due political process but on the basis of pleasure of the coterie that worked for her.

In yet another anti-democratic and completely immature move, she decided to introduce her elder son Rajiv Gandhi into active politics. Rajiv Gandhi was happy as a simple pilot with Indian Airlines. Politics, especially of the Sanjay variety, was completely alien to his thinking. She also brought in Arun Nehru, a distant cousin of her, to help her out in dealing with party matters. Her council of ministers was an absolutely clear statement about the total lack of talented people or men with experience in day-to-day affairs within the Congress. Purely in terms of some technical grounding, R Venkataraman filled the bill of a senior minister. As for the others, men like Pranav Mukherji may have had some individual merits were completely rootless in terms of mass support. There were few others who also had no ground support in their state even though they were considered to be the seniors.

She perforce had to include those loyalists who had stood by her when the Shah Commission and other inquests were on to nail her for Emergency excesses and other misdemeanors. This being their only major qualification, the loyalists were just men of straw. They had nothing going for them except for Indira Gandhi's patronage and blessings. The Congress suffered enormously in the period 1980-84 because the presence of just one Indira Gandhi could hardly substitute for the lack of a party structure of political beings at different levels. In fact, Congress had ceased to be a multi-layered entity. All the earlier think tanks like the Nehru Forum and the Socialist Forum had vanished from view. There were none around who could dare and protest against the wrong decisions as it used to happen before she had imposed Emergency. With a splintered opposition groping for ideas and platforms, Indira Gandhi presumed that her own inadequacies at the organizational end would not matter much. She was being typically shortsighted.

What a major transformation this was from Indira Gandhi of yore can be had from the fact that unlike in1971, she took months and months to even consider revitalizing the party in any manner at all. Rajiv Gandhi had been made a general secretary in 1982, and that year, while on a visit to Hyderabad, he insulted and trivialized chief minister T. Anjiah so badly at the airport itself that the latter had no option but to publicly cry over his humiliation. Arun Nehru was asked to intercede in the Kashmir political crisis where he made one blunder after another. The sheer stupidity with which the Andhra crisis was treated showed adhocism at its worst. The emergence of N.T. Rama Rao as a political entity was a result of Indira Gandhi's characteristically disdainful attitude towards usurpers. Little did she realize that NTR, who personified of several myths and legends, also commanded a personal equation with the people of the state. That equation was built over several years of popularity in the most effective mass medium like cinema.

Indira Gandhi's own theatre of the absurd was little better than NTR's antics. She also resorted to low histrionics and high-pitched melodrama when the need arose. Indira-amma might still have had, and actually did have, a very transparent and tangible following. But as far as the party went, it only mattered during election time. In fact workers moved like a contractor's well fed and well provided gangs. For the rest of the period, state units were sleeping; the CWC and wider forums like the AICC had become rubber stamps required merely to endorse continued faith in the vision and charisma of one leader. The Congress had ceased to exist as a party; it became an extension, an appendage, of Indira Gandhi's angularities.

Periodic interactions were limited to pre-session pep talk to MPs and some increasingly rare public meetings. Unlike in the late sixties or the early seventies, Indira Gandhi was now for some reason totally disinterested in meeting people, interacting with Congressmen or taking the party and the country into confidence on policy issues. Few knew what was going on in the leader's mind. Her earlier, principled opposition to foreign aid had given way to meek acceptance of World Bank and IMF prescriptions.

Meanwhile, as Punjab saw senior police and para-military officials being eliminated one after the other in early 1984, Indira Gandhi was totally clueless about how to handle the situation. The Punjab police had been rendered almost ineffectual by terrorist-infiltration. By March 1984, the situation had become intolerable, especially after Bhindranwale used a threat that Hindus would not be spared if any Sikh were killed in Punjab. His statement aroused passions to such an extent that the Opposition members wrote a blank cheque to Indira Gandhi for any action to curtail the terrorism in Punjab when the issue was discussed in the Lok Sabha on March 4 1984. Madhu Dandavate was the most impassioned exponent of harsh measures to curb Bhindranwale.

Arif Mohamed Khan, who was then considered close to Indira Gandhi as a minister of state, that very day walked into her chamber in Parliament House after the heated debate got over and asked her what was preventing an immediate crackdown, especially since even the Opposition had given her a carte blanche. Indira Gandhi remarked, "Arif, let the public outcry simmer some more." The decks were being cleared for a more sustained and organized crackdown on Bhindranwale and his cohorts now holed up inside the Golden Temple.

Elsewhere in the country, Indira Gandhi's preoccupation with Assam and Punjab got reflected in a series of electoral set backs, especially in Karnataka and Andhra Pradesh in January 1983. This happened in spite of enormous resources available with the Congress. Utter novices had replaced flunkies of the old order. The Congress member from Gujarat Jaideep Singh Baria wrote to her a strong letter blaming the defeats on her action of closing all forums of healthy discussions within the party when members could tell her what the popular perceptions and problems were. She was shocked to receive such a letter and invited him to meet her. He explained that he had not sought an appointment but wanted to tell her that she must devote time to listen to members in party discussions instead of shutting them out completely. But Indira Gandhi did not follow it up because her attention was diverted to other pressing problem of rising terrorist activities in Punjab.

Another reason for the declining fortunes of the Congress party was ideological incoherence. After her return to power, Indira Gandhi shifted the focus of her economics without seeking a national or even party consensus. She went for her trip to the United States in July 1982 and took Rajiv along. There, as the new lexicon of liberalization impelled by Reagonomics and Thatcherite shifts towards privatization was made clear to them, the mother and the son were totally at a loss to respond with the kind of solid aplomb that the Indian leadership had till then consistently displayed on the emerging international economic order based on out-and-out globalisation. While there, Rajiv made a statement that indicated concurrence with the changes suggested. India was prepared to "open up" in the name of liberalization, without having either the structure or the necessary thinking to supplement a radical economic shift.

At this stage, the Leftist intelligentsia had given up all hopes of making Indira Gandhi becoming once again interested in their rejection of the new economic model. A new breed of World Bank certified bureaucrats and academicians became increasingly close to Rajiv. Indira Gandhi, on her part, was enmeshed in the Punjab quagmire. Indira Gandhi, who during her "radical" days paid little heed to the exhortations of the west to discard the existing economic model was now a silent supporter of the change dictated by the Breton Woods' twins.

In 1971, her thinking was also influenced by the response of other third world economies that similarly resisted capitulating before the World Bank-inspired agenda. Indira Gandhi had also broadly adopted the concept of Dr. Mahbub-ul Haque, a leading economist of Pakistan. Dr Haque had opined that the growth of GDP due to increase in production of items of class consumption did not reflect the true picture if there was no growth in production of items of mass consumption. However, in actual fact, Indira Gandhi had moved in to increase production of items of class consumption. She encouraged the Maruti car project only because her son Sanjay was initially associated with it. While the automobile boom captivated the urban middle classes, the ordinary man on the street felt diminished by the lack of concern shown towards shoring up the public transport sector.

The shift in economic focus was affected even without any serious discussions in any forums of the party or outside. The Working Committee was also not taken into confidence when Rajiv Gandhi made what amounted to a virtual policy statement, which he had no authority to make in the first place. At best, it was his personal view; but the way things were, his personal view was superimposed on the party and the country to the detriment of both. Indira Gandhi had misread both the electoral debacle and the consequences of blindly accepting western advice on the economy. The upwardly mobile sections within the middle class thought that Indira the Liberaliser would provide them the kind of leverage in policy-formulation that economic reforms which held no meaning for the vast majority of the people save a tiny segment would get focused and implemented. The corporate sector, which had shown no anxiety or inclination in the crucial infrastructure sector thought that a series of macro-economic changes would somehow alter existing economic paradigms. The Congress became a party without focus; a party so completely unable to formulate its own thinking on such a vital issue that the interests of the country were mortgaged without a thought.

The personality-driven party now had a leader who had lost her sense of priorities. This distanced the party from its traditional vote banks. If an election were to be held then, Indira Gandhi's suicidal economic policies, coupled with the failure to tackle terrorism and growing social discontent, would have resulted in a massive defeat for the Congress. At this stage, destiny was to intervene—in a cruel manner, which ironically turned out to be a resounding return of the very same Congress.

Operation Blue Star has been discussed at length in various tomes. Its disastrous consequences as well as the reasons, which left Indira Gandhi with no option but to undertake the unpopular move has also been discussed threadbare. Suffice here to say that Rajiv Gandhi's ascent had led to a series of immature responses, which helped neither Indira Gandhi nor the party. But no one could point it out to Indira Gandhi or her son. Even when Rajiv Gandhi used the Andhra Governor Ram Lal to dismiss the Rama Rao government and install a pro Congress defector Nadella Bhaskar Rao, who was the deputy to the chief minister Ramarao as the chief minister in August 1984 the party could not protest. Rajiv Gandhi also had another achievement to his credit when he got the Farooq Abdullah government dismissed in Kashmir and install his brother in law Gul Mohmed Shah as the chief minister in Kashmir a month later. Indira Gandhi had to correct the situation by sending Dr. Shankar Dayal Sharma to Andhra Pradesh as the governor so that he could reinstall the Ramarao government in the state in place of the defector's government. But she could not undo what was done in Kashmir and had to live unhappily with the immature political actions of her son.

Regular scandals and scams kept surfacing all along. She was embarrassed beyond measure by the manner in which a private trust was floated and nursed in her name by then Maharashtra chief minister Abdul Rehman Antulay. Till today, Antulay maintains that he did nothing wrong and became a victim of media-propaganda. That may or may not be the case, but Indira

Gandhi was getting increasingly caught up in a vortex of scandals that increased the credibility gap even further. Loyalists and ministers were made to face the music while Indira Gandhi vainly searched for a face-saving device. Her government faced, and survived, two no-confidence motions. She left it to Venkataraman to defend the government when the second one was brought up. So much for her concern for retaining her waning popularity!

This book is categorical in its assessment that Indira Gandhi just before her death had become very slow in her reflexes to respond in any cogent manner to the several posers that kept cropping up. Her indifference extinguished any chance of the Congress galvanizing a suitable strategy to confront mounting disaffection. The mere recapping of various scandals during Indira Gandhi's twilight phase will be of no help here. After all, these were just a manifestation of a leader who had allowed the grass to grow under her feet. She had little time to reflect on the deleterious impact all this had on the Congress. The person who had revived the Congress from assured oblivion was now herself fading into a pale shadow of her former combative self.

Corruption in high places has always struck an emotive chord with the Indian electorate. The electorate is prepared to overlook corruption till such time that the leader concerned has at least some solid support in his or her favour to offset allegations of sleaze. But when the leader becomes just a silent spectator of mounting rot, the people at once realize that a change is called for. Indira Gandhi did not understand this fact in spite of her sharp and astute assessment of the Indian psyche. Was her "oversight" deliberate, or had she become reconciled like some others in the South Asian neighbourhood to let those intent on fleecing the system make the hindmost as long as the electorate does not wake up to the sordid goings-on at the top.

Meanwhile, in India's most populous state, Uttar Pradesh chief minister Viswanath Pratap Singh had caused another embarrassment to Indira Gandhi and the Congress. V.P. Singh dithered when the powerful Thakurs in the state avenged casteist scores through engineered violence. When the Behmai episode, in which 22 people from the lower castes were butchered and Phoolan Devi was brutalized in more ways than one, V.P. Singh took shelter behind false modesty and handed in his resignation. He quit his post merely because he was annoyed that Arjun Singh, the Madhya Pradesh chief minister had worked out a deal with the bandit queen, who agreed to surrender before the Madhya Pradesh police. VP Singh could not understand the politics of Arjun Singh who wanted to win over the Other Backward Classes to ensure the victory of the Congress in Madhya Pradesh in the subsequent election. Arjun Singh needed to expand his vote base in the state since both the Congress and the BJP that were the main and only rivals in the state could not win over on the basis of support from upper castes alone.

There were other indicators of strife; Chandra Shekhar's Padyatra from Kanyakumari in Tamilnadu to Raj Ghat in New Delhi, traveling 4500 kms distance on foot, convinced him and those whom he interacted with that the system in Delhi was insensitive to the core to the aspirations of the people in the periphery. The political wind was clearly pointing towards renewed disenchantment with the Congress. The Padyatra captured public imagination because it reflected disaffection with the rulers in Delhi.

A new nucleus of Opposition to the Congress, with a set of both old as well as new leaders, was building up. This could have crystallized into a more tangible form because Indira Gandhi had lost the will to resist. But destiny had charted out a different course for the Indian polity that was to result in a complete decimation of the new nucleus.

In May that year, just a month before the Operation Blue Star became an inevitability due to her weak leadership, Indira Gandhi invited state Congress leaders for group discussions to evolve new ways to revive the party. But it seemed that the time for such cosmetic exercises was over. The Congress had become a boneless monolith devoid of strength because the people who sustained it through popular support were getting increasingly restive. A moot point is whether any of the state leaders had the guts to directly tell Indira Gandhi that? The Congress appeared to be "living " just because Indira Gandhi was a physical representation of that; in essential terms, the party had declined inexorably. Internecine warfare in state units such as in the Gujarat

Congress were allowed to fester. There was no Indira Gandhi left in the person responding to that name now.

There indeed were some perfunctory meetings called by the Prime Minister to resolve inter-state disputes. She had become more of a CEO in the boardroom of a sinking company rather than an upbeat political manager of rampant contradictions.

Purely in terms of historical record, Operation Blue Star had conclusively proved how ineffective Indira Gandhi's political instincts had become blunt over four long years of cynical manipulation. The incapacity of the state apparatus to comprehend the consolidation of separatist tendencies was an intelligence failure. But to attribute it to be the failure of designated wings of the government to keep track of terrorist consolidation will be tantamount to explaining off the tragedy in very convenient terms. The intelligence failure was primarily on part of Indira Gandhi herself; she had not realized that her attempt to counter Akalis by devious intrigue and political manipulation was not taking her anywhere near the ostensible goal of eradicating terrorism. In actual fact, the real battle, which Indira Gandhi never joined, was to convince the people in the state about how a separate theocratic state was an untenable, dangerous and extremely bigoted idea which in essence spelt the beginning of balkanization of the Indian nation-state.

The stupid and even juvenile strategy to combat the Akali Dal which only succeeded in forcing that party into adopting the controversial Anandpur Sahib Resolution was a product of Zail Singh's consistent and deliberate attempt to undo the attempts made by Darbara Singh to limit the battle to political confines. Zail Singh thought that by discrediting Darbara Singh on the one hand and making the Akalis irrelevant by allowing Sant Bhindranwale to establish his own network of terror will leave the field clear for him to emerge as numero uno in state politics. This naïve approach not only stoked the anger in Punjab on a daily basis. It also effectively ensured that the Congress as a political entity became completely suspect in the eyes of the broad masses who thought that their interests had been sacrificed at the altar of expediency of the worst sort.

A vast majority of the state's Sikhs were in agreement with the majority of Hindus that a cynical game of brinkmanship had only succeeded in legitmising the separatist agenda in the eyes of those sections of the state's upper peasantry which was always highly suspicious of the Congress approach to neutralize Akalis. The Sikh Jats who dominated the Akali top leadership were utterly apathetic to the rise of separatist terror because they thought that it was a conscious attempt by the Congress to undermine the Akali social base. The rise of terrorism was abetted, in an increasingly brazen and unconcealed manner, by the feudal elite in control in Pakistan. But that was a consequence of Indira Gandhi's failure to find a workable strategy to resolve problems that she and her misguided minions were simply too inadequate to provide.

In terms of knee-jerk reactions to the fast-deteriorating Punjab crisis, Indira Gandhi went through the tepid exercise of trying to involve other political parties to see what could be done to neutralize the terrorist threat. Whether she herself was listening to the advice emerging from these meetings is doubtful.

It was a first-rate crisis alright. The Sikh extremists under Bhindranwale's sway had converted the historic Golden Temple into their fortress. Sections of the Punjab police were reportedly aware of the fact that huge consignments of arms were being sent inside the Temple in trucks ostensibly carrying rations and food grains. The terrorists had already succeeded in subordinating the wireless and telecom network; and, in an absolutely unforgivable response, Indira Gandhi did not care to understand why sustained attempts by the paramilitary forces in the phase immediately prior to Operation Blue Star were being stymied from within the establishment which had been suborned by the terrorists with increasing success.

While discussions about the likely costs a counter-terrorist response did take place, there was little appreciation of the fact that the already troubled psyche of the state would suffer even greater damage if Delhi continued to perceive the Punjab crisis purely in terms of a law and order approach. Contemporary accounts of the phase indicate that Congressmen were getting it from both sides—from the broad masses, who thought that their party was simply playing games, and from the central leadership, which in its allegedly superior wisdom thought that the state unit was deliberately not carrying out its orders. But in actual fact, Indira Gandhi had not cared to even discuss with state leaders what measures they thought, were urgently needed to be taken to expose Akali duplicity and rising militancy.

Indira Gandhi was unable to comprehend any logical way out because she mistook the entire disaffection in the state as an attempt by forces inimical to Indian sovereignty to project their agenda forward. Darbara Singh and after him, some other relatively sober and concerned elements within the Congress were simply aghast why Indira Gandhi had so willingly played the game which her opponents both within and outside the country wanted.

From the ridiculous to draconian, several suggestions were given to meet the militant challenge. Indira Gandhi fluctuated between indecision and over-reaction; there was no sense of proportion in her approach to the problem as it had assumed the sinister form it did in the last four years. Certain so-called progressive elements of the Left, like the valiant Communist leader Satyapal Dang, kept trying to convince Indira Gandhi that the broad masses of Punjab were not in any manner supportive of Bhindranwale and his cohorts. Except resorting to the extreme step of storming the holiest shrine of Sikhs, Indira Gandhi had left herself with no other option. And the option she had been forced into believing as the only available one made her an instant casualty of dangerous myopia and worse.

The Sikh reaction, especially in the Armed forces to the storming of the holiest shrine the Golden temple went along predictable lines. Desertions and insubordination in the Armed forces created an unprecedented crisis, since this was perhaps the first time in the long and mostly uncontroversial history of the Indian Army and other wings of the security apparatus that rank indiscipline had become such a rampant phenomenon. There were suggestions after the Operation Blue Star that some of the security personnel should be shifted out from the immediate proximity to her. Indira Gandhi did not agree with the advice. On October 30, 1984, a mock drill was carried out at her official residence in New Delhi for checking the security system and responses of the personnel manning different locations while she was away to Bhuvaneshwar for a public meeting. It was here she had said that she would be happy and proud if every drop of her blood came to serve the cause of the nation.

The very next morning, Indira Gandhi was assassinated. Two of her own security guards, who had sworn protect her, emptied their automatic guns on her body in her residence. The politics of countering terror with state-terror, if that could be termed as politics at all, had been shown to be what it was: a cruel device which could only have tragic results. Her assassination became the starting point of a ghastly communal backlash, on a dimension unseen in post-Independence India. Indira Gandhi had sacrificed her life. But whether the sacrifice was the logical (if indeed tragic) consequence of her own creation is something that can be answered straight-off; Indira Gandhi, during her comeback years, first destroyed the party apparatus; subsequently, she trivialized the real hurt and anguish of the people of Punjab; thirdly, she remained captive to patently idiotic advice; and finally, her tragic assassination in one stroke removed from the scene a brilliant yet scheming; sharp but manipulative; courageous but insecure; democratic but authoritarian, personality from the Indian political scene. With her, the last hope of any resurgence within the Congress also died.

The stage had thus been set for a succession that had been forced on the Congress and the nation by the party's own ineptitude. It is possible to retrace the events that took place in those few hours, which finally resulted in Rajiv Gandhi assuming charge. The story is important in itself; the manner in which it was executed also showed how bereft of cogency the Congress was. Rajiv's ascension was both accidental and premature. He had done nothing at all to deserve the prime slot, except for the obvious dynastic factor that went in his favour. But even that can be termed just a marginal factor when it is seen in the context of how, within a matter of just a few years, the Congress had become nothing but a living example of a party without vision, clarity, leadership and maturity. The inner-party dynamics that contributed to this degeneration have been fleshed out in some detail through this book. What should however be stressed here is the simple fact that a proud and independent country, as also its foremost political party, had been reduced to a collection of rudderless cronies who had over the years mushroomed around Indira Gandhi and her sons and some completely apolitical, rootless elements of the techno-managerial elite who thought that everything could be reduced to seeking answers not from the people but from inputs derived from fancy institutions and esoteric models which the ordinary man in the street was completely at a loss to understand or comprehend.

Indira Gandhi's departure, especially the tragic facts of the immediate incident, provided Rajiv Gandhi a powerful platform that he had no role in either erecting or shaping in the first place. The Congress edifice had become too rickety for Rajiv and his advisers to be of much consequence. There were, however, a few attempts by the new leader to work out a new idiom to suit the mindset he represented. Not everything that Rajiv tried in his first few weeks can, in hindsight, be described as either mischievous or essentially wicked. However, the lack of political finesse was evident from day one. Opportunists around him, and even Indira-baiters like Ramnath Goenka, began thinking in terms of using Rajiv Gandhi's search for a new ethos to govern the party and run the Congress, as a chance to indirectly control the direction of national policy.

Rajiv Gandhi's unprecedented success in the polls that followed was mistakenly attributed to his "Mr Clean " image. Maybe, the affable and gentle aspects of the Rajiv persona, and his youth, helped in investing him with a halo. But looking at it as something more than a mere adjustment at the top of the ruling classes will be to question inevitable ironies that accompany specific historic conjunctures.

The decimation of what constituted the traditional Opposition to the Congress is a story that needs to be understood with one key element in mind: Rajiv Gandhi was not a product of Congress politics, but a striking rejection of all that the party had stood for.

Some of the things he rejected, as became apparent when he gave a thundering call to rid the party of power-brokers in his famous centennial speech in Bombay, were undoubtedly welcomed as an indication of a historic necessity. Unfortunately, however, the new leader threw the baby (the Congress) along with the bathwater!

9

Charm vs Chasm

He has left off reading altogether to the great improvement of his originality

Charles Lamb

There is nothing new under the sun

The Bible

The young have aspirations that never come to pass, the old have reminiscences of what never happened

H. H. Munro

Young men have a passion for regarding their elders as senile

Henry Adams

Rajiv Gandhi brought about a complete turnaround in the structure and values of the Congress. He changed the character of both the party and government. Most of the old stalwarts who had worked closely with Indira Gandhi were removed from places of influence or were totally marginalized. Pranab Mukherjee, who had worked in total cooperation with Indira Gandhi since 1974 and virtually was her number two, was left out of the first Council of Ministers that Rajiv Gandhi formed on December 31 1984. Obviously, Mukherjee had fallen a victim to the rumours that he was representing a major corporate house that wanted him to become caretaker leader after the assassination of Indira Gandhi. There was no way that Mukherjee could have scotched rumours since there was no amount of money could have got him the position in the circumstances in which the country was caught after the assassination of Indira Gandhi. The President Zail Singh could not have installed anyone but Rajiv Gandhi even as an interim arrangement.

Beneath a façade of continuity with the earlier era in the shape of men like PV Narasimha Rao, B. Shankaranand, P Shiv Shankar and Shankarrao Chavan, a brand new breed of corporate advisers and image-makers took control of India's destiny. It was obvious from day one that Arun Nehru would be the major domo of the Rajiv establishment. It became an open secret that even the formation of the government was his brainchild.

But more than the removal of traditionalists from the decision-making process, Rajiv Gandhi intended to effect a techno-managerial coup within the Congress. That this would incur the wrath of the ordinary congressman or even the man on the street did not matter. For him, it was just a matter of cost-overruns in the realization of his dream project. Unlike any of his predecessors, Rajiv had grown up in a very protective and secluded environ. Struggle or interaction with anyone outside his social class was unknown to him. Only a few select friends and those with dazzling utopias to offer were attractive to a man who had little education and had no intellectual background whatsoever. He was completely removed from the real world that the ordinary Indian lived in, and prime ministership became some kind of a Bharat Darshan exercise for him. For him, a ride around Teen Murti house with Nathu cook's cycle, carried tremendous exotic appeal. He was a naïve, simple and impressionable young man, who could be manipulated any which way sharp minds like Arun Nehru wanted.

Thus, it was not at all surprising when he confided, in an extensive interview with journalist Dhiren Bhagat, that he had read only adventure stories, and sometimes, Harold Robbins novels and Groucho Marx type humour to relieve his tedium. While this lack of intellectual pretensions could be a pardonable luxury for others from his class background, the seriousness of his new assignment demanded much greater depth of knowledge from Rajiv Gandhi, which he simply did not possess. The political, social, cultural and historical background of even the Nehru-Indira family would have helped him know a lot more than he actually did. As his great-aunt Vijaya Lakshmi Pandit told Tully and Masani (From Raj to Rajiv: 40 Years of Indian Independence), Rajiv valued his own profession (as an aviation- pilot) much more than politics, which he openly admitted to know little about. While Indira Gandhi and Sanjay were close to each other and shared political work, Rajiv voluntarily kept himself aloof from such concerns. It was a matter of routine that when visitors came calling to see him in is capacity as party general secretary Rajiv was often engrossed in reading popular thrillers. He preferred to cosy around with his former school-mates, and often appeared to resent his new responsibilities.

He was very fond of new gadgets and innovations that were presented to him. When he was presented with a cordless phone, Rajiv was thrilled to the core. It so happened that one of his junior ministers called on him just when he was discovering the uses of the new contraption. Rajiv at once got down to explain to his perplexed ministerial colleague the way the device worked. A precious half an hour went into this initiation exercise. Many others had similar experiences to narrate when they first 'saw' the new leader.

He also introduced a new style of annual vacation away from the capital. He always carried his family and also his friends to the security bound areas where they would not have access otherwise. The fun, frolic and revelry that went on during such vacations found space in media columns. Rajiv came out as a happy-go-lucky, carefree man who was fond of fast driving, and enjoyed safaris and holidays. It was a culture so different from the old culture of governance.

Everyone is entitled to his or her personal lifestyle, and Rajiv valued his own. But the fact is that neither his party nor the country at large identified with this way of living. It became a matter of national concern when several decisions were taken in an apparently cavalier spirit. It may not be fair to judge Rajiv by his lifestyle alone. But both Indira Gandhi and Jawaharlal Nehru had made conscious attempts to make themselves identifiable with the ordinary Indian, because they were political beings sworn to preside over the most important political office in the country. Rajiv Gandhi took a long time to understand how important it was to understand the roots and connectivity that ran through Indian history; and by the time he did, it was perhaps too late both for him and the Congress. Rajiv Gandhi came as a culture-shock to the ordinary congressman; and he himself did not understand the values that permeated through the land. This failed interaction became a major national problem, and for the Congress, it meant a steady dilution of its traditional support-base.

Indira Gandhi used her daily meetings with ordinary people from all over the country as a forum for educating herself. Even when out of power, she never lost touch with the masses. Rajiv Gandhi, quite unwittingly of course, responded differently. Right from the people with whom he interacted with to his constituents at large, a broad cultural gap divided the young prime minister from the social reality at the ground level.

Within a short span in office, Rajiv became the pet delight of satirists and caricaturists. As tales of his innocence that he displayed when he visited a tribal village in Madhya Pradesh or the Indira Gandhi canal in Rajasthan spread, so did his extensive aura in a section of the middle class. But essentially, Rajiv was an innocent person who had not seen Indian reality closely enough. He was readily impressed by the westernized urban elite, that believed that the "socialist" pattern for creating a just and prosperous society was a mere pipedream, which had dragged India down all these years. In his eagerness to change the way things were, Rajiv Gandhi showed a complete inability to understand why his mother or grand-father had laid so much value to the ideological structure enshrined in the Congress party's organizational values.

Rajiv Gandhi's half-baked ideological makeup was reflected in everything; his governance was marked by a bewildering inability to grasp essentials. His cosmetic leaps became a major hindrance in giving firm direction to the functioning of the new polity he envisioned. Thus, promises such as ridding the Indian economy of bureaucratic shackles and also liberate it from legal hurdles, licensing constraints and limits of labour laws and the grip of trade unions were both tangible and lost. Parallels were not too incorrectly drawn with the autocratic Shah of Iran, whose anxiety to modernize presaged a revivalist backlash which took Iran back to the era of Ayatollahs. Rajiv's India became a favourite theme for discussion in elite circles. Almost everybody in the upper middle class was completely mesmerized by the young man's apparent honesty and intensity of purpose.

It will be a complete travesty to deny Rajiv credit where it is due. Several novel and in some ways, excellent breakthroughs were made through the six technology missions which were started during this phase. The remarkable strides in the telecom sector, envisioned and implemented by the brilliant Satyam Gangaram Pitroda, are there for all to see. However, the concept of "opening up" was not clear to Rajiv, and as subsequent history has shown, the manner in which this sector as well as the Indian economy has been globalised has led to further intensification of existing inequities. The Congress as a party suffered immeasurably because of the ideological fuzziness of its promoters.

Rajiv Gandhi had sincerely believed that the country needed a quantum jump into the next century in just a matter of few years. He had unfolded his ideas and his dream when he had addressed the Centenary Session of the Indian National Congress at Mumbai in December 1985. He could not understand that only a minuscule segment of the Indian population believed in his ideas and dreams and agreed that they will work. The majority of people were struggling even for two square meals a day. For them any "quantum jump" meant fulfilling that humble requirement first. Most of his ministers were too servile to even think of telling Rajiv Gandhi that his dreams were fine, but unrealizable till such time that the basic needs of the people were not met. So eager to please the ministers were that they left it to Rajiv to do the thinking for them; Rajiv had left that to his favoured few. At the end of the day, there was nobody to think either about the party or the people.

A senior minister had even suggested at the same Centenary Session that he wanted every hut to have a computer by the turn of the century. A realist in the audience quipped, "Why not first provide electricity in every hut before you take a computer there?" At the same meeting in the August Kranti Maidan of Mumbai, mikes failed and an angry Rajiv Gandhi publicly remonstrated Bombay Pradesh Congress chief Murli Deora: "Why couldn't you make proper arrangements?" Incidentally, the same story was repeated the next day—the mikes failed yet again, as Rajiv was in the middle of his historic address!

However, the address itself was very well received. The AICC reverberated to the call to remove the power-brokers, which electrified the nation too with a new sense of hope. Rajiv Gandhi in this instance was referring to the party structure and the chieftains who had come to occupy seats of power, which they clung on to, because actually their writ in the party depended on the seat.

There were two types of power crises. At the party level, the satraps were ruling the roost. In actual day-to-day existence throughout the country, shortage of electricity for interminably long hours was the more immediate power-crisis. Most states were in no position to supply power on regular basis and were plagued with shortages. In Uttar Pradesh, most urban areas did not have power supply in the morning for six hours. Imagine doctors in state hospitals waiting for all those hours for electricity supply to be resumed, so that they could start "normal" treatment of patients!

Rajiv's impatience with people reminded old timers of his grand father's temperamental outbursts. But whereas Jawaharlal Nehru's frequent lapses into bad temper were always followed by quick, decisive action to undo the damage, not all the Nehrus Rajiv knew turned out to be men of such resolve and determination.

Rajiv often chose the right people for the wrong reasons. Sometimes, he did not pay much heed to the right advice. In his relationship with friends and colleagues, Rajiv Gandhi often miscalculated to his own detriment. His implicit trust and faith in Vishwanath Pratap Singh turned out to be a political disaster. 'V.P.' was, in the early years, a Sanjay acolyte; subsequently, when Rajiv Gandhi assumed ascendancy, V.P. is on record as saying that in Rajiv, he had found his "true leader." The two of them got along well in the beginning. Rajiv entrusted V.P. Singh with the crucial finance portfolio. In his overzealous exercise of ministerial power, V.P. decided to inaugurate a 'raid-raj' of a kind unprecedented in recent Indian history. His targets were ostensibly those in the industrial and corporate sectors who had fleeced the nation of crores through subterfuge and stealth. V.P. Singh was highly selective rather than objective in his attempt. At a time when the country was agog with the full-scale war between two corporate houses and its consequences on the politics and economics of the moment, V.P. Singh chose to take sides in the battle rather than act as an impartial arbiter.

In his first budget, Viswanath Pratap Singh announced abolition of estate duty. He justified its abolition as a measure to do away with red tape. He did not realize that estate duty was not an instrument for earning revenue. It was an instrument for maintaining control over the wealth and wealthy. Since wealth and wealthy were far more among the former ruling princes and princesses as well as among those who controlled the monopoly business, it was essentially a political instrument to maintain a control over them. VP Singh had released them from the political control in one stroke. After listening to his first budget speech, Sitaram Kesri was the first Congress leader to remark, "Today he has put the Congress party on a downward slide." These proved to be prophetic words because the Congress never recovered from it nor could climb back to its past glory. Rajiv Gandhi's unprecedented majority in the Lok Sabha elections of1984 did nothing to change the lives of those who voted for him. Another leader had betrayed the led; the Congress had flattered to deceive yet again. But more of that later.

To Rajiv's chagrin V.P. Singh's obsessive streak often got the better of him. He was given to needlessly verbalise his fascination for some and hatred for some others. His strong likes and dislikes did not suit the sensitivities of the finance portfolio. His much-touted, "relentless" campaign against the dirty practices of the rich often yielded completely different results than desired. He once explained to MJ Akbar, the famous author-journalist, that what he was trying through the raids was to punish those "modern Ravanas "who were destroying the country's economy. For V.P. Singh, several industrialists were all rogues and they needed to be punished. This kind of gimmicks won him instant popularity, but for the Rajiv government, such obsessive zeal became a major credibility problem. When SL Kirloskar, the octogenarian industrialist of Maharashtra who is universally regarded as among the great pioneers of Indian enterprise, was arrested on flimsy charges and detained in prison, there was shock and disgust throughout the land. Industry circles made much of this crucial lapse of judgment by the finance minister's super-charged bureaucrats. The country's image was dented by this one episode to an extent that whatever good that V.P. Singh had intended proved almost completely counter-productive. According to industrialist Hari Shankar Singhania, one German industrialist asked him in the wake of Kirloskar's arrest: "What is wrong? Is the government bad or Indian laws are so antiquated? Or, were all Indian industrialists that bad?" The query met with a swift response. "Something has to be bad otherwise how could an 80 year old industrialist be put behind bars?"

Rajiv Gandhi and his finance minister were obviously working at cross-purposes. On advice from captains of industry, Rajiv Gandhi wanted to introduce reforms in the economy so that productive and creative energies of the urban oriented, vibrant and educated middle class could be exploited to a fuller extent. V.P. Singh was behaving like a finance minister possessed by an unwarranted zeal to set everything right in one go. There was no logical continuity in his actions as finance minister. He made the principle of natural justice stand on its head. Unbecoming power to the bureaucracy could only result in miscarriage of justice. V.P. Singh did not realise that, and Rajiv Gandhi did not have the required will to make him understand that. As a consequence, a perfectly valid weapon available to the state to get even with errant industrialists and others who misinterpreted laws to their benefit was grossly misused.

The great Indian middle class had found a new hero in Rajiv Gandhi. But within the same set, Rajiv had also emerged as a villain in a soft man's guise. For the Congress, all this flurry of activity at the top led to confusion worse confounded. As a party avowedly committed to socialism and by definition against monopoly houses, the Congress could have made vital gains through intelligent policy initiatives. But there was no Indira Gandhi to translate economic policies into good politics. For the electorate at large, Rajiv Gandhi's real moment of reckoning was to come, not because of the raids but because of certain dubious aspects associated with key defence deals.

Bad politics made Rajiv Gandhi reject the idea of starting mid day meal schemes for children all over the country when such a specific suggestion was made to him. He had then said that it was a waste of resources to start such an unproductive scheme that did not generate creative assets. He disliked what he termed were "populist" projects. In later years, he had also said that only 15-paise actually reached the targeted audience out of each rupee sanctioned for developmental projects. Earnest Congressmen tried to convince him that more money was spent in meeting administrative costs than actualizing developmental gains.

Another example of good intentions going haywire was the manner in which the anti-defection bill was shepherded. Madhu Limaye had opposed and thwarted the attempt of the Morarji Desai government in 1978 to introduce a similar bill to put a halt to defections. His good friend Madhu Dandavate had seen visions of Jawahar Lal Nehru in Rajiv Gandhi when the Bill was introduced in the Lok Sabha. The Bill spelt out a new definition of electoral and by inference, political, morality by arithmetical considerations. The logic was not too quaint: If thirty-three persons out of a given hundred crossed the floor in Parliament or state legislatures, it was immoral act and was to be punished with disqualification. If thirty-four persons preferred to part the company with the original group, they were to be rewarded with recognition as a separate group.

This was to change the entire complexion of politics. Horse-trading had a new meaning now. Enticements and inducements had to be substantial to meet the requirements of the new law. Quite contrary to stated intentions, a seemingly foolproof ploy to discourage floor-crossing has since become a handy tool for political destabilization and worse. Any crossing over ought to have been recognized as an immoral act in itself as it was an act of betrayal of the electorate. To get elected on one agenda, one promise, and then revert sides ought to be punished with compulsory resignation and the need to seek re election from the same set of constituents. In the absence of such correctives, the Act has remained a cruel paradox.

By the time the Bofors scandal erupted in all its fury, much of the gloss that surrounded Rajiv had already got corroded. His government was unable to deliver, and with the party no longer providing either impetus or ideas to the leader, Rajiv Gandhi was orphaned twice over. Like his mother, he had signed his own exit policy. But the exit was to come on most disagreeable and tragic terms. What the Bofors scandal did was to directly bring Rajiv Gandhi in the focus of kickback allegations in the deal and thus, into the ambit of corruption. To this day, it is still not established that Rajiv Gandhi himself was a beneficiary from the alleged kickbacks. But the Bofors scandal succeeded in kicking Rajiv out of the hero-mould, which the middle class had so assiduously put around him. The nitty-gritty of how the Bofors scandal was first "broken" by a Swedish radio network and how through V.P. Singh it became a cause celebre has been told and will be told. Some controversies have this indelible touch to them.

For the record, Rajiv Gandhi had shifted Viswanath Pratap Singh from the finance to the defence ministry in January 1987, much to Singh's annoyance, who took it as a rebuff from powerful corporate giants. Rajiv Gandhi had to in any case pay a heavy price for removing V.P. as well as for the Bofors deal. The mist around the deal killed the 'Mr Clean' part of Rajiv Gandhi. A set of horrendous circumstances was to actually lead to his actual assassination. But it was Bofors that started it all. Not the defence minister VP Singh but the Prime Minister Rajiv Gandhi was put on the mat by the opposition for it was known that Rajiv Gandhi had hurried the signing of the agreement after his visit to Sweden and discussion with the Swedish Prime Minister Olof Palme. Narsimha Rao was shifted out of the defence ministry in September 1985 and Rajiv Gandhi had taken over when the negotiations for the Howitzer Guns with three foreign firms were at the crucial stage.

In March 1986 the agreement was signed with the Bofors firm. VP Singh had cleared the agreement as the finance minister in March 1986. But VP Singh was not the target of the opposition onslaught. It was Rajiv Gandhi who became the prime target. Rajiv

Gandhi also denied that he or his family had received any kickbacks in the deal instead of claiming that no one was paid in India. He could have easily taken a stand if any payments were made elsewhere (to individuals or the party) the government would enquire into it. He could have then shifted the blame elsewhere but Rajiv Gandhi, surrounded by rootless wonders as his advisers and strategists, did not understand the logic behind such a course. He admitted in September 1990 that he was badly advised over the controversy by his advisors. He was amused when a group of journalists told him in September 1990 that he was surrounded by rootless wonders as his advisers. He wanted to know whether the journalists meant rootless or ruthless. He was told that all those who surrounded him were not elected from their own states but from states other than their own. That was one way to define their "rootless" status. Rajiv just smiled.

The thick wall of security around Rajiv had made him more distant from his constituents. He was as usual flippant and often made the securitymen feel sheepish. But the fault was more often than not Rajiv's own. His decision to rush the Indian Peacekeeping Force to Sri Lanka, though he did that on Junios Jayewardene's express requests to that effect, was to prove suicidal.

Why did Rajiv Gandhi break the cardinal principle of management that says that no manager should carry the monkey of others on his shoulders? Why did he forget the elementary fact that everyone should be given enough rope to hang himself? The compulsions that drove Rajiv into embracing Jayawardene's proposal remain obscure till date. That is why no one has been able to understand the compulsions that had driven Rajiv Gandhi to fight the LTTE in Sri Lanka even though it was primarily the task of the Sri Lankan government to do so. There was a time when V. Prabhakaran was Indian government's guest in a major New Delhi hotel. It is well known that the LTTE got material and moral support from their patrons in other countries, including those in Tamil Nadu. Hundreds of IPKF men were killed, several lost their limbs or were maimed for life.

If that was done with ulterior, political purposes, than neither Rajiv—who was to be killed by a LTTE suicide bomber on May 21,

1991- nor the Congress benefited much. But that is running ahead of the story. In 1989, the Indian electorate had reserved another kind of lesson for the Congress. Though it remained the single largest party, the Congress got 197 seats in the Lok Sabha. Not enough to form a government, and Rajiv judiciously did not press the claim. He had been asked by President R Venkataraman whether he would, as the leader of the single largest party, explore the possibility of forming a government. Rajiv politely, and to his democratic credit, declined.

Rajiv Gandhi effected a record number of 139 changes through several cabinet and council reshuffles in four years. No minister was certain when the axe would fall on him or he would be shunted out to another department. Not even the seniors were certain how long would their stay be in a given ministry. The immediate gainers were the bureaucrats in the PMO, who had managed to wrest an upper hand vis-à-vis ministers to an extent they never imagined. They could reject proposals or seek an amendment that would change the entire nature or complexion of proposals forwarded by a minister to the Prime Minister's Office. The ministers could not protest for the fear that they would be shifted out. Ministers tried to short-circuit the bureaucrats by seeking direct access to to Rajiv Gandhi himself; but on a given day, practical considerations of the leader's availability undid most of such attempts. This amounted to nothing but humiliation of the ministers in the eyes of the bureaucracy that they had always taken for granted in earlier epochs.

His dealing with party affairs was equally bewildering. He had appointed the veteran, Kamlapati Tripathi as the working president without giving him any power for functioning as the party's operative chief. Rajiv was incensed when Tripathi wrote a nasty letter to him pointing out serious lapses on Rajiv's part. Pranav Mukherji who was left out of the cabinet was suspected to have drafted the series of letters under the signature of the working president. So he was pushed out of the party. Then Rajiv Gandhi suddenly changed and brought Arjun Singh to take over as the vice president of the party and also removed all general secretaries and brought in a new set of general secretaries in January 1986; why he did it was never fully explained. There was another change of party functionaries in April 1987, the beginning of Rajiv's own downhill tide.

The Punjab accord with Sant H.S. Longowal of the Akali Dal has been hailed as one of the main achievements of the Rajiv Gandhi era. But the terms of the agreement were worked out surreptitiously and in total secrecy as if it were a merger between two corporate giants. The governor of Punjab, Arjun Singh had worked out the details without involving the due and open political processes that are necessary for acceptance of such an agreement. The Indira Gandhi government had worked overtime to destroy the personal image of Sant Longowal and Prakash Singh Badal by planting the stories in the media that both had surrendered to the Armed forces at the time of the Operation Blue Star. Rajiv Gandhi, by inference, had generously agreed to sign an agreement with such a leader of Punjab whose image stood sullied. The inevitable happened. Sant Longowal, while addressing a public rally, was assassinated, even before the ink had dried on the accord.

Assam Gana Parishad boys were deep in sleep when they were asked to pack up and be ready to meet Rajiv Gandhi, sign an accord with him, and thereby, add another feather to Rajiv Gandhi's cap. Arun Nehru, his major domo and internal security minister had warned against signing such an agreement but Rajiv Gandhi would not listen to Nehru's counter-arguments which compromised the work and hardship faced by the Army which had braved the agitation's fury. According to Arun Nehru, that marked the beginning of his rift with Rajiv Gandhi. Though the immediate cause was considered to be their disagreement on the agreement with AGP, the real cause was somewhere else. Rajiv Gandhi was constantly being told on the household front that Arun Nehru constituted a danger and a threat to him as Nehru had ambitions of replacing Rajiv. Thus, in September 1986, when Rajiv Gandhi reshuffled his Council of Ministers the fourth time since January 1985, he divested Arun Nehru of his internal security portfolio. Arun Nehru came to meet Rajiv Gandhi at the official residence of the Prime Minister. Vithal Gadgil and a few junior ministers were present in the main hall when Arun Nehru walked in while Rajiv Gandhi emerged from his anteroom. Arun Nehru asked him bluntly,

"Will you reconsider your decision?' Rajiv Gandhi said: "No."Arun Nehru walked out without uttering another word. Their rift was cemented by that one word. Later, when Arun Nehru lay in a Srinagar hospital recuperating after a heart stroke, his close friend had no time to visit him. The personal touch had gone out of the relationship forever.

Perhaps the spreading cynicism made Rajiv Gandhi desperate enough to buy the proposal that was put before him for defaming Vishwanath Pratap Singh by involving his son Ajeya Singh who was working in a foreign Bank in United States. As per the CBI case that was filed later the main perpetrator of St Kitts conspiracy was the controversial Chandra Swamy. He had got involved a private detective agency to prepare the forged documents of a numbered bank account with an St Kitts Bank to say that Ajay Singh owned it. Generally numbered accounts do not reveal the identity of the holder in any document because they are operated on the basis of code given to the account holder. But this document specified that it belonged to V.P.'s son. It was a crude attempt to malign VP Singh through his son. But the conspiracy theory was obviously far fetched. Narasimha Rao who was then the foreign minister got involved in the controversy because of his close association with Chandra Swamy. Narasimha Rao is said to have issued instructions to the Indian diplomat to assist Chandra Swamy though the case that CBI filed years later did not make any substantive progress.

Rajiv Gandhi was enmeshed in another controversy with the President Zail Singh. Rajiv Gandhi made a statement in the Lok Sabha on March 4 1987 that he had kept the President Zail Singh fully apprised of all developments and his visits to other countries. Zail Singh was peeved over the fact that Rajiv Gandhi had not called on him for months or informed him of his decisions. Giani Zail Singh had sent back the controversial Postal bill that was enacted to provide powers to the government to intercept and screen postal communications for checks whether it was a communication between terrorists. He did not approve of providing such sweeping powers to the government to encroach on privacy of citizens. In this context the debate was raised in the House and Rajiv Gandhi had replied to the opposition charge with the assertive statement. But was only to invite a rejoinder from the President within the same week

On March 8 1987 the President wrote that because the Prime Minister had not divulged the whole truth to him, the former unwittingly did not tell the truth to the Lok Sabha. The onus was on Rajiv to keep the President apprised of developments, which he did not honour. A meeting of the Union cabinet was summoned to assess the fall-out of the President's letter accusing the Prime Minister of misleading the Lok Sabha. It was a serious charge. The story was broken on March 9, two days before the Indian Express claimed it as an exclusive. The Express also alleged that there was a hand of the controversial God-man Chandra Swamy behind the letter. It was a part of a large conspiracy

In the midst of the raging controversy over the Bofors deal, VP Singh found another accusation in a message that had come from a German government firm that it was unable to pay the kick back demanded of it for supply of two HDW submarines. It was in the government files in the defence ministry. VP Singh promptly ordered inquiry in to the accusations on April 9 1987. He was asked to submit his resignation for his action of ordering the inquiry without prior consultations with the Prime Minister. The action was construed as political misdemeanor. VP Singh was suspected by many party stalwarts since 1986 when he had played out a drama of injured innocence over a report published by Raviver, a Hindi weekly brought out by the Anand Bazaar Group which accused him of amassing huge amounts by counting bushes for trees. The land deal was also brought into close scrutiny. It is widely known that H.N. Bahuguna supplied the relevant details to Mulayam Singh Yadav, who, in his capacity as the leader of the opposition in the U.P. Assembly, made a great hue and cry over it. V.P. Singh's intention to involve the Opposition to certify his Innocence alienated him from those Congressmen who thought that he should have clarified his bona fides before the party first.

The parting of ways between V.P. Singh and Rajiv is still wrapped in mystery. It is said that VP Singh never wanted to leave the Congress and was ready to serve even as the party secretary. However his plea was not accepted. Arun Nehru and Arif Mohamed

Khan goaded him out of the party. Arif Mohmed Khan had a score to settle with the Prime Minister for making him a sacrificial goat over the Shah Bano controversy. At Raja's instance, Arif Mohmed Khan had defended the Supreme Court verdict and the government for Indira Gandhi had amended the Criminal procedure Code in 1972 to provide same benefits to Muslim women as, were available to others for maintenance after divorce. Under pressure from the Muslim leaders, Rajiv Gandhi had agreed to enactment of a new law for the divorced Muslim women and deprive them of a right to maintenance as was demanded by the Muslim clergy. Arif Mohmed Khan could not agree with the decision and had sent his resignation and it was accepted also promptly. A bitter Khan joined hands with the already embittered Arun Nehru.

He also had to take care against another charge that he had prompted Rajiv Gandhi to throw open the doors of the Babri Masjid that had remained locked up since 1949 after a communal riot over the puja at the temple inside the Masjid. Arun Nehru has always maintained that he was not responsible for the advice but others who were acting as his advisers. He had merely dialed the telephone number of the then UP chief minister Veer Bahadur Singh and handed over the receiver to Rajiv Gandhi to issue the instructions to the chief minister as he pleased. The phone call was an invitation to a controversy that was to harass the normal life in the country for years as the Kashmir issue has. It became one abiding great source of the tension between the two religious communities. The Babri Masjid controversy has remained a live controversy for years causing the communal tension and providing a ground for the fundamentalists to reap political benefits out of it.

Now Arun Nehru and Arif Mohamed Khan goaded VP Singh to come out in open against Rajiv Gandhi and the Indira Congress. Incidentally, there was a fierce debate before the Centenary Session of the party at Bombay in 1985 whether the Indian National Congress should continue to use name of Indira Gandhi in its title. For years it was known as INC (I). Many howled when GK Moopanar suggested that there was no point in using Indira's I in the title since Indira Gandhi was no more alive. After three hours debate, it was decided that capital I be converted to small I.

So the trio decided to fight the party with a small I. They formed the Jan Morcha with many others who had fallen way back from the Congress also decided to join the new bandwagon that was to be driven by the honest (?) politician VP Singh. Harikesh Bahadur Singh young Congress leader has said when VP Singh came out of the Congress that VP Singh's honesty was strategic and not instinctive. The events later were to prove that he was right.

But the formation of the Jan Morcha did electrify Indian politics. Other parties were also mesmerized by the public support and response that VP Singh and his Jan Morcha received in different parts of the country. Rajiv Gandhi and his advisers desperately tried various moves to get out of the defence deals controversy but each move entangled them further new knots. Krishna Chandra Pant was given charge of the defence but he proved to be unequal to meet the opposition challenge. In the midst of it, Arun Singh who was earlier made the minister of state for defence stepped out of the Rajiv Gandhi government over his differences with Rajiv Gandhi. To intensify its pressure the opposition members had even submitted their resignations from the Lok Sabha. It was an unprecedented political step in a hope that it might force Rajiv Gandhi to seek a fresh mandate.

It led to rumours that President Zail Singh was approached by a senior Jan Morcha leader to dismiss Rajiv Gandhi and install someone else as the Prime Minister since Rajiv Gandhi was caught up in allegations of receiving kickbacks in the defence deals. The tension was apparent and perceptible though it was not known whether or not Giani Zail Singh had even considered such a possibility. He was advised by several senior political leaders that he should not indulge in the conspiratorial politics as the country was still suffering from politics of conspiracy that was carried out by one previous President Neelam Sanjiv Reddy who had refused to accept the legitimate claims of the Janata Party and installed Charan Singh as the prime minister. Nothing happened except that Zail Singh retired in July 1987 and R. Venkataraman was elected in his place to occupy Rashtrapati Bhavan for next five years.

Though the opposition had resigned from the Lok Sabha, its members continued to be on the Joint Parliamentary Committee that was appointed to inquire into allegations of the kickbacks in the defence deals. A sub committee had even attended the field trials of the Bofors gun and certified that it was the best gun that had been purchased by the Rajiv Gandhi government. Such a certificate was essential because some opposition leaders had begun to campaign in Punjab and Haryana to incite the masses with claims that while their children were being sent to the defence forces to defend the honour and borders of the country, the government was purchasing inferior defence equipment in order to earn the ill-gotten wealth. Such a campaign would cause demoralization in the defence forces and also in the rural areas.

In 1988 and 1989, Rajiv Gandhi became the butt of many political jokes. Sharad Joshi, the Hindi satirist had written many a satire at Rajiv Gandhi's expense; especially after his visits to tribal areas in Madhya Pradesh where he had even asked villagers whether they had to pay rents for huts in which they were living. Rajiv Gandhi had made honest efforts to change the country. There was no doubt about it. He had come as a great hope to the educated population of the country and also entrepreneurs. However his advisers had led him to make several mistakes and political gaffes. Ultimately he was advised to go in for the Panchayat Raj for villages and districts so that he could directly reach the masses in rural areas. A committee was appointed to draft a bill for introduction of the Panchayat Raj in the country. However members who had never lived in villages nor did know what the village life was like laded the committee. They were sons and daughters of the persons who had held high offices in urban areas of the country. And their acquaintance with the villages was their occasional visits. Rajiv Gandhi decided to call in for the early elections in October 1989. The man who had won an unprecedented majority only five years earlier had decided to go to polls without any substantive issue in hand. He had decided to take on the challenge with the opposition that was laced with the inflammatory arsenal spelt as Bofors.

The formation of the Janata Dal provided a joint opposition platform. It was born out of the merger of the Janata party with the

Jan Morcha with VP Singh becoming its leader. Despite the fact that it was beset with many problems due to personal differences among various leaders, it was ready for battle with the Indira Congress, which had already lost its vote banks due to disenchantment of the poor with the policies of the Rajiv Gandhi government. Rajiv Gandhi made fitful attempts towards the latter part to reach the poor in rural areas directly, by allotment of funds that bypassed local bureaucrats. But it proved to be of no avail. The Shah Bano controversy had become a scarecrow for the Congress party. The defence kickbacks issue also was a great wall between the Congress and the victory in the Lok Sabha elections. To add to the injuries was the understanding that the Janata Dal had reached with the regional parties like TDP in Andhra Pradesh, DMK in Tamilnadu and Akali Dal in Punjab and Assam Gan Parishad in Assam to form the National front that was launched in Madras in October 1989 when Rajiv Gandhi was preparing for the elections.

Amid all this, the Janata Dal and the Bharatiya Janata party reached an understanding to give one to one fight with the Congress in the most parts of the country. During the election campaign, Rajiv Gandhi ordered Buta Singh to attend the Shilanyas (Foundation Stone laying ceremony) at the controversial site near Babri Masjid in October 1989, much to the amusement of the BJP leadership and to the horror of others. The move was only to whet the appetite of Hindu fundamentalists. Opinion polls had clearly indicated that the Congress would fall short of a majority by a hundred seats. Even the internal assessment of the Congress predicted great surprises. The party was on a steep decline, which was clearly indicated by the final results that came. The Congress party that had won 412 seats in the December 1984 elections was reduced to winning only 162 seats in December 1989 elections even though it had emerged as the single largest party. It had lost 250 constituencies to the opposition. What could be more tragic?

The five-year term of Rajiv Gandhi was summed up by Kalpnath Rai, former minister of state during the election campaign of 1989 in one sentence. His leader completed a full term without achieving any thing (except one). He had cleared the path for the others to take over because the social and political reach of the

Congress had begun to shrink due to the economic policies of the Indira Congress since 1980. The political ball game had changed completely.

Charisma as the defining factor in party politics has run its course. Rajiv Gandhi was perhaps the last of the charismatic breed; V.P.Singh also wore a halo around him, but it faded a bit too soon for the messiah's own good. Rajiv Gandhi may have had all the ingredients of a pleasing personality; he was perhaps handsomer than even his grand father, and was a man who was at all times affable and courteous. Stupid advisers distanced him first from V.P. Singh and then, from Chandra Shekhar. Towards the end of his innings, Rajiv appeared to have learnt from some of his earlier follies. He was trying hard to undo the 'immaturity' tag during the 1991 campaign. He was also drawing reasonable crowds, which meant that his politics had not been entirely denuded of all charm. But beyond his essential charm, Rajiv Gandhi remained a naïve practitioner of politics whose ignorance of several key components of leadership was unpardonable. He was not as clever as his mother, which was perhaps a quality. But in politics, if the one and only one leader of an otherwise rudderless party turns out to be completely devoid of statecraft as Rajiv often proved himself to be, the end-result had to be drastic and tragic. Rajiv Gandhi's tragedy was not just in the fact that he died young. The much greater tragedy was that unlike his brother Sanjay and mother, he was by and large open to suggestions and could still have evolved into a remarkable leader of men.

10

The Failed Messiah

" If there was no V.P. Singh, we would have had to invent one..."
George Fernandes

" He is as good as his word—and his word is no good."
Seumas MacManus

"A man must not swallow more beliefs than he can digest."
Brooks Adams

What was the essential message of the 1989 elections? Did the verdict mean unqualified rejection of an individual—Rajiv Gandhi—and the acceptance of another, Vishwanath Singh? If politics could be reduced to such objectivities, the world would be so much simpler.

Let us try and see the 1989 elections more closely. For one, the verdict spelt the end of single party domination; but that was only an arithmetical aftermath. Was there a concrete alternative that emerged to the Rajiv dispensation? The answer has to be in the negative. The Congress, for one, was still the single largest party. And only an inherently contradictory and hence rickety combine replaced the Congress at the Centre. Vishwanath Pratap Singh had individually symbolized the collective disillusionment with Rajiv's 'Mr Clean' persona. His acceptability to both the Right and the Left of the political spectrum was only because he symbolized the anti Congress sentiments that had catapulted him to the high office.

There was an unusual, typically melodramatic moment before the transition. From nowhere, as it were, the name of Chaudhary Devi Lal cropped up to lead the new conglomerate. Although the 'Tau' had indeed shepherded the gradual build-up against Rajiv through a series of conclaves and meetings, the verdict in 1989 had gone in favour of the kind of disillusionment, which V.P. Singh's break from the Congress represented. Both L.K. Advani and Somnath Chatterjee for once agreed on that fact.

For effect rather than by design, V.P. Singh was not elected as the party at the first meeting of the Janata Dal in parliament in December 1989. Instead Devi Lal was unanimously elected; Devi Lal then grandly declared that he was gifting the post to VP Singh. Even the Returning Officer Madhu Dandavate did not protest or found anything irregular in this kind of gift at the party meeting. It was prearranged at a meeting organized by Biju Patnaik. Several other leaders were privy to the ploy. The man who was left groping in the dark was Chandra Shekhar, who took the overall exercise as a sleight-of-the-hand.

Thus VP Singh had begun his term as the Prime Minister on a false note. He set up his term on the crutches provided by the Left and the Right as well as other regional parties that had become a part of the National Front in October 1988. Devi Lal accepted the post of the deputy Prime minister but Chandra Shekhar refused to associate himself with the government. He later told others who were pressing him to accept the offer and join the Singh cabinet that they were asking him to undermine the VP government after he had declared his reservations in the leadership of VP Singh. Earlier in the Janata party government in 1977, he had spurned down the offer of the cabinet post that was made by the Prime Minister Morarji Desai. He refused because he had not accepted leadership of Morarji Desai and had in fact told the Sarvodaya leader Jai Prakash not to make Morarji the Prime Minister.

Rajiv Gandhi and others in his party silently watched the spectacle. The Congress could not have hoped for a more farcical opening to the unfolding chapter. It was clear that V.P. Singh would have to forever undertake a 'left, right, left' drill to satisfy diametrically opposite supporters as well as due to desperate conglomerate that had assembled in the National Front. Compromise with a capital 'C' was writ large over the entire arrangement.

In the hurry that it was formed, the Janata Dal 'forgot' to have any ideological moorings of its own. It had no economic programme worth the name. Nor leaders who were desperate to grab power had even thought of a need for such a commitment. The first sign of acrimony became apparent when the Rajya Sabha was debating the Motion of Thanks on the Presidential address. The statement revealed no original thinking. The Janata Dal was formed without any serious commitment to an economic programme worth the name. Allocation of portfolios had been agreed upon, and party office bearers were in place: but there was no programme in sight. In a sheepish reaction, Chandra Shekhar was requested to prepare an economic blueprint. In five minutes flat, his draft programme was adopted! The new leaders had even not bothered to read the draft carefully to find out what commitments were made by one who had written the programme.

This made it a lot easier for the Congress to hold proceedings on one issue after another. The Congress thought it was repaying an old debt; the Opposition had been similarly nit picking during the uproar over defence deals. Endless hours were spent on generating noise. The ensuing one-upmanship diminished the quality of the debate to abysmal depths. A shouting brigade in the Rajya Sabha was complemented by a similarly vocal segment in the lower house; effectively, the joke was on the institution of Parliament. Sanity became an instant casualty.

There were several occasions in the first session itself when the shouting brigade defied senior leaders. The brigade sought, and got, sanction from Rajiv Gandhi; some veterans like P. Shiv Shankar did complain, but their voice was lost in the all-pervasive cacophony. The loss to their credibility hardly mattered with the new ring-leaders of the Opposition benches. Rajiv Gandhi's quixotic silence did not help matters. What exact purpose did he propose to achieve by blocking serious debate remained a mystery about which only he could answer. He did not, and the tamasha was thus licensed to go on. A mature response from Rajiv would have shown the gaping contradictions between the Janata Dal's promises and their actual reality. If the government was blocked in every manner and on every issue, there was no way that democracy could function in a healthy atmosphere. Even this much was not clear to the stormy petrels of the Opposition. Rajiv Gandhi was content with the trouble the shouting brigade caused to Arif Khan and Arun Nehru. After all, they had betrayed him, hadn't they? Both were specifically targeted though both managed to overcome the Congress onslaught. Arif had by then become an astute parliamentarian having learnt all tricks of the trade on the Congress bench earlier.

For the first time in four decades, an unprecedented number of amendments were moved to the Motion of Thanks. Normally, a customary address by the President to the Joint session of parliament hardly attracts such attention. Prime Minister VP Singh was not allowed to complete his reply to the short debate in the Rajya Sabha for five days because of heckling, interruptions and heated exchanges. The shouting brigade was determined not to allow him even a couple of sentences in one stretch. Since the brigade was determined and not amenable to any kind of persuasion, it was a futile exercise from within and between the parliamentary affairs minister and the brigade members to bring about a compromise. The brigade had deleted the word compromise from its lexicon precisely because Vishwajit Singh was the main instigating force. His close proximity to Rajiv Gandhi helped him enormously.

While pandemonium became the norm in Parliament, every important (and sometimes, not so important) decision had to satisfy both the Right and Left supporters of the ruling Front. To appease his promoters from the Right, V.P. Singh okayed the appointment of Jagmohan as the Kashmir governor. The Bharatiya Janata Party had insisted that he was ideal man to solve the problem of increasing terrorism and violence in the state. Chandra Shekhar had warned the Prime Minister that it was a wrong step because Kashmir chief minister Farooq Abdullah was opposed to it. VP Singh showed his helplessness, because his home minister Mufti Mohmmad Sayeed also wanted the same man. They had their way but only to compound the confusion.

Terrorism had grown in Kashmir largely as an offshoot of the rigged elections in March 1987. The National Conference and the Indira Congress had fought the elections in alliance. Several voices in the party, like Dr Najma Heptulia's, had warned against the techniques the two sides had used to ensure that the Muslim United Front was not able to even file nominations. Farooq wanted the deal and his friend Rajesh Pilot was in total agreement. Rajiv Gandhi acceded to their demand. As a consequence, a large number of nominations from sources outside the two allied parties were summarily rejected. Only eight members could make it to the Assembly's Opposition benches. Since the Congress and the National Conference were allies, there was a total vacuum in the opposition. Frustration and disappointment within a large section naturally diverted embittered youth towards terror. Pakistan was only waiting for any such opportunity to present itself.

The situation needed careful and delicate political handling. State terrorism was no counter to the misgivings among the youth. Jagmohan's sledgehammer approach worsened things greatly. Farooq Abdullah's resignation paved the way for untrammeled governor's rule. He had locked himself in a high security fortress and began using the security forces to deal with the situation instead of opening the doors for a dialogue with the people who mattered and who could have prevailed with their sane approach. The confrontation between the security forces and the terrorist groups merely encouraged the other side to look for desperate measures to bring the governor to his knees and one such was abduction of daughter of the union home minister Mufti Sayeed Mohamed with a demand for release of three terrorists who were held by the government.

The country would have lauded the union home minister if he had taken a firm and adamant position of refusing to concede demand of the terrorist group. It would have set a new equation between the two religious groups in the country. Instead, he allowed himself to be persuaded by others to agree to the release of three terrorists in return of Dr Rubbaiya's release.

Yet another knee-jerk response from VP Singh was grounding the entire fleet of new Air Bus planes that had then joined the Indian Airlines fleet, after an Airbus was hit by a mishap at the Bangalore airport in February 1990. It was clearly a human error by the Commander of the plane. But VP Singh ordered grounding of the entire fleet for rumours were making rounds that kickbacks had changed hands in the deal. The fleet remained grounded from February 1990 to September 1990 leading to a colossus financial loss to the Indian Airlines. Eagerness of the civil aviation minister Arif Mohmed Khan to cut the losses by taking off the grounded fleet had invited suspicion that he was an interested party to help out the Airbus Consortium to retrieve its lost credibility due to the grounding of the entire fleet. There was no medicine for the suspicious minds.

Even though Arun Nehru and Arif Mohmed Khan were the main architects and designers of the Janata Morcha and had propped up VP Singh, a line of mistrust remained between them and V.P. Singh. Their relations were never easy as VP Singh always thought that he was being used for ulterior motives. Their differences surfaced after the VP government faced mayhem at Meham in Haryana during the bye-election to the state assembly. The violent incidents in Mahem were instigated and inspired by Om Prakash Choutala against the Congress candidate was the allegation. So Arun Nehru and Khan got an opportunity to bring the uneasiness in their relations with VP Singh to the surface. They penned a missive to the Prime Minister, giving him the option to either retain deputy Prime Minister Devi Lal or them in the Council of Ministers.

The Congress was just waiting for this kind of a development within the Jan Morcha that had become a part of the Janata Dal but had not merged as a cohesive force. It was behaving as a separate group within. Their ultimatum left VP Singh with little choice and he sought resignation of the deputy Prime Minister. The demand was the beginning of the collapse of the VP Singh government.

Several other pointers, like a completely World Bank inspired new industrial policy; the tumult and worse surrounding the removal of Devi Lal; the steady dilution of the draft economic programme; the growing disaffection for V.P. 's individual style of functioning and many such small and major inputs removed the myths that surrounded V.P. Singh. This was a big opportunity for the Congress to score politically. V.P. Singh added fuel to the fire by pretending that he was the victim; wronged by contending interests. In actual fact, he allowed contradictions to manage him, as he candidly admitted a few crucial months later.

As if internal contradictions were not enough, V.P. Singh's equivocal stand on Ayodhya encouraged the saffron brigade to turn it into the single most volatile issue, which has divided communities in post-Independence India. Devi Lal, who felt humiliated at his unceremonious eviction from the government, decided to strike back. He organised a major rally of farmers at the Boat Club lawns. V.P. Singh sought to preempt the consolidation by resorting to accepting the Mandal Commission Report for reservations in government jobs and entry into the higher technical educational institutions for other backward castes. The report had been submitted way back in 1980, but no party either opposed it or implemented it. Sensing the great counter-effect the acceptance of the Report will have on both Devi Lal and the BJP, V.P. Singh embraced the controversial report, which led to immediate, and rather uncalled for, reactions from the younger generation of the upper castes, especially in the north.

Since positive discrimination as a means of state policy had almost run its course, and the Mandal Commission's report could only have had very marginal effect on the exact employment pattern in the government sector, much of the brouhaha that accompanied the report was clearly misplaced. Neither Mandalisation's proponents or its critics were very right in opposing the recommendations for the reasons they did. But purely in tactical terms, V.P. Singh had for the moment diverted public attention from Devi Lal. But the events that followed also had the attention of all focused on him alone.

But Ayodhya turned out to be his nemesis. The failure to convince the Hindutva brigade about the highly explosive and dangerous dimensions of raking up the issue cost V.P. Singh heavily. His political martyrdom was inbuilt into the situation he had created. But he was playing the game of perpetuating his position by creating his own constituency among the other backward classes as he could not consolidate his position in the traditional vote banks of either the Congress party or the BJP. He had to seek a different and new constituency. He chose the other backward classes of the north.

The Congress failed to capitalize on an excellent opportunity to clarify its stand on Mandal and its opposition to the Ram temple demand in Ayodhya. In the election campaign that followed a year after the collapse of the VP Singh govoernment, Rajiv had the kick-start of his campaign from Faizabad- the place of the major controversy, promising to usher in Ram Rajya. His advisers had thoroughly misread the public mood once again. In the guise of introducing social justice, V.P. Singh was playing a game, which could only result in several volatile forces getting unleashed in one go. One such was the younger generation of the upper castes that had begun to react with self-immolation on streets in the northern states. It caused revulsion though the reaction from the younger generation was uncalled for and unjustified.

Self-immolations as political protest were hitherto confined to the Southern states only. They spread like wild fire in the North India. The Congress was stunned by the sharp reactions by the younger generation that believed that it had been deprived of the economic benefits by denying them number of jobs in the governments, but that was only a reaction rather than a political way out. The urban middle class, the constituency of the BJP was rudely shaken by the steps initiated by the VP Singh government. The BJP leadership was thrown into a desperate spin for it had to take counter measures to control the political damage it would suffer due to the step announced by VP Singh. And it chose the dangerous cynicism of the Ram Janambhoomi issue to create political space for itself. Inversely, V.P. Singh had helped in this sordid denouement.

The Congress leadership strangely preferred silence to enunciating where it stood. Rajiv Gandhi admitted to a group of media persons who had met him on September 29 1990 for nearly two hours that the issue was fraught with a political danger because VP Singh had created an explosive situation in the country by his step that was bound to lead to a sharper caste division. He also agreed that the benefits of the reservations were merely circulating and not percolating. The fact that it was the very weapon that had helped the Congress to retain power for forty long years was lost on Rajiv. He could have easily pointed out that VP Singh was playing unfair with the backward classes by not including the reservations in admissions to the higher technical education for the other backward classes as provided for the schedule castes and tribes. Without the preferred and discriminatory privileges also for education, the reservations would not make any dent on providing social justice to them. His advisers told him to prefer silence since endorsement to the decision would go one way and the opposition to it would go other way and the Congress would not derive political mileage from either endorsing or opposing the step taken.

The BJP could not have remained silent, because it thought that Mandal's sway will sweep the Ram temple issue out of the picture frame. L.K. Advani's Rath Yatra from Somnath to Ayodhya that was set to pass through several states and was slated to raising the communal temperature and tension as naked swords and trishuls became a part of the entourage that accompanied him. Young bands danced with open swords and trishuls in their hands and saffron bands tied to their heads before his chariot raising the provocative slogans. Even more provocative speeches were made while Advani heard them out patiently. His purpose was being served. Tactica ; BJP said that it was the Mandal Report that made it withdraw support to the V.P. Singh government. In actual fact, it secretly welcomed the opportunity to unleash the Ram Mandir issue to keep its Hindutva plank together in face of possible casteist realignments.

The Congress had been accorded yet another opportunity to set its house in order by taking a clear-cut stand on issues of casteism and communalism. Instead of doing that, Rajiv Gandhi wanted the other players to make mistakes. The Congress was prepared only to gain from the confusion; it did nothing to end it. This is where the absence of a strong leader with defined ideas and a party, which was committed to supporting him became glaringly obvious. While each and every segment of the political class, except perhaps the isolated Leftists, were scoring cynical brownie points out of the situation, Rajiv Gandhi and his party preferred to wait and see. This proved to be as suicidal a course as the one his mother had adopted in the wake of the Allahabad high court verdict. Instead of facing political crises frontally, the Congress had been reduced to a spectator.

The Congress was the single largest party in the Lok Sabha. Hence contacts were established with Chandra Shekhar whether he was willing to form a government in order to avoid an early election to the Lok Sabha. The Congress under Rajiv Gandhi was yet not ready to face an early election. When Devi Lal had tried to persuade Chandra Shekhar to accept the offer of the Deputy Prime Minister in the VP Singh government, Chandra Shekhar had told him, Choudhary saheb aap apani pagari kisike hathme rakh sakate hai par mai itana bewqoof nahi. (Chodharyji, you can hand over your turban to some one but I am not that fool). VP Singh did not send in his resignation. Instead he preferred to face the vote confidence and accept the defeat on the floor of the House. For he was obviously keen to register his last statement as the Prime Minister. He registered his last statement for the records of the Lok Sabha on November 7 1990 and was soundly defeated. He became the first Indian Prime Minister to be defeated on the floor of the House. Morarji Desai had earlier faced a similar situation in July 1979 but had preferred to step down gracefully than get defeated. Charan Singh had sought the dissolution of the Lok Sabha rather than face a losing vote of confidence in August 1979.

But he had set the country aflame and ensured that the caste divide and religious divide of the country was accentuated sharply. It would be decades before the country could recover from such a deep divide. Only historians would be able to evaluate his policy and his role in evacuation of a million Indians who were stranded in the Middle East when Iran's Saddam Hussain had decided to gobble up Kuwait as a part of his territory and unleashed an unprecedented war in the region. Obviously the large implications of the war that had come closer to India were missed. Only concern shown was how to evacuate the stranded Indians.

The BJP had by then established a new identity by targeting the minorities as its political enemies. Till then the BJP had not taken an overt anti minority stand. But the caste-divide introduced by VP Singh in the Indian polity had forced it to take an open stand of bashing the minorities. It was to provide a new strength to the Vishwa Hindu Parishad that had come to be the aggressive wing of the Sangh Parivar by leading the movement on the Ayodhya issue. The country was caught in a sharp wedge between the caste-divide and the religious divide. The religious divide was used by the BJP to bash at the Congress by accusing it of appeasing the minorities as its vote bank through pseudo secularism. The regional parties had begun to cut the vote base of the Congress and thus grow at its cost as the next election to the Lok Sabha has shown. Thus a difficult situation was prevailing when Chandra Shekhar was sworn in on November 10 1990 on the front courtyard of the Rashtrapati Bhavan with the conditioned support of the Indira Congress that it would provide support for a full year. No one else but the President R Venkataraman had sought such an assurance from Rajiv Gandhi for he knew how difficult times were when he also had contributed in persuading Chandra Shekhar to accept the challenge.

11

Shotgun Marriage

If you don't know where you are going, you will probably end up somewhere else

Lawrence J Peter

Even if you are on the right track, you will be run over if you just sit there

Will Rogers

To my extreme mortification, I grow wiser every day

Lord Byron

The man who had tried his best to give a veneer of ideology to Indira Gandhi was also one who had few doubts that his exertions would prove transient. He was also the man who tried hard to make a distinction between his usually cordial personal rapport with Indira Gandhi and the objective reality that was inexorably distancing the two. He had also realised that his hitherto self-preferred rejection of accepting political high office had rendered his mass-appeal a bit incongruous: Why should anybody stick it out in politics one silly season after another, if the idea is not to convert that into a tangible platform which went beyond correcting others when he felt they were going wrong and making spirited, but sporadic, interventions in a given parliamentary debate or another?

These thoughts may not have come readily to his mind when Chandra Shekhar, in a bizarre twist of events, found himself in a position to occupy the most important political seat in the land. After what must have been a protracted forethought, Chandra

Shekhar undertook the responsibility of a tenuous arrangement where he, with just fifty-four Members of Parliament in the Lok Sabha, happened to become Prime Minister on November 10 1990. It was an accident, which, apart from its very obvious arithmetical dimensions, also implied an acceptance on part of the Man from Balia that he was inviting more problems for his own credibility than win any fresh honours. In his heart of hearts, Chandra Shekhar knew that even when the Congress was forced by circumstances to back him, the support that he got from that party was premised on highly temporary foundations. A political one-night stand, or playing as night-watchman to ensure that there was no further loss to his team (in this case, the political system) than what had already been inflicted by a series of predecessors who knew what they wanted but did not know how to get the desired results. As consequences, they had built up an aura of confrontation within the system.

Among his close friends, Chandra Shekhar had rather carefully clarified that his decision to accept the challenge was because he sincerely felt the credibility of the system had nose dived to such an extent that playing the lone-ranger would not be enough. He simply did not have the mandate to back any radical or substantial breakthroughs. He had come to occupy the office through a split in the Janata Dal and with the support of the Congress party from the outside. The split was not effected with a desire to occupy the high office but the prevalent danger to the political and economic system had beckoned him to invite trouble by pricking of his thumb so that he could apply the bold correctives to pull the system from the brink of collapse. The politics of confrontation that his predecessors had followed for more than a decade had pushed the Indian parliamentary democracy to the brink of an imminent collapse. Indira Gandhi had continued confrontation with the Akali Dal, Rajiv Gandhi had his hands full in Kashmir with a confrontation and Vishwa Nath Pratap Singh had opened a caste confrontation in order to perpetuate his own constituency. None had given a clear thought to the consequences of their politics of confrontation. So he risked his reputation by forming the government with such a shaky support. He knew that he had a short time to do what he could and he would without hoping to have much of a back up to his programme for salvaging the situation so that the parliamentary democracy could once again be put back on rails.

Rajiv Gandhi would not accept the plea that the Congress should join the government to give the new team better cohesion. The general credibility of a small group being helped along by a numerically much larger ally from the outside could never have been high at any rate. If the critics felt that Shekhar had succumbed to the lure of office, his supporters wondered whether their 'Adhyakshji' (the honorofic for 'Mr. President 'which had become some kind of a nick name for Chandra Shekhar from the time he accepted to be the Janata Party chief in May 1977) will have the necessary elbow-room to fashion out anything resembling his often stated vision of using state-power as a means to further certain egalitarian ends. Neither the critics nor his friends had understood either the man closely enough nor had studied his politics spanning four decades to reach any credible conclusions.

From the word go in his political life, Chandra Shekhar had wrestled with two subjective inclinations. He had striven hard to create a separate niche for himself as an anti-establishment rebel. But his rebellion was not of a kind that excluded the possibility of intervening, if so required, at critical junctures when the political class found itself uncomprehending in face of contradictory pulls and pressures. The long years of political tutelage under Acharya Narendra Dev had convinced Chandra Shekhar that the corridors of power were made of such hard granite that the "leader" often became deaf to the unstated but always eloquent distrust of the ordinary man about the "real" person behind a given persona. Maybe not in so many words, but that is what being Prime Minister had come to mean when Shekhar cynically accepted the opportunity that was his in a set of totally fortuitous circumstances.

Nobody who knew him ever doubted the man's credentials for the job; a left-of-centre profile, an impressive understanding of politics and economics and also, and that is very significant to state here, the essential hollowness which characterized most political parties. Shekhar knew that the Congress under Rajiv was neither a party attuned to the need of the times nor was it any longer the kind of please-all platform which drew sustenance from the once genuinely pan-Indian, national base to confront political challenges. He was deeply suspicious of the direction of economic policies, which had been adopted more under duress from imperialist diktat rather than evolved through national consensus and dialogue.

The Congress was obviously compelled to support him more out of political compulsions rather than any ideological considerations. During his long political innings, Chandra Shekhar had learnt the art of getting along with even those with whom he may have disagreed on ideological or other issues. Rajiv Gandhi did not know what to expect from the conditions that operated at the time when he struck a deal with Chandra Shekhar. The deal was not a result of any newfound realization in the Congress that Chandra Shekhar will be the man who could bail the party out of its internal morass. There was, however at least one thing which both Shekhar and the Congress knew; if at all their mutual arrangement were to have any chance, its longevity could only emanate from good and sensible governance. The Mandal and Masjid divides had already done enough harm to the social fabric for it to withstand an onslaught from cynical successors to a process of systematic dilution of credibility of the polity as a whole.

That the politics of convenience that had catapulted him into the hot seat would continue to bedevil him all through the time he had at his disposal. He became Prime Minister not because he was doing the country or himself any favour. He had seized upon an opportunity, which he reckoned could give him at least some scope to translate often disparate thoughts into a cogent policy. It is said that those who do not expect any miracles often find themselves becoming party to creating one. Chandra Shekhar the Prime Minister had not lost sight of all these essentials when he departed from his till then established stylebook of playing agony aunt here and a well-meaning if a trifle too stern elder statesman at large. The tag 'Young Turk' implied a radical orientation and a sense of strongly felt disenchantment with the prevailing political atmosphere. Chandra Shekhar had two choices; he could either go down as an insignificant footnote, a mere also-ran in a race which nobody in the fray had the chance of winning. Readers would perhaps detect that this book has been very accommodative in trying to locate the importance of Chandra Shekhar in a given historical epoch. Some could say that this kind of accommodation was something that Chandra Shekhar does not deserve, because he has often appeared to be happier in the role of a distant but shrewd observer rather an active player in the political akhara. So, Chandra Shekhar's first choice, which he rejected, was to keep the seat warm before someone with greater numbers replaced him.

The second choice was to accept the challenge and give it the best shot. Opinion is bound to be considerably divided whether Chandra Shekhar actually succeeded in reinforcing the second option. If he actually did, he could have easily and naturally inherited a Rajiv-less Congress as his political springboard. The relations between the two gentlemen had to be polite and politically correct; what is more, it was up to Shekhar to so orient the task he faced that individually and politically, he would not lose out in the long run just because he had courted short-term celebrity. This is of course not to imply that India's most reluctant Prime Minister in history was afraid of taking risks or initiating policies that could leave at least some of his own individual impress on events over which his control was at best tenuous. The arithmetical factor had to be forgotten and in its place, positive thinking, which could resolve, at least immediate problems was needed. It was obviously of some help that Chandra Shekhar had a vision and a set of ideas; after all, not many in the political game had such elementary credentials backing them.

To those inclined to take the view that Chandra Shekhar represented a sense of principles and probity, and often chose to take up an unpopular stand even when others reveled in simply coasting along with the wind, Chandra Shekhar's background provides some references. He had the nerve to take on Indira Gandhi when she ruled supreme in the Congress party in 1971 and win the election to the Central Election Committee of the party, even though she was opposed to him and his friends had deserted him at the crucial hour. He had raised voice in the Central Election Committee in support of even those who were not his friends but who were to suffer injustice by denial of the party nomination. He could take on Morarji Desai and also the formidable Birla empire over the issue of their monopolistic practices; and he did not apologise to Morarji Desai for taking such a stand even when Indira Gandhi insisted. Closer in the context of this narrative, Chandra Shekhar had not sought to build bridges with Rajiv Gandhi even when both may have wanted to see the back of V.P. Singh. It is said that he had not even met Rajiv Gandhi for any length of time for him to think on those lines. Initially, he had reservations himself about efforts to bring them together for a meeting. He said he did not want to embarrass Rajiv Gandhi, who during his stewardship of the country had dubbed him "anti-national."

For someone who often gave views about individuals and made value judgments rather easily, his unease while V.P. Singh held centre-stage was often sought to be exploited by the media, forever hungry to get an angry riposte from him. Just because somebody was in power did not mean that Chandra Shekhar would accept the person as his leader simply because of that reason. And, his anger at the way his friend Devi Lal had become a party to the "deceit" that installed V.P. Singh in power was genuine and transparent.

The best that Chandra Shekhar could hope to do in circumstances, which were far-too-complex and problematic than he could handle, was to remain a realist first and last. He knew that the post Mandal, post saffronisation epoch had divided society too much for piecemeal solutions to work. He did not have the mandate to back him if he at all wanted to fight the challenge posed by either scenarios. Even temporary palliatives often seem to do magic. Chandra Shekhar was looking for those very palliatives when he looked around himself to find a surfeit of terror amid very little sanity. On the economic front, the highly precarious balance of payments situation could not be ignored. For all the smart trappings of reforms, they had done nothing to alter the grim imbalances facing each and every aspect of economic functioning. Foreign exchange reserves were not enough even to last a week, while repayment dues and defaults had mounted inexorably. The Rajiv Gandhi government had depended heavily on market borrowings; this entailed higher interest rates and greater outflow of foreign exchange. Emergency or contingency operations could not be carried out with empty coffers. The Iraq war spelt further economic doom. The narrow support base of the new economic policies adopted by his immediate predecessors had fueled large-scale disenchantment.

The Congress was prepared to play along when the going was good, but bore no responsibility for things getting out-of-hand. Shekhar was thus open to all forms of blackmail. He had in place a bureaucracy that had got accustomed not to tell their political masters the bitter truth even when they themselves knew it. Bureaucrats functioned in a sort of vacuum, which demanded no accountability. He did try to tell some senior bureaucrats that he wanted their cooperation at least in terms of streamlining the national response to the challenges the country faced. All he got were blank stares and seldom, if any, cogent answers. Statistics were thrown at him that could hardly have impressed a seasoned veteran to assume that things were fine. His message to industry was simple: the country faced a fiscal imbalance of Rs 1200 crores, and the big business groups had to help in tiding over the crisis. When the corporate sector did not oblige, Chandra Shekhar immediately imposed new duties that were to fetch him Rs. 1250 crores.

The Congress tried its own version of back seat driving when it wanted specifics. Its first demand was that TN Seshan should be appointed as cabinet secretary; Chandra Shekhar refused. Subsequently, Shekhar did agree, under pressure, to appoint Seshan as Chief Election Commissioner. He had to make do with the available, and extremely limited, talent at is disposal while finalising his council of ministers. He knew that his opponents both to the Right and the Left of the divide were pre determined to scuttle any attempt to rope in talent from outside the narrow group of MPs under his command.

On Ayodhya, Chandra Shekhar opted for seeking a mutually acceptable settlement from the contending parties; to an extent, he met with some success in this direction, but others in the political fray were too envious to give him the kind of support and longevity to see the negotiations reach a logical end. He also tried to reason with belligerent groups in both Kashmir and Punjab with the idea to secure a political way out. As signals of intention, these were on par; in actual terms, these represented abstract attempts to resolve what had been allowed to become an intractable situation.

Pragmatism can only be a partial response. Chandra Shekhar had erred in forgetting this basic fact. Sometimes, because of his equation with individuals at the personal level, Chandra Shekhar could act as an honest arbiter. But that role was better suited to someone not in power; and not when you are in the hot seat, as Chandra Shekhar discovered during the period he had to ease out Tamilnadu chief minister M.Karunanidhi. To begin with, Shekhar tried to have a one-to-one interface in order to tell Karunanidhi that his tacit support for the Liberation Tigers of Tamil Eelam went against national interests. When Karunanidhi did not listen, and the Intelligence Bureau informed Shekhar that there existed direct links between LTTE and the state government, and the tigers knew exactly what had transpired between him and Karunanidhi word by word, the Prime Minister immediately got in touch with state governor Surjit Singh Barnala, and asked for a report of action taken against those who had been guilty of compromising national interests by being in cahoots with the LTTE. When Barnala failed to send the desired report, Chandra Shekhar dismissed the Karunanidhi government and brought the state under central rule.

The first indication about Congress getting edgy about the ongoing arrangement was available when that party insisted that Union finance minister Yashwant Sinha should not present a full budget but seek a vote-on-account instead. Rajiv Gandhi was obviously getting restive and disinclined to honour his promise made to President Venkataraman that the Congress would support the Shekhar government at least for one year.

In the face of mounting popular pressure, Chandra Shekhar conceded one major demand. He agreed to stop refueling facilities, which were being extended to American warplanes during their Iraq campaign. Rajiv Gandhi could claim that it was under Congress pressure that a tacit form of support to the American war on Iraq had been withdrawn. Rajiv had, as a matter of record, planned to visit Baghdad to meet Saddam Hussain. Chandra Shekhar immediately asked Digvijay Singh, minister of state for foreign affairs to accompany the former Prime Minister on his visit to Moscow and Baghdad to facilitate the protocol requirements so that Rajiv Gandhi was able to accomplish whatever his political mission was. Ultimately, the Rajiv gambit turned out to be a bitter fiasco that soured the Shekhar-Congress equation even further.

Rajiv Gandhi's decision to increase mass contact through sadbhavna yatras militated against the type of security cordon that surrounded the Congress leader. He preferred to ignore the security constraints, while being Prime Minister Chandra Shekhar could not have done so.

The mist surrounding Rajiv's assassination persists, and it is for history to punish those who were responsible for the tragedy. Two months before the Rajiv assassination, the Congress charge that two constables from Haryana police had been asked to keep a watch on movements around 10, Janpath raised a huge uproar. Chandra Shekhar offered to get the matter enquired into, but since the Congress had chosen to use this perceived surveillance as the reason for parting ways with Shekhar, it hardly came as a surprise when the Congress party pulled the rug from Shekhar's feet. When the Congress leaders informed him that the party would not support the Motion of Thanks to the President for his conventional address to the two Houses meeting for the budget session, he opted for the only way that was open for him of handing over the resignation and dissolving the Lok Sabha. The Congress leadership was given to understand that he would wilt under the threat and be obedient to meet demands of the party. The Congress managers strived for two days to make him stay as the Congress president was willing to provide him unqualified support but he would not budge from his position as he knew that his acceptance of the Congress proposal would expose him to blackmail by the Congress. He preferred to go out rather than stay at that price. The coterie around Rajiv Gandhi had grossly underestimated the man.

Objectively, Chandra Shekhar had taken a calculated risk in agreeing to become Prime Minister, and the move had backfired. It did not help the Congress to get enough time to recapture its lost élan. Chandra Shekhar had made the cardinal error of expecting much too soon; Rajiv Gandhi thought that he will get what he wanted without paying a heavy price. In the event, both lost. Rajiv Gandhi was assassinated; Chandra Shekhar had to quit his job in far-from-pleasant circumstances. An illogical arrangement inflicted on the people came to an abrupt end.

12

A Dithering, Withering Rao

"How did I get there? Somebody pushed me..."
—Anonymous

" Nothing is interesting if you are not interested..."
Helen MacInness

There was one veteran politician who was completely oblivious of the din and bustle that surrounded the rest of his tribe. He had seen some of it all; he had also been party to some of the best and worst moments that had preceded May 1991. The story was very simple: the nation had been pitch forked into another election. P.V. Narasimha Rao, leisure personified, was contemplating retirement from active politics. Nobody came seeking his advice; he did not feel compelled enough to move very far from where he was—in the quiet of his study, trying hard to concentrate and be interested in what he was doing, but the mind had already decided that politically, the post-election scenario held no charm for him.

A politician from the old school he may have been, but Rao was not the usual kind of servitor that the Congress had spawned over the years. He was at the same time no radical either. He was simply a man out of the race, looking at it disinterestedly as Rajiv Gandhi and others slogged it out in increasingly difficult and trying physical conditions to make political sense for their campaign trails in May 1991. For Rao, the trail pointed to a return back to his home state, as a Congressman who had served the party in various capacities without ever entertaining even the faintest notions of what destiny had in store fore him.

On 21 May, Rao, like the rest of the world, learnt that Rajiv Gandhi had been assassinated, while he was giving finishing touches to a frenetic election campaign in a hope that it would bring him back to the seat of power. Two short-lived governments that succeeded Rajiv Gandhi had become victims of their own internal contradictions. Rajiv's demise, at a time when he was desperately trying to author a political comeback, came as a boon to the Congress in one tragically ironic sense: the assassination could, and eventually did, add a few more seats to the Congress kitty.

But at the end of the 1991 elections, the Congress was still quite some way short of the magic figure that would have automatically catapulted it to power. Rajiv was the only leader; his death meant that nobody was visibly available as a popular alternative to him. P.V. Narasimha Rao became the unlikely choice, after a proactive big business initiative to hoist Sharad Pawar to the political hot seat was aborted from within contending lobbies within the Congress. Rao was acceptable not because he had won that acceptability in terms of popular legitimacy; he became a choice out of compulsion.

It is easy to suggest that as Prime Minister, P.V. Narasimha Rao did much better than what was expected of him. He did not waste much time in understanding the meaning of his ascension; he was everybody's stop-gap arrangement. For the Congress, with Sonia Gandhi still studiously aloof from an active political profile, anybody who could give a semblance of continuity with its past was acceptable. Since Sharad Pawar, by far a more crafty politician than Rao but still somewhat hemmed in by the regional tag he carried, was only a brief hindrance before India's most reluctant Prime Minister was thrust upon uncertain circumstances, or whichever way the reader would like to surmise from a scenario where the party (the Congress) had emerged at the top of the heap, but not with a majority clear enough to form a stable government. Rao had to forget notions about returning to his home state and pursue a more relaxed life than Delhi afforded him.

For the record, the Congress had won 232 seats, and was short by 40 seats of majority in the Lok Sabha. Rao was never a popular rallying point for the Congress; he was at best an able and competent minister under previous dispensations. Since no political party was prepared to go to polls so soon after having faced the second election in two years, there was nothing to show to the people. They had nothing either their gains or opponents negative achievements to display during the campaign if an early election was invited by their actions. The BJP built up Narasimha Rao as the next best Prime Minister to Lal Bahadur Shastri because the BJP knew well that the Congress was on the death blues. Even for the BJP, Rao was only an interregnum. The so-called Third Front was completely routed and the Left parties were marginalized and were out of picture. Thus fear of other parties to face the elections immediately became the strength for Narasimha Rao to continue in the office.

But the year, which saw him assume power was very crucial for both the Congress and the country. The Congress needed artificial respiration; the country needed direction and leadership. Rao was, in the event, neither suited for this role nor did he lobby for it. But once it came along, the implications were clear.

In order to make the Rao transition appear more tangible, here is a brief recap:

*** The country's economy had reached a stage where the World Bank-IMF prescriptions to rejuvenate growth meant a through reversal of several key inputs that had marked earlier Congress interventions. For one, unlike in the past, the state sector was to be gradually deprived of its prime status, because most of the public sector undertakings had by then become either unwieldy or were blunted instruments of ordering economic direction. The fact that the Congress had as a party failed to comprehend the full meaning of the new 'mantra' of globalisation meant that the new leadership was thoroughly captive in the hands of "others" to set the pace.

Rao was not the kind of proactive leader who could either articulate new aspirations, or was he the one who could readily reject the road that had been laid out before he joined the race. But he knew what was expected of him since he had chosen Dr. Manmohan Singh to be his finance minister to implement the prescription that was prepared by the officialdom in anticipation that the new government would implement it. The liberal economic reform programme was not even discussed at the various party forums before or after the new government took over.

*** Thanks to a set of circumstances quite beyond the comprehension of the country's economic managers, the country's stock markets provided an opening for those who could dare to challenge red tape, interpret existing rules to their liking, avail of aid from banking and financial institutions and chart out individual entrepreneurial dreams. One such character who happened to be around at the right place at the right time as far as playing the markets was concerned was a Mumbai stockbroker Harshad Mehta, then in his late-thirties. Mehta's acumen became extraordinary because he had been around the circuit longer than several other players. But more than that, he had the necessary understanding of the loopholes and the opportunities that existed in the system to "work" them in favour of those who knew that the market could open up fresh investment possibilities at risks, which even the lower segments of the middle class could afford. Harshad Mehta was no miracle man; but he was a shrewd market-player. Within months, as he acquired the tag of 'Big Bull' for himself, Mehta slowly but surely managed to get access to the kind of credit facilities which he could recycle into the market for immediate returns. But that was not all. He also had the vision to realize that several within the country shared his dream, who had some resources to invest but not enough to become rich overnight.

*** The securities scandal was a product of this widespread desire on part of an increasingly interested section of market-players to use the system to their own benefit. Harshad Mehta's individual credibility was of a high enough order for financial and banking institutions to trust him with easy money. Mehta used the money he got to transform the very face of the stock exchange; his bulk-purchase of shares gave him the leeway to create a bullish environment, which everyone in the market latched onto, for relative benefits to themselves. Mehta's ability is not material here.

The fact of the matter is that when the multi-million securities scam took the shape it did, the country's economic managers were both pleasantly surprised but severely jolted. This is an obvious contradiction in terms, but it can be understood in the logic of what happened. The sudden emergence of the Big Bull, his ability to use the system to facilitate his rise, and his immediate success encouraged thousands of medium and small-term investors to trust Mehta's instincts and ape his success story to the extent they could. The big boom was artificial; the consequent crash was very real. Thousands of dreams turned into nightmare when it became clear that Mehta had defaulted on several very serious counts, and with him, the entire system had received unanticipated jolts.

*** The parliamentary probe was held and responsibilities fixed. However the biggest question that has remained unanswered is: Where is the Rs 93000 crores that was mobilized through public issues by various industrialists during the boom? Harshad Mehta had devised an ingenuous method of mobilizing resources to industrialists, which many copied because they now need not go to banks or financial institutions and fulfill attendant commitments. Instead they could mobilize resources through the public issue route, without ever having to worry for repayments. Thousands of public issues hit the market in three years; most of the promoters who had mobilized resources on the basis of the sale of golden dreams vanished into thin air without the promised projects nowhere in sight. There was neither procedure nor law baulking the unscrupulous. Investors were in the dark about the antecedents of new promoters.

*** Rao and the Congress were perhaps not so clear as Dr Manmohan Singh was, when he correctly and honestly admitted that the scam signified "systemic failure." Mehta was chased by economic agencies for the several frauds he perpetrated. He died in 2001.

The Rao regime had to face several other scandals; the Jain 'hawala' scandal, the telecom fraud , the urea scandal and several others. While other scandals did not affect him politically, he was affected by the Jain Hawala case because of the more than ordinary interest shown by the Supreme Court in the scandal.

Rao was forced to ask for papers of his six ministers when they were named in the charge sheets under the directions of the Supreme Court though they were eventually exonerated from the charges of receiving the bribes because the diaries found of the Jain brothers were not admissible under the Evidence Act. Some of those named in the diaries chose their kin as proxies to fight the subsequent election.

Even as the dust has settled on some of the scandals and a few others remain faintly alive, the short point is that in less than 40 years of freedom, democratic India had become privy to corrupt, unscrupulous, criminal and opportunist elements out to make quick money. Was it because Rao patronized them? Did he inherit a system, which was waiting to be milked? Was he, as an individual, a corrupt man who was satisfied with an alleged payment to him by Mehta? These questions are relevant. But in the context of this book, what is more relevant is the fact that through systematic brutalisation and rape of its dignity and ideology, the party that had spearheaded the movement for country's freedom had itself become a decrepit, unruly, corrupt and completely discredited entity.

Rao's biggest failure lay elsewhere; his absolutely unpardonable lack of either initiative or understanding to defuse the time-bomb called the Ayodhya dispute. He was perhaps overjoyed by the fact that the BJP was singing paeans in his praise; little did he realize that the communal forces were only using him to remain satisfied in his fool's paradise even as they systematically maneuvered and planned using the Babri Masjid demolition as a central point of their political advance. Rao had erred, and erred most grievously. He had presided over the virtual decimation of the Indian state structure, its values of secular and democratic functioning, and its pride of place as a pluralist, multi-cultural, secular, democratic republic. The failure was both individual and collective. The gleeful, shameless perpetrators of the act are there, savouring the ill-gotten fruits of their politics of hatred. Gujarat in 2002 saw the same tendency erupt again. It is a moot point whether the Congress, in its shape under Rao or now under Sonia Gandhi's dispensation, can alter the grim tidings facing it and the country. The Congress may or may not learn the right lessons. But the country should not be punished for its myopic vision. That is the clear, central message which politics and civil society have for the once truly great, genuinely democratic party called the Indian National Congress.

But Narasimha Rao alone can not be blamed for the mess of reforms and scandals of the five years of his regime because more ambitious persons within the party who had thought that they would be able to run him as the Prime Minister soon found that it was not easy to push the old man around even when they were holding the threat of Sonia Gandhi to terrorise and manipulate Narasimha Rao. Systematic campaign was run against him within the party so as to weaken him. On and often he was accused of doing nothing to bring the culprits who had conspired to assassinate Rajiv Gandhi. It was more a move to provoke Sonia Gandhi to lash out at Rao than anything else. In fact she was made to lament publicly that she was disappointed that the Rao government did nothing to bring the assassins to books.

When the sustained campaign failed to move Narasimha Rao to give up one of the two posts he was holding, the foundations were laid for bringing him down from one of the posts. Since 1978, Indira Gandhi had held both the offices, of the party and the parliamentary party without any one raising even a murmur. Rajiv Gandhi had continued the tradition without anyone objecting to his holding the two offices. However leaders who were instrumental in his installation as the Prime Minister, wanted him to give up one post. When he refused to bow to the pressure, a split was effected. For Sonia Gandhi the splintered group became the real Indian National Congress. Her dislike for Narasimha Rao could be easily traced back to an incident when the Kerala leader K. Karunakaran had made it clear that Sonia Gandhi had no place in the party position. In fact he was asked in 1994 whether the party would make Sonia Gandhi the party president, Karunakaran had quipped, "There was no vacancy at the top." The break away group had high hopes but these high hopes were dashed ultimately during the Lok Sabha elections. The break away group could win only two seats in Uttar Pradesh but had done considerable damage to the Congress in several seats.

There was no doubt that the Narasimha Rao government had succeeded in pulling the Indian economy from the brinks of a certain collapse. There were greater achievements to its credit but it could not communicate these achievements in political terms. The then minister Madhavrao Scindia had once correctly observed when he said, "Our difficulty is in the lack of communications. We do not understand what Manmohan Singh says because he speaks only in economic terms and he does not understand what we say in political terms. Thus there was a total break down of the communications within the cabinet and in the parliamentary party."

But is the party over? We shall see, as we wind up the narrative over the next section, that the ball is in the party's court. If it fails, the people are going to give it an even more severe drubbing that the historic lows it has yet achieved.

13

Unity of Opposites

"Politics begins where the masses are, not where there are thousands but where there are millions, that is where the serious politics begins."

"All our lives, we fought against exalting an individual against the elevation of a single person, and long ago were overindulgent with the business of the hero, and here comes up again: the glorification of one personality."

"You cannot make a revolution in white gloves"

V.I. Lenin

After Narasimha Rao resigned to make way for Atal Behari Vajpayee to take over the reign for thirteen days, it was apparent that the Indian National Congress would remain out of power for a long time since the politics of coalition had come to stay for a longer duration. It was also a time when the Congress leadership would have to look forward to putting back the party on the rails. Narasimha Rao had already prepared himself for retirement from politics five years earlier. It was now time to give effect to his plans of retirement from active politics and sit down at leisure to write what he had intended for a long time and had already begun in spare time while he was still holding the office of the Prime Minister. He had to hand over the charge of the party to some one. Sonia Gandhi had yet not made up her mind though she was more active in public life. So Narasimha Rao chose Sitaram Kesri who was the senior most in the party. The man was worldly-wise, but somewhat pedantic and no visionary, though practical and pragmatic. No one in the Congress quite believed his claims of having made great sacrifices for the party during the freedom struggle; similarly, the claim that he had lent his shoulders to Jai Prakash Narayan to scale the wall of the Bihar jail (where the latter was lodged) finds no corroborative evidence.

Sitaram Kesri was chosen by Rao in the belief that he would remain loyal to him for Kesri had laid prostrate before Narasimha Rao soon after the election results spelt out an electoral disaster for the Congress party. So Narasimha Rao told his charmed circle that it was a loyalist supplicant in the form of the rotund Kesri he needed as head of the party. Kesri, however, was a slimy kind of politician; he knew how to please, and was willing to crawl when asked to bend. He had little understanding of economics and government functioning, but excelled as a treasurer. Being from Bihar, he knew caste dynamics well; and favoured "social engineering," a term that had become fashionable to describe the various social and caste combinations for the political assertions. Sitaram Kesri had favoured the alliance with Laloo Prasad Yadav in Bihar and also wanted similar kind of arrangements with Mulayam Singh Yadav in Uttar Pradesh. He was the only notable Congress votary of the reservations policy that Vishwanath Pratap Singh had adopted on August 7 1990, and had taken pains to ensure its implementation when he was taken in the Narasimha Rao government as the social welfare minister.

He set before himself the task of winning back the Muslims for the Congress party and made some announcements that were aimed at cutting the umbilical cord of Narasimha Rao with the party. He announced that Narasimha Rao would not be nominated for the party in any election, as he was mainly responsible for the destruction of the Babri Masjid. He inducted three Muslims as party functionaries to his team. He thought that these measures would ensure the return of the Muslims to the Congress fold. But his antics did not have the desired effect. He did succeed in bringing back the Narain Dutt Tiwari faction to the Congress fold even though he did not like Arjun Singh anywhere around him.

Arjun Singh had tried to move closer to Sonia Gandhi even when she was far away from Indian politics and was playing the role of a widow who was busy protecting her two children, by raising the issue of slow progress of the inquiry into the conspiracy for assassination of Rajiv Gandhi that was enthrusted to the MC Jain Commission. Even though the Commission was appointed in 1991, it made no progress at all for two years and had made complaints that he was not given proper accommodation or cooperation from the Narasimha Rao government. Another cause for complaint was that Narasimha Rao government had refused to hand over the sensitive documents that the Jain Commission had demanded. Even though Arjun Singh was the human resources development minister in Rao cabinet, he had insisted that the Jain Commission should be supplied with documents that it had demanded though he ought to have known that no government could part with the sensitive documents that were directly connected with the national security aspects and put them in hands where they would become easily accessible to wrong hands. These were attempts to ingratiate him with the Sonia camp. Why was he making such efforts was to be clear later, on when Sonia Gandhi assumed command of the party. Arjun Singh fancied himself in the role of the trusted adviser to Sonia Gandhi.

Sitaram Kesri managed to get himself installed as the leader of the Congress party in parliament and then he decided to get the approval of the AICC to his elevation as the party chief. So he announced the organizational elections that were to culminate in the election of the Congress president at the session to be held at Calcutta. The last presidential election was held in 1952. Sharad Pawar and Rajesh Pilot decided to contest the election even when they knew that the system was loaded heavily in favour of the incumbent. Pawar and Pilot did not combine their strength against Kesri, for both of them wanted to emerge as independent centers of power in their own light.Jitendra Prasad remained undecided. The ultimate result was as predicted but Kesri had managed to ensure that Rajesh Pilot was also defeated in the election to the Working Committee. The mischief was done at the time of counting. Votes in favour of Pilot were credited to Vijay Bhaskar Reddy who had thought that he had lost the election and was on his way to Hyderabad when he was called back from the airport.

The BJP government could not sustain itself in the office, as it did not receive support from any quarter. So Vajpayee resigned in 13 days, and the other parties engaged themselves to raise coalition government in the place so as to avoid the immediate elections. Several names were considered. Even the possibility of supporting the Congress was also considered but no suitable candidate was available from within the Congress. Hence Harkishen Surjit managed to install the former chief minister of Karnataka HD Devegowda as the Prime Minister even though he was not a member of either House of parliament. The country was surprised when an absolute dark horse was installed to run the most difficult coalition front with the Indian National Congress as the main constituent as both the vanguard and the rearguard, as it had 160 members while others contributed only 100 members to facilitate the transition.

Even though the Congress was forced to support the Devegowda government from outside, the equation between Kesri and Devegowda was never sure or settled. Their relations were to remain uneasy as the Prime Minister refused to meet several demands that came from the office of the Congress president. It was also a time when Kesri had also begun to acquire a new ambition. If Devegowda could become the Prime Minister, why couldn't he, was the predominant logic on his mind. But his immediate task was to handle the needs of Ashok Jain, chairman of the Bennet Coleman, a company that owned the Times of India group of publications. Ashok Jain was facing a criminal case for violation of the Foreign Exchange Regulations Act for some omissions relating to transactions marking the group's centennial celebrations. Ashok Jain had tried to reach the Prime Minister through various avenues, to seek squashing of the inquiry and the case against him.

The then Director of Enforcement BM Bezbarua was not willing to oblige the newspaper magnate. The Prime Minister refused to remove the Director who was unwilling to relent in this case even though he was approached to from various quarters. He continued to provide political protection to the bureaucracy. When Devegowda refused to meet the demand of Sitaram Kesri, he decided to use the authority was vested in him by the Working Committee.

Since the dramatic return of Indira Gandhi, the Indian National Congress had undergone a radical change in its functioning. All power and authority was vested in the party chief. In every meeting of the Congress Working Committee, (the instrument of the Parliamentary Board was abandoned for it was never constituted since 1985, though it was the main decision making body on the political and economic issues in earlier periods) the sycophants initiated the debate on any issue. Only on few occasions a differing note was sounded but it was squashed immediately as sycophants pounced on the differing member. Then the Working Committee meetings always ended with authorization to the party president to take necessary decision. Thus the party chief became the sole repository of all authority and could take the final decision without a need to consult others.

Suddenly Kesri decided to withdraw support to the Devegowda government with the allegation that it had failed to meet the challenge of the communalism. He had taken his entire party by surprise with his sudden move. He went and submitted the letter of withdrawal to the President Dr. SD Sharma on March 30 1997. The whole country was taken by surprise because there was no indication of the prevailing uneasiness within the party over the Devegowda government or it's functioning. There was no immediate issue also to provoke the Congress president to make such a drastic move and unsettle the national politics. If Kesri had hoped that he would be invited to form the government at New Delhi, it was to remain his pipedream. Devegowda refused to resign. Instead he sought to face the vote of confidence as was directed by the President, after the Congress pulled the rug from under his feet.

Devegowda was in his element as he demolished Sitaram Kesri and his move as an old man in hurry. It was a devastating performance by the Prime Minister who had earlier shown that he was not comfortable in either English or Hindi, though he did attempt to address the nation in Hindi from the ramparts of the Red Fort on the Independence Day. But his reply to the confidence vote debate was a superb revelation of cultivated cynicism. The Congress members were left speechless for they had no defence for the action of their party chief. It was the most embarrassing moment for them. As expected Devegowda became the second Prime Minister to lose the vote of confidence on the floor of the Lok Sabha, because the BJP was hardly expected to miss such a great opportunity afforded to it. In his usual, satirical style, Devegowda had taken a dig at Inder Kumar Gujral whose name was on the top as the successor to Devegowda. Turning to Inder Gujral who was in the next bench, Devegowda said, 'you want to be the Prime Minister with support of this old man in hurry? Beware, he would ditch you also.'

Inder Gujral was the least unacceptable candidate after Harkishen Surjeet had committed a historical blunder when he, egged on by the younger elements within the CPI-M politburo, ruled out Jyoti Basu as a deserving successor to Devegowda, and named Inder Gujral instead. Jyoti Basu had a vast experience in handling coalitions, having done that for a record two decades and more in Bengal. Basu had an impeccable reputation for probity and administrative aptitude. But men within his own party (the CPI-M, untrue to its claims of having no gender bias, has always been rather discriminatory in putting women at the top of the party's decision-making structures) conspired to deprive Jyoti Basu a befitting finale to a grand political career. Even the Congress would have fallen in line, but for Surjeet and co.'s inexplicable coyness. Inder Gujral had to face an unusual storm when the Jain Commission report on the conspiracy to assassinate Rajiv Gandhi was released. The Congress leadership led by Arjun Singh demanded that the United Front ought to dismiss the DMK ministers from its ranks as the Inquiry report has strongly condemned the DMK chief Karunanidhi for his role in the state politics that had led to assassination of Rajiv Gandhi.

The Arjun camp's first demand was to remove the DMK from the ruling coalition. When the demand was firmly rejected by the coalition leaders, it was reduced to asking the DMK ministers to step down at least. But the coalition leaders preferred a fresh election to meeting demands of the Congress party. Once again the President had to ask the two Houses to endorse the appropriation bill before the House was dissolved and fresh elections ordered. In two years, this was the second election to the Lok Sabha and the "dream budget" that P. Chidambaram had presented as the finance minister was reduced to a horrendous nightmare only because of the Indian National Congress. If the Congressmen had hoped for a better performance from their own party, they were in for a greater shock because the party had ended with same tally as it had in the earlier elections though its vote base in Uttar Pradesh had further dwindled

But the change of the Prime Minister due to haste of Sitaram Kesri and the electoral disaster that the party had faced now, forced a widespread rethink within Congress ranks. Three members of the Working Committee led by Jitendra Prasad decided that a change was inevitable and in the interest of the party. Jitendra Prasad received support from three members including Pranab Mukherjee. The Working Committee held in the most unusual fashion decided to sack Kesri and installed Sonia Gandhi as the party chief. Her choice was obvious because she had made her first appearance on the Congress stage at the Calcutta session of AICC and had received a standing ovation from the AICC members. Her stepping into the shoes of the Congress president was clearly under-written in that ovation.

Sitaram Kesri's term as the Congress president was also marked by several litigations in which the party got involved. He was the party treasurer when the party had received donations from abroad to the tune of Rs. 3.6 crores from three different sources. The party had failed to account for it or seek the permission from the Home Ministry for receiving such donations from abroad. Hence Public Interest Litigation was filed against the Congress party. There were suspicions also that he was someway connected with the murder of an young physician Dr Tanwar whose headless body was found though no charges were officially framed. He was also involved in two other litigations.

The Working Committee members marched from the AICC office to her residence in the adjoining bungalow on Jan Path for the brief installation ceremony. They were made to wait in the main reception room for half an hour before a messenger came to invite them to the drawing room where Sonia Gandhi waited for them. It was a new experience for the members of the Working Committee, for they were not treated to a cup of tea even as one of the members was to reveal later. They were disposed off in a business-like manner and were told to disperse as soon as they handed over the resolution appointing her as the new party chief. Sonia Gandhi had already involved herself in the election campaign for the Congress candidates during the 1997 elections to the Lok Sabha though she had not held any position in the party. While Sitaram Kesri was blamed for the dismal performance, she was given the credit for bringing the tally to the same level as the 1996 elections.

Sonia Gandhi was hardly well versed with the national politics, nor did she know much about issues that were confronted the nation. She fumbled while taking questions, which she ever did so reticently. She avoided looking straight into the eyes of TV cameras, and badly needed an image advisory. Several people wrote her speeches, delivered deadpan. It was clear that the lady was only carrying out a disinterested ritual. But she had begun to emulate the style of Indira Gandhi in her dress, her style of walking and waving at the audiences from the stage. But she lacked the verve of Indira Gandhi in addressing the audiences and avoided meeting their eyes. Her first brush with the media persons was on the lawns of the bungalow of Dr. Najma Heptulla's official residence was an eminently forgettable, given her hesitant style. She had already broken the rule established by her husband of not sponsoring the candidates for the Rajya Sabha who had lost the elections to the Lok Sabha. She had fielded Oscar Fernandes in Karnataka and Santosh Mohan Dev for Assam even though both had lost the Lok Sabha elections. She admitted when she was asked on this violation and asserted that a similar mistake would not be committed in the future. Arjun Singh who was also present at the function concluded that the question was framed so as to keep him out of the Rajya Sabha because he had also lost the Lok Sabha election. In fact he was told not select Hoshangabad constituency for his election to the Lok Sabha as it was a difficult constituency that had always preferred a socialist to anyone else. But he was confident that he would overcome the difficulties. He could not.

It was on these lawns when Sonia Gandhi was facing the media persons on that day, Jitendra Prasad was asking his close friends in media circles, "Will she be able to revive the Congress?" He was responsible for bringing her to the center-stage of the party but now even he was expressing doubts on the move he had made. What had happened to make Prasad so unsure only two months since Sonia Gandhi was installed is not known because he never revealed that disillusionment. But that he had fallen out with Sonia Gandhi became clear after complaints reached Sonia about how Prasad had handled the election campaign in the previous Lok Sabha elections. Jitendra Prasad had made a valiant attempt to fight an election against Sonia Gandhi for the party post through it was known that he would lose. But he wanted to make his presence felt since Sonia Gandhi had ticked him off within weeks after she had taken over.

The Congress suffered three heavy losses in the death of three aspiring and promising leaders; in Rajesh Pilot who died in a road accident, Jitendra Prasad who died of a stroke and Madhav Rao Scindia who died in a plane crash when he was rushing to attend a public rally of the party in Uttar Pradesh. All three died in a span of few months after Sonia Gandhi had taken over as the party president. She could not convince GK Moopanar either, who had formed a regional party Tamil Manila Congress- Tamil People's Congress after he had parted over differences with Narasimha Rao over the issue of joining hands with Jaylalitha for the 1996 elections to return to the Congress fold. Nor could she convince Mamta Banerjee who had broken away in Bengal to form her Trinamul Congress. Sonia had succeeded in allowing the great Indian National Congress become the 'B' team to Mamta Bannerji in the state assembly elections in 2001 but the end results was that both the parties failed in making even a dent on the hold of the Marxists in the state.

Moopanar had played a vital role in holding operations during the Indira Gandhi's time as well as in Rajiv Gandhi era. He was a shrewd politician, even though he may not have been very articulate. He had a robust common sense to understand the rest of India and made up his lack by asking the right kind of people their opinions when he had to face a difficult political problem pertaining to any state.

Sonia's first acid test came when three states, Rajasthan Madhya Pradesh and Delhi were to go for Assembly polls in November 1998. Madhya Pradesh was under Congress rule while Rajasthan and Delhi were held by the BJP. In fact the BJP had removed the Delhi chief minister Sahib Singh Verma and installed Sushma Swaraj as the chief minister though she was reluctant to accept the post in October first week when the elections to the state assembly were due in a month's time. But she was forced to accept the change. Digvijay Singh had to overcome the anti-incumbency factor that had destroyed several other state governments. He sought the last minute changes in the candidates that were approved by the party high command earlier. He was frank enough to tell Sonia Gandhi that he should be given the authority to change or else some one else should take the responsibility of leading the campaign. Sharad Pawar had fully backed him and got her endorsement for the change in the list, as suggested by the chief minister. The BJP was trounced in Rajasthan and Delhi while it could not overthrow the Congress government in Madhya Pradesh since it could not avail of the anti incumbency factor due to the last minute changes that Digvijay Singh had effected and had fielded the new faces who did not have to account to the constituencies for the non- or bad performance of previous legislators. Sonia Gandhi had passed the acid test and had established herself as the leader.

On her election as the party chief, she was appointed as the leader of the Congress parliamentary party as Kesri had managed to install himself previously. However she had to depute Sharad Pawar as the leader of the Opposition in the Lok Sabha and Shankarrao Chavan in the Rajya Sabha. This was a new introduction that one person hold two posts and it had endorsement from the senior members who had sought only three years earlier to remove Narasimha Rao from one of the two posts that he had held. She or her personal aide, Vincent George was controlling the Congress performance inside the two houses of parliament. Even though Sharad Pawar represented the party at the conferences convened by the Speaker to sort out the knotty problems that the Lok Sabha faced and proceedings were barracked, he could not give his assurance that his party would remain bound by the agreements reached because he had to have the prior approval from her to any such agreement. There were occasions when the list of the Congress participants in any debate in the Lok Sabha were suddenly changed and without consultations with him. New names were given to the Speaker or the presiding officer by the party chief whip PJ Kurien who was used to taking instructions from Vincent George. Pawar also often found that he was not able to have direct communication with Sonia Gandhi as her phones were routed through her office only.

On one occasion, few weeks before the Jaylalitha became active and nursed new ambitions of playing a vital role in the national politics, he could not get in touch with Sonia Gandhi though he had rang up her residence six times in the span of few hours. Each time he was told that she was not available. Ultimately when he was able to reach her, he suggested that the front offices on both side should be kept out of the conversation between them on vital and important issues. She readily agreed and gave him the private number that he could access without the formality of the front office. Sharad Pawar had used the number only on one occasion. And that proved to be vital in demolition of the Vajpayee government in April 1999. But V George did not know that he had now a direct access to her.

The controversial person Subramaniam Swamy had been working on the Tamilnadu leader Jaylalitha that she had a role in the national politics especially after the spat between the defence minister George Fernandes and the Naval chief Admiral Bhagwat over the selection of an officer for a particular command. He brought her to New Delhi in March 1999 for three important functions including one to address an international gathering only to display her skills in handling even the international skills and diplomacy. She was being presented and projected as the perfect candidate who could handle the national affairs more skillfully and adaptively. He also organized a tea party in honour of Jaylalitha while she was on visit to New Delhi and had also invited the Congress president Sonia Gandhi. After a great hesitation, Sonia Gandhi made a brief appearance at the tea party, said hullo to Jaylalitha and left the party without much debate. But the brief meeting had led the foundation for a great political upheaval in April when Jaylalitha announced withdrawal of her support to the

Vajpayee government as he had failed to meet her demands for the change of the defence minister. It came as a bolt from the blue when Vajpayee was least expecting. He grabbed it of course, knowing that the jinx which had undone him a few months earlier would not come his way again.

His party managers were confident that they would sail through the confidence vote that the President KR Narayanan had asked him to obtain from the Lok Sabha after Jaylalitha had withdrawn the support of her party reducing the Vajpayee to a minority. Their confidence depended on the declaration by Mayawati of BSP that her party would remain neutral and abstain from voting during the confidence vote. But the BJP managers did not realize that Sharad Pawar was working in tandem with Arif Mohammad Khan holding fort for the BSP. Khan was able to convince Mayawati that this was a great moment for her to establish herself; that she was also genuinely against the Manuvadi (wedded to the varna, caste-system) forces. It made the task of Sharad Pawar easy to convince her to vote against the Vajpayee government. He succeeded in his attempt at midnight, previous to the scheduled voting during the next day. Mayawati told Sharad Pawar that he kept on speaking to her, but his leader Sonia Gandhi never spoke to her. Sharad Pawar took Mayawati to his office in Parliament House, rang up the private number of Sonia Gandhi and made her speak to Mayawati. The deal was complete but except four, Sonia Gandhi, Sharad Pawar, Mayavati and Arif Mohmed Khan, no one else was aware of what was being cooked behind the scenes.

Just before the division on the confidence motion, some misapprehension that Mayawati would abstain as she had declared earlier made Arif to rush to Sharad Pawar who came out to fetch Mayavati to the Inner Lobby of the Lok Sabha and get her assurance again. She explained only to keep the BJP managers in suspense that she had indicated that she would abstain from voting. Just before the division was to start that she declared her intention to vote against the Vajpayee government and brought down the BJP government by a single vote. There was some confusion in the vote of the leader of the Anna DMK party. The indicator was green though he had voted negative. Others in the party came to know of the midnight deal that Sharad Pawar had stuck with Mayavati.

Soon after the fall of the Vajpayee government, the process of forming the alternate government was initiated and Sonia Gandhi took the command of her party initiatives. However Sharad Pawar was deliberately kept out of strategy formulation Sonia had begun in consultation with other leaders. Pawar was either not conveyed the timings of the meetings or was deliberately given the message at the last minute so that he would not be able to reach in time. She met other leaders also and gave a clear indication that she was in the game. The opposition had belatedly decided to correct the historical blunder and proposed the name of Jyoti Basu as the next Prime Minister while the Prime Minister and his entourage of advisers and managers waited with anxiety to find out the developments in the other camp.

Without consulting the seniors in her party or others whose support she expected, she rushed to Rashtrapati Bhavan to stake her claim to form the government. The President KR Narayanan asked her to produce the names of 272 members who would support her government. Only then he could invite her to form the government, he told her. Beaming with her success, or at least that is what she thought, she declared before waiting media persons that she had support of 272 and she would produce their names. On the previous night, Jaylalitha and Laloo Prasad Yadav had come to her residence with a proposal that she should support Jyoti Basu. She was reported to have told both of them that it was either she or no one. The talks finally broke down when Mulayam Singh Yadav and other non-BJP parties (barring the Marxists and the communists) refused to support her claims to form the government. There was a sigh pf relief in the heart of the Prime Minister Atal Behari Vajpayee who was in communication with the former Prime Minister Chandra Shekhar. Both had also met at the residence of Digvijay Singh over a dinner that the junior minister had organized in honour of the birthday of Chandra Shekhar and had a brief talk on the future. Mulayam Singh refused to budge even an inch in his adamant stance. His studied indifference was to leave permanent rupture and bitterness in their relations.

Sonia Gandhi had gone by the advice that "others" had no alternative but to support her government. Only the alternative was to face yet another election in two years that was a risky proposition. But her advisers had miscalculated the games of Mulayam Singh or underrated him. He was prepared go through yet another election because he had seen improvement in his vote base. He was certain that the Muslims were returning to his fold and not to the Congress fold. Many congressmen were under the illusion the Muslims were turning back towards the Congress. He was certain that he would improve his performance in the election. Hence it was less risky for him than for the Congress. The dye was cast for another election.

Sonia Gandhi decided to contest from two constituencies, one Amethi in Uttar Pradesh and second Bellary in Karnataka. Her party was believed that she could bring 230 members to the Lok Sabha with her intense campaign because the people were disappointed with the Vajpayee government. They would derive the benefit of the anti- incumbency factor in their favour. Once they crossed the hump of 230, no one could stop Sonia Gandhi from getting into the saddle. But she was yet to cross the main hurdle of the issue of her foreign origins. So far she had been successful because at the stake was not her leadership but the stake was of the choice of the chief minister. In the Lok Sabha election, the stake was on selecting a person who would occupy the office of the Prime Minister. Mulayam Singh had made the issue of her origins already and the BJP was all set to certainly take the issue to the electorate with all its might and intensity. But the Congress did not have convincing answers. So the question needed to be debated and answers found.

With this intention, Purno A Sangma raised the issue of her foreign origins and said that he did not know anything about her. Sharad Pawar and Tariq Anwar also said that the issue needed a debate in the party. No one had expected that such an issue would ever be raised in the Congress Working Committee for it tantamount to questioning her leadership credentials. The crestfallen Sonia Gandhi stormed out of the meeting with a declaration that she would resign. Sitaram Kesri tried to block her path with a request not to leave the meeting because majority was on her side. Three members had touched her raw nerve.

All hell broke out soon as messages were conveyed to different state units to rush with strength to support Sonia Gandhi as she was in trouble due to irrelevant issue raised in the Working Committee, they were told. Several delegations were rushed to persuade her to relent as the majority of the party was behind her. But she refused to meet though the seniors persuaded her to attend the Special AICC that was to be convened to endorse her election once again but after expulsion of three members who had raised the issue at the Working Committee. At the meeting at the Talkatora Indoor Stadium in Delhi, every one waited for an hour for her arrival. No one dared to take to mike and say anything. No one was certain of the final outcome. Only junior functionaries reached the mike to announce that Sonia Gandhi would arrive soon. She came and accepted the endorsement without a word and the meeting was dispersed after laying foundations for the formation of yet another offshoot of the Indian National Congress.

The Congress party went through yet another organizational election when Jitendra Prasad decided to contest against Sonia Gandhi for the post of the party president. The result was a foregone conclusion but his intention was merely to show that there was a section within the party that had not approved of her style of functioning and her dependence on a close coterie that had surrounded her and did not allow an access to her.

As the Congress was fighting the internal battle within the government was forced to attend to a large-scale intrusion by the militants in the Kargil sector with a support of the Pakistani Armed Forces. The infiltration had begun much early because the difficult terrain at the high hills and heights is vacated by the Indian Armed Forces during the difficult winter season that makes the terrain unapproachable and inhabitable. Infiltrators had reached the bunkers of the Indian side as well soon as snow had begun to melt. The infiltration was noticed soon and the government ordered the clearance of the region while the issue was taken up with the Pakistan authorities. The Vajpayee government was determined for a full-scale clash with Pakistan as it denied any hand in the infiltration. Only in February the Prime Minister had undertaken a peace journey in a bus to Lahore and signed a peace agreement with the Pakistan Prime Minister Nawaz Sharif. So this blow was much more painful as it had brought the peace initiative to nothingness.

While brave officers and jawans were sacrificing their lives to ensure the clearance of the borders, the Congress found an issue to pick holes in the government performance over the Kargil misadventure by Pakistan. The Congress may have been technically right, but was politically wrong, because it conveyed a wrong message. Every day official Congress spokespersons found new words to criticize the Vajpayee government while the ministers of the Vajpayee government were attending the somber ceremonies when the dead bodies of the killed martyrs were brought to Delhi for dispatching them to their native stations for the last rites with the state honours and winning sympathies. The Congress party did not understand that the popular sentiment was with the government over the confrontation with Pakistan over the large-scale infiltration. Any different approach on this issue was hazardous and politically dangerous. But there was no way the party men could make their high command to understand what were the popular sentiments over the issue. The high command was under the illusion that its campaign on this issue was getting popular support and exposing the Vajpayee government thoroughly. But the trends were entirely in an opposite direction; even if the Vajpayee administration had allowed a crisis to develop, the first task was to secure evacuation of Pak forces. The net result of this myopia was to be reflected in the final tally after the elections results were known. Only few men in the party admitted that they had committed a big blunder in taking a different line over the Kargil issue.

The final tally of the Congress party came as a rude shock. Sonia Gandhi could win only 112 seats in the Lok Sabha. Even the rather dyspeptic Sitaram Kesri had brought fifty more seats to the Congress tally. She had won from both her seats though Sushma Swaraj who was a surprise sprung on Sonia Gandhi in Bellary had succeeded in reducing her victory margin to a comfortable level. Only upset caused in the opposite camp was defeat of Arun Nehru in Raebareili constituency where Prianka Gandhi had campaigned against Arun Nehru. The Congress leaders were expecting any thing above 230 seats under her command. What was the basis of their optimism was not known nor could they articulate the basis of their optimism. They were also not willing to accept that the people had a choice between the "home bred" Atal Behari Vajpayee who was on the national scenes for the past 40 years and Sonia Gandhi.

Yet many could not understand why the Congress party was voted to power in many states subsequent to the Lok Sabha elections. Or why the Congress was routed elsewhere (and of course, most tellingly in the Lok Sabha polls) even though it had fought the assembly elections in Bengal and Tamilnadu as B teams of the regional parties. It was a dismal performance by any standards. The Congress was by now (January 2003) ruling in fourteen states. She had half the number of chief ministers under her command. So it is taken that credit for it must go to Sonia Gandhi. The party was on the recovery bend they claim by avoiding the inconvenient question then what happened in Uttar Pradesh? Why the party was pushed to a fourth slot in the state assembly? Even in the assembly elections in Gujarat in December 2002, the Congress leadership was confident of trouncing the BJP and coming to power. Sonia Gandhi had intensely campaigned in the state. Yet the result was devastating for the Congress. The BJP had sprung back from the certain defeat to win back the state with the two thirds majority. Why did it happen so? In other states it had got the benefits of the anti incumbency factor. Her charisma was not enough to win the Lok Sabha election is not getting down their throat because it is a bitter pill and they are unable to swallow.

Another indication that the party was not on the recovery curve is provided in the reading by the industrial houses that had earlier flooded the Congress coffers with funds and had never allowed the party to feel the resources crunch during the election times and also for running the huge party apparatus. However the sources for funds began to dry up after the initial period of Narasimha Rao government. The inflow further dwindled with Sitaram Kesri at the helm of affairs. But after Sonia Gandhi took over, there was some improvement. But the Bombay clamped a tight screw over its funding after Sonia Gandhi decided to make the Calcutta industrialist Rama Prasad Goenka, a loner in industrial circuits, a Rajya Sabha member on the Congresss nomination. He had helped Sonia Gandhi to mobilize resources for the Rajiv Gandhi Foundation though he contribution did not equal what Dhirubhai Ambani alone had contributed to the Foundation.

There is a rivalry in the industrial world between Calcutta and Mumbai. She annoyed them even further when she decided to field Khosla, another industrialist of Delhi who was connected with the Nehru family for the Rajya Sabha from Uttar Pradesh. He could not win because of the smart moves by a journalist who had obtained support of the Congress faction that had broken away from the Congress to join the Kalyan Singh government. It also caused an annoyance in the industrial circle. The leader has to know what would be the overall impact of the selection of particular candidates. She did not know and experienced hands were not at hand to give her correct advice. Hence she had to depend on chief ministers to collect funds for the party. But there was a limit to which the chief minister can exert his influence. They all go by what had happened to Chimanbhai Patel in 1974 when the accusations were leveled against him that he mobilized funds from the oil traders of Gujarat for the party. There was no truth in the charge but Chimanbhai could never shake off the label that got stuck on his head. There was yet another problem beset the Congress funding. Every PCC president and heads of different wings of the Congress party also rushes to Mumbai to collect funds from the chief minister. When he refuses to oblige he invites the wrath of the party chief who is narrated the tales how the chief minister insulted them on their simple demands. He is so unpopular a figure that the Congress president ignored his protests and nominated two persons for the Rajya Sabha elections, who had no kind words for the chief minister. The fate of other Congress chief ministers was no different when it came to select the candidates for the Rajya Sabha or for bye-elections in the state. Party men were not able to understand why she tried to ignore the protests from the chief ministers when she depended on them for the resources?

The stage was set for the saffron brigade to romp home. Vajpayee, chastened by the earlier experience, was somber and rather subdued. But he knew that the jinx that had undone him was well and truly over—at least for the time being.

No, it was not over for time being but for a full five years. Vajpayee was able to complete the full term of the 13th Lok Sabha in the office of the prime minister without facing even once a serious threat to his government from the Congress Party under the stewardship of Sonia Gandhi as the leader of the opposition in the Lok Sabha. The Congress Party could never push the National Democratic Alliance to fight her with their backs to the wall. Even on the unprecedented communal carnage in Gujarat following fire in a bogie of the Express train at Godhra station in Gujarat on February 27 2002 that burnt down more than 50 passengers was not used effectively by the Congress party to push the Bharatiya Janata Party to fight in desperation to survive in the office.

On issues, the Congress succeeded in becoming a stone wall but it could never pose a serious threat because of the comfort of numbers behind Vajpayee and its ability of the Congress to raise serious debates in either house. There were strange strategies that the Congress had adopted during the five years which made no sense. The continued boycott of the defence minister George Fernandes by the Congress remained inexplicable strategy. The Vajpayee government was forced to roll back some if its economic decisions but it was due to pressure that came from within the NDA and not because of the Congress Party sitting comfortably on the opposition bench.

The victory in the state assembly elections in Rajasthan, Madhya Pradesh and Chhatisgarh in October 2003 gave ideas to many within the Bharatiya Janata Party that it would be able to win easily the Lok Sabha elections by advancing it by a few months. Pramod Mahajan, a practical politician was able to convince the party leadership that it would not win the elections on the planks of the Hindutva. The assembly elections in Uttar Pradesh had proved it because two anti Ram Janam Boomi issue had secured first and second place in the assembly polls while the BJP was pushed down to the third position. He also pointed out that more than half the electorate was constituted by men and women who were under the age of thirty. Their aspirations were rooted in economic betterment. Hence he convinced the party to push the Hindutva issue to back burners and tag on to the shinning Indian slogan. It would have worked but for the strategy change that

Mahajan's subordinate Sudhanshu Mittal decided to adopt of putting Atal Behari Vajpayee's voice on to the mobile phones all over the country.

It received wide publicity and the poor construed from it that BJP was talking to only rich who could afford the mobile phones. In any case the NDA had pursued the economic policy that was initiated by the Congress party during the Narasimha Rao regime and for which the party had paid a heavy price for two elections. The BJP could win earlier elections as it did not have sufficient time between two elections for the people to see what kind of economic policies it would pursue.

The identity crisis was real and its effect was for every one to see when the final count of voting became apparent. The BJP that had won 52 Lok Sabha seats in Uttar Pradesh was reduced to third position with only ten seats to its share. Its allies in different states also did not fare better.

Chandrababu Naidu could not overcome the anti incumbency factor in Andhra Pradesh though Navin Patnaik managed to overcome it because he had, unlike Chandra babu Naidu in Andhra Pradesh, not tried to turn his state into a global one. SM Krishna of the Congress Party also paid the price for his efforts to convert his state Karnataka into a part of the global phenomenon. The Congress could come back to power only after alliance with HD Devegowda and his Janata Dal (Secular). The Congress had to fight for the post of the chief minister by enlisting services of Sharad Pawar. It was a compromise.

The NDA was confident that it would win 300 plus seats in the 14th Lok Sabha but it could not understand why it failed nor could it come to terms with the unexpected defeat in May 2004 as the Congress also could not understand why it won in the election. For BJP it was not merely a shock of loss of power but the trauma was caused as it had lost its identity that had propelled it to power for previous six years. As the BJP could not come to terms with its defeat, it refused to cooperate with United Progressive Alliance government. The tragedy was in its inability to comprehend the success of the Sonia Gandhi phenomenon. So also the Congress was unable to understand it.

14

The Slide

A rich man purchases a Rolls Royce and drives off. After some ten kms, the car comes to a grinding halt. He gets a mechanic to find out what had gone wrong. The mechanic opens the hood and tells the owner: " Sorry sir, but there is no engine inside." The perplexed owner asks the mechanic." Tell me, how did it run this far? " Prompt comes the reply—" On the company's reputation, sir."

The Indian National Congress had its jaunty run since the Indira Gandhi years largely on its earlier reputation earned through struggle, strife and power, as also because it was the only party which had a truly all-India character. The vehicle may keep changing one driver after the other, but depreciating brand equity had to take its toll. The engine that propelled it was becoming suspect; the energies that had driven it seemed half-exhausted. But still, only the most puerile would have concluded that the wagon needed to be condemned forever.

The Congress through the years evolved first as a rather fortuitous premonition of certain Raj civil servants who smelt a sense of impending revolt in the air. It then assumed the form of a well-meaning, educated but still rather moderate debating-hall. The 1920s necessitated a makeover to a platform, which initially attracted only a limited clientele. The subsequent shifts and turns, all engineered from the top, defined the broad parameters, like tackling poverty through a socialistic pattern of economic development, redistributive justice and other egalitarian impulses.

Nehru introduced the concept of economic development through the instrument of centralized planning which implied commanding heights to the state sector in preference to a greater role for the private sector. The concept was both sophisticated and alluring, and also very much the need of the times in which India found itself caught at the dawn of freedom. It is by now an established fact that the fault-lines lay in the implementation of policies that were a product of an ideological package devoid of cohesive content. Indira Gandhi admitted as much during her conversations with author Fritjof Capra in 1972 that left to herself, she would have liked a different launching pad but she could not throw away what had been achieved.

Interestingly, when Capra asked her why did India not follow the Gandhian prescription for economic advance, she simply said: "If I could start from the scratch, I would do things quite differently. But I have to be realistic. There is a large industrial base in India which I can't throw away." The definite conjuncture arrived in 1969, but Indira Gandhi herself was not equal or serious enough to tackle the task. She then changed her strategy and decided to take-on the old guards in the party in 1969.

She promised the poor two square meals a day for each family, as it was their right to have the two meals. She had broken their spell of fatalism under which they had eked out their livelihood for centuries without complaining and accepting their plight as the desire of the Almighty. When she promised them the dignity of two meals a day without fail, the response was electric. Indira Gandhi had emerged as the personification of the solution, and in creating that persona around her, both she and the masses who invested in her erred. Historical processes, imperceptible as they are, follow a definite pattern.

The larger-than-life, feudal-democratic profile that the chosen leader acquired was in essence the very deception that undid not only individuals within the Congress but the party itself. Clues towards that abound through the party's chequered advance. Indira Gandhi gave respectability to the aspirations of the poor; but she was unable and incapable of getting the aspirations fulfilled just because she had the individual vision closer home to the masses. But all along, those who invested their hopes in the Congress—the myriad underclass as a whole— also turned against the Congress party as the democratic process has unfolded.

Indira Gandhi could not, may be did not even want to, deliver on the promises she made to the poor. Hence there was a gradual build up of discontent and anger among the masses. They expressed their discontent in various ways and supported the Opposition parties that had taken up their cause after the failure of Indira Gandhi to keep her electoral promises and running her government in the opposite direction. Informed sections of the Opposition had successfully demonstrated that monopoly houses had grown rapidly. Their resources and assets were growing at a much faster rate than earlier periods when there were restrictions on their operations but the poor have not improved their positions. It was enough to cause the disenchantment with the Indian National Congress within two years after the masses had put Indira Gandhi on a high pedestal of their hearts and minds and voted her massively.

The successful Railway strike of 1974 was one early indication of the disenchantment and disillusionment. The complete derailment of the giant railways graphically illustrated the popular mood. But Indira Gandhi seemed neither to care nor see. There were food riots in the tribal belt of Madhya Pradesh that had brought the movement on the Central Railways to a grinding halt for a week in 1974. Never before were food riots so rampant in the country and that too down to the remote tribal areas. It was unimaginable that the tribal would rise against the government for food. They believed in fatalism even more than others in Indian society because they suffer vagaries of nature in every way. The scarcity conditions had driven them to desperation. Even the Nav Nirman movement in Gujarat was nothing short of a food riot though it was engineered for a different political purpose. She played her card but in the end she was the great loser because the logic of the event that she had created had overtaken her intentions. She could not control the logic that emanated from her designs. She could not win back the state only a year later.

Jai Prakash Narayan could lead a successful movement known as Total Revolution in Bihar after a young postgraduate had triggered off a student movement in the state only because the resentment within the youth found an outlet. The anti-establishment mood was enough to bring the resentment to the fore, and maybe, it was this amorphous character that led to the concept's eventual dilution. But that is rushing ahead of the story. There was no mistaking one point: there was a distinct anti-Congress sentiment. Indira Gandhi initially thought that the sentiment would subside after a while; that was a crucial political error. Because she may have been right about the character of the movement but mistook it purely as a transient phase that was a costly error. The reason why such movements could sustain for long durations was due to the dwindling mass support of the Congress. It was no more a recognizable political entity, as the people had known it earlier. For three years, they had waited patiently for the government to deliver. Instead, the resultant chaos only confirmed that the Congress central leadership had singularly failed to judge the mood of the people, which was only a reflection of their rejection of the ineptitude of existing governance.

After her decisive triumph in the 1971 elections, Indira Gandhi had almost forgotten her promises of expediting land reforms, increasing the minimum wages for landless labour and other such vital aspects of the promises she had made to the country. The essentially radical character of the change visualized needed institutional renewal and a different political approach. This was forsaken and forgotten to attend the new requirements because the farm lobby had become more powerful around her. Even the operations for providing relief and succour to people during scarcities like were merely turned into a political weapon used as a polemic against non-Congress governments in the states.

The discontent did not have a specific dateline. It did not erupt all of a sudden. The roots of disenchantment were inherent in the system that Nehru had conceived with sophistication without giving much thought about how the socio-economic impetus could be translated in actual terms. There was thus a pronounced hiatus between perception and the reality. The state as a prime mover of change required from the apparatus, sensitivity and understanding which it lacked. To retain such a massive power for intervention, the political leadership was compelled into relying on the license and permit Raj, which permeated every sector and aspect of the edifice. The cost-intensive nature of this policy framework inhibited the creative urges and desires of people in general and dampened individual enterprise in particular. The mechanics of the system were full of such gaping loopholes that they only meant an open invitation to the corrupt and the unscrupulous. The absence of a defined structural back up which minimized the possibility of corruption meant, at another level, uneven and unbalanced economic growth that limited the benefits of development to a select few. It was thus inevitable that such profligacy as an inherent element would breed mass anger and also help the ideological Right (like the Swatantra Party) to define its ideological counterpoint. The unchecked growth of the license-permit Raj undermined the efficacy of state interventionism.

The true and most effective picture of existing inequities felt at all levels by those at the receiving end was depicted by Salman Rushdie in a documentary 'Midnight Riddles' to project issues, affecting the man on streets who is ignored and peripheral considerations given free-play. What had irked the establishment much more to ban its broadcast was the starkness of the depiction of day-to-day life, like a woman on a Mumbai footpath making rotis on a temporary chulha of loose bricks, while her toddler son is playing in the sewer. The TV camera then shifts to focus on a modern kitchen in a posh home where a housewife is making kebabs. Her pet dog comes, pulls her sari by mouth so that apiece of kebab falls down, dog grabs it and runs away.

The meaning of the 1971 mandate was lost on those who won it. If only due consideration had been given to the socio-economic content of the new politics which people sought, things would have been different. Indira Gandhi's inability to sustain the economics of her political platform defeated her. The Opposition only utilised the opportunity it was given by a feckless ruling class utterly incapable of internalizing the logic of initiatives such as the 20-point programme, announced with such fanfare on July 1, 1975, less than a week into the Emergency. The electorate gave her a resounding defeat because it felt cheated on every single front; the economics of the Emergency was as cynical and manipulative as the politics of authoritarianism. The limitations of an individual's personal charisma were decisively exposed in the 1977 elections. The same individual was acceptable six years earlier because she held out both promise and hope; the story was completely different once the true character of the hypocrisy behind the charisma became clear to the vast masses.

That Indira Gandhi was brought back to power in January 1980 can be attributed to the failure of the Janata experiment to cohere on all fronts. Individual clashes and angularities were focused because personal ambitions and desires toyed with the aspirations and hopes of the people who had rejected authoritarianism in favour of democratic functioning. The 1984 election was a slap on the face of people who were talking of a second partition of the country. Punjab voted for the Akali Dal in 1985 after the Rajiv-Longowal Accord. The accord was acceptable and was vindicated; the Congress party's insensitivity during preceding years was not. Even Rajiv Gandhi was compelled to remark that the Congress had lost the election but the people of Punjab had won.

The fluctuating fortunes of parties reflect different variables. It is by now established that the mind of the Indian voter is acutely attuned to the variables at work. Inputs like caste and ethnic considerations are not independent of other variables, as the political class has grudgingly discovered for itself over the years.

The transition from Indira Gandhi's cynical gamesmanship to Rajiv Gandhi's over-exuberant attempts to dismantle the edifice that had slowly lost touch with the masses was a half-baked response to a first rate crisis. The party organization had been eroded so deeply that it dare not question either the mother or the son. The party was no longer a springboard for chalking up ideas and schemes—the ubiquitous Congressman had left the process of thinking entirely to one leader. The party had become wholly subservient to the whims and fancies of the high command. Indira Gandhi's personal frailties apart, it was this culture of subservience that she had succeeded in installing in the party that devalued all efforts towards rejuvenation.

Party workers at the ground level were simply in no position to think or act on their own. As the country plunged from crisis to chaos, the party was in a state of such advanced sclerosis that nothing seemed to move until this or that committee nominated by leaders sitting in Delhi cared to go through the motions of contriving a response to the all-pervasive rot. In 1987, when Gujarat suffered the worst drought in four decades and relief camps were opened on a massive scale, why was such frantic shuttling between Delhi and Gandhinagar? The response to such a query was cryptic: "Nominations are decided in Delhi and not by people in the relief camps," they said.

This was another significant reflection of how people nominated from the top rather than thrown up from below began to dominate the party and lead to its decay. The structure of the party had been turned into a nominated one where every decision and every appointment depended on the perceived intelligence and satisfaction of "the leader." Others had no say nor could they protest unless they were ready to invite punishment for any act of defiance.

The managers of the leader surrounded her with a wall of sycophants. The leader could not see or hear what the suffering masses had to say and show because sycophants were not willing to relay it as they were themselves incapable of understanding or were not willing to invite the displeasure of the leader by conveying the hard realities and truth. There was thus an inbuilt communication gap, which no intelligence agency could bridge, and help the leader come out of the self-imposed barriers between the leader and the people. In subsequent years, the communication gap was only widened by the security net that divided the ruler and the ruled. The Special Protection Group and other allied security forces impeded the free movement of even legislators. There was no question of a common man getting through the claustrophobic security and reach the leader. The security cover deterred democratic interaction, with the leader imprisoned within a high walled fortress. Even at electoral rallies and public meetings, the leader was expected to speak from a "safe" distance exemplified by bulletproof platforms. The distance made it impossible for both the speaker and the audience to read each other's body language to understand whether the intended message was conveyed or received.

This break in the communication channels between the leader and the electorate was further compounded by the fact that the upper castes and rich had easy access to the leader. At the behest of monopoly houses and big business, the party's socialist protestations suffered. Several schemes designed to reinforce the party's egalitarian base were sidelined. Instead, the marauders of big business captured the mindset of an increasing number of Congress leaders from urban areas. The urban middle class was happy with the change, but the Congress party's strongholds were not confined to that segment alone. It was much wider. For a multi-class, multi-cultural party, the changes proved detrimental. There was thus a clear demarcation between the leader and the shifting character of the intended audience. This eroded the fundamentals of policies and objectives. The masses were no longer the primary target of planning or the policies. They had gone out of the leader's focus. The upwardly mobile, techno-managerial elite, bubbling with fresh ideas imported from abroad spoke a language that was alien to the common voter. In the name of rapid economic growth, a parasitical class had usurped the political apparatus.

For instance, even when the successes achieved by several technology missions like the Telecom Commission in its specific context were dazzling and immediate, the political advantage of using such technological breakthroughs were beyond the comprehension of rootless bureaucrats and experts who had wrested the initiative from the earlier political elite. The facility of expanded telecom services could yield dividend only if they helped during sudden emergencies like rushing doctors to those areas that had earlier been inaccessible. A telephone call could reach a doctor; but could the doctor respond by reaching the village in absence of the linking road? Such incongruities of a technological mismatch were highlighted on an increased level. General awareness levels had been raised, but the mindset of those who controlled the levers of power had not had a corresponding shift. The infrastructure needed to sustain technological inputs was not in place—roads, to name one elementary part of the required backup to ensure easier access between the new technology and those it was expected to benefit.

The tarmac bias of politicians and bureaucrats is even now ruling supreme in the country. This bias has still kept many thousand villages beyond the reach of safe drinking water and access by roads because politicians and bureaucrats are loathe to ride on roads where their automobiles cannot travel at a greater speed due to inaccessible road. The leaders do not have a clue; their advisers are busy implementing multilateral agendas and schemes thought out by the Bretton Woods sisters. The leader can listen only what he is told by his advisers, who are in turn looking over their shoulders for advice from their mentors in the World Bank or wherever. In this scenario, the gap between the political leadership and the ruled can only widen. After all, technology does not function in a vacuum.

> It is not that Congress leaders have been completely lost in the maze of contradictory advice. Indira Gandhi had said in 1969: "the western countries are pressing India to modernize by importing their new technology. In fact they were trying to pass off to us their technology that had become obsolete for them and would soon become obsolete for us as well. So there is no point in importing what they were trying to pass on to us. We should develop it ourselves through our efforts and research so that we can continue to renew it continually." Twenty years later, her son was doing precisely what Indira Gandhi had warned against—enslavement to borrowed ideas without understanding how to make them effective tools for change. His ministers even wanted to carry a computer to every hut as a part of what they perceived constituted modernization but, in this process, they had completely overlooked that they would first need to provide electricity supply to those huts. Can any party lead the people up such a garden path, and for how long? Intellectuals might not have found an answer but the electorate has replied, in no uncertain terms, in election after election.

Politics cannot evolve into a meaningful discourse when its practitioners, who abound in the Congress and other sections of the political class, refuse to see the writing on the wall. The electorate wants change, but of a variety which involves them. From Nehru downwards, except for Indira Gandhi in some patches, the Congress as an exponent of politics has failed to relate to the people because they are blissfully ignorant of what constitutes the political mind of the Indian voter. The variables and aspirations, ambitions and demands of successive generations have been misunderstood and mislaid by politicians who have reduced the democratic system to a game of numbers alone. The evolution of a new idiom, language and grammar over generations has been lost on an increasingly insular and self-centered ruling class. For two successive generations, the Congress has become consigned to history and is no longer a part of their day-to-day experience. For them the fluctuating fortunes of the Congress are merely a page of history that they have not cared to read. The failure is not theirs; it is basically the historical failure of the Congress to keep in touch with the changed idiom that is primarily at the root of its present crisis. For the burgeoning and ambitious middle class, material improvement is the immediate goal. Polemics and promises of removing poverty and deprivation have become empty catchwords bereft of a meaning beyond rhetoric. Their search for status, power and dignity has been misinterpreted by the Congress, that is only reduced to reap benefits from the blunders of its rivals. The Congress has failed to understand why it has been reduced to a mere spectator because its leadership has failed to read the popular mood and its requirements. Issues that could attract the younger generation to the party's ideological platform are not clear to those who control the party's destiny. It is this failure that has made the Congress to appear to be a party out of sync with the changed aspirations of people.

The Congress response has been static. It talks in a language that has lost all meaning. It has failed to grasp the need to raise issues that are important and relevant today. The party cannot live in the past; what was relevant fifty-odd years ago has little relevance unless the party is able to logically understand why it has failed to be an attractive proposition for sections seeking fresh social and political space. Unless the Congress leadership is able to bridge this communication gap, it would find itself out of its depth.

For the first two general elections in the country, a clear majority of the electorate was a participant in the freedom struggle. For it, the Indian National Congress under Nehru was a living phenomenon with roots in a past they had themselves experienced. But by the time the third general elections came along, a new generation had come to the fore. The Congress had to change its focus and reorient itself to this emerging class of people. The 1971 elections marked a watershed. From thereon, the Congress has consistently failed to reflect the popular sentiment. Indira Gandhi had changed the structure and nature of her politics; she had made grand promises to the poor masses and had rid them of their sense of fatalism and blind acceptance. As long as she could do that, she continued to occupy the political centre-stage. Her triumphs reflected her sensitivity to the needs of the masses. The moment she started her downhill curve by ad-hoc decisions and authoritarian impulses, her decline was only a matter of time. She had flattered to deceive. She made the mistake of taking the Indian voter for granted, who will continue to support her even if she continued to make one serious concession to powerful interest groups after another. She became a captive of a corrupt coterie busy milking the system. The presumption that the electorate will continue to keep investing in her individual charisma and appeal was rudely shattered by a combination of forces which may have lacked her style and élan but were certainly more firmly rooted in reality. The ordinary voter had realized his strength in the ballot paper that he held in his hand.

An interesting conversation was heard between a young man who was preparing bhang and the Sadhu who was apparently his guru at the Ganga Ghat early morning one day when the 1977 elections were on. The boy asked, Guriji Kya hoga is election me? Sadhu replied badlav lana hoga. The disciple asked once again, per Guruji naye log achhe nahi nikale to? Guru replied to unhe bhi badal denge agale election me. (A young disciple asked what would happen in this election. Guru said that change would be brought. The disciple asked but if the new proved to be bad? Then we will change them as well said Guru.) This conversation only reflected the mood and realisation of people what they held in their hands as a ballot paper. It was their power for bringing and ushering in the change. They know what they hold in their hand. No one can fool them.

To many, Rajiv Gandhi had played a masterstroke when he proposed a reduction of the voting age from 21 to 18 years; in actual fact, he had made a grave error. In doing so, he unconsciously expanded the element of anti establishment in the electorate. Generally, the threshold years signify rebellion and change from existing norms. Existing family, social and cultural ties face doubt and challenge. This defiance of existing norms is in-built, and it was truly a measure of Rajiv Gandhi's immaturity not to have factored that aspect into his schema for change. In retrospect, the expansion of voting rights has given a greater scope to the skepticism and curiosity of the impressionable. For the first two generations since Independence, elections meant a deeply reflective and crucial exercise for which they had the time and leisure to spend long hours awaiting their turn to vote at polling booths. Subsequent generations have been depoliticised by a globalised environment to which the Congress has responded only in terms of gross economics and abstract growth rate figures which to the uninitiated are just statistics and no more.

But the Congress history is not all a terminal decline precipitated by an increasingly bankrupt leadership. It is some thing much more than that. The key to understanding the Congress decline lies in the socio-political profile of those who have gained at its expense. In terms of its failures, the Congress party's cardinal error lay in the reorganization of states on a linguistic basis in the wake of the recommendations of the States Reorganisation Commission of 1955. The Congress party succumbed to sectarian fires emanating from the South after Andhra Pradesh had been carved out of the Madras state in 1953. After initially taking a posture against divisions based on linguistic considerations, the Congress made the costly error of succumbing to the virus which at once gripped several regions which also began seeking statehood based on the language formula. The issue became a matter of fierce debate at the national level, and within the Congress, there was no unanimity of views.

At a vulnerable moment, even Nehru lost his usual cool. This was after the first self-immolation in Hyderabad over the demand for a separate state based on the language. He responded by appointing a commission to work out an acceptable formula based on linguistic considerations. This, however, only stoked sub-national fires that a "please-all" party like the Congress was in no position to douse politically. From a position where it envisioned a casteless society, the Congress had plunged into a snake pit. The pluralistic vision was severely dented by short-term gains. The reorganization, and subsequently, carving out of fresh states on the basis of language had severe repercussions. For example, the SRC had categorised the Bombay state as bilingual. The Nehru government had to face a fierce agitation in both sides of the state and had to ultimately agree to creation of two states. Years later, it also had to agree to the bifurcation of Punjab. The northeast was divided into seven separate states on the basis of their ethnic identity. The phenomenal growth of regional parties was a direct consequence of political short sightedness reflected in conceding to linguistic chauvinism. The sons-of-the-soil movement, which spread in several states of the Indian Union, was a corollary of inflamed aspirations. Regionalism as an entity was thus a by-product of Congress ambivalence.

Unwittingly, a blueprint to change the agrarian landscape of the country through the introduction of better technological inputs acted conversely on the politics of the Congress. In itself, starting from the Zamindari Abolition Act of 1951, the Congress had consciously chosen to act as an agent of change in the country's still highly feudal land structure. However, by taking this and other measures, the Congress lost control over the very forces it helped unleash. The so-called Green Revolution was not just a matter of introducing high yield varieties (HYV) through increased institutional and structural support. It radically altered the social base of the countryside, and several sections who had hitherto been comfortable within the Congress began entertaining increasing doubts about the real intent of the changes introduced. Politically, the Green Revolution introduced in 1966 (the year in which Indira Gandhi took over) created a new class of ascendant peasant proprietors who were now poised to stake a greater claim to political power sharing. The intermediate or middle castes till then were economically mobile but politically largely subsumed under the umbrella-structure of the Congress.

The onset of the Green Revolution heralded a paradigm shift. The shift that occurred in the pattern of land-holdings was to be reflected at the political level as well. "Bullock-capitalists" emerged as a new factor in the regions where the Green Revolution was introduced in separate doses. The most palpable difference was witnessed in the north, where in Uttar Pradesh, Punjab, Haryana and in parts of Rajasthan, a brash new breed of political wannabes appeared on the horizon. In 1959, Dr Ram Manohar Lohia had split the socialist movement on the question of backwards vs. forward castes. The impact of that movement had vertically split the social structures in several Indian states, especially in the north. Now, with the Green Revolution creating a new category of the rural-rich who could afford the benefits of better technological inputs, the Congress party's support base underwent drastic changes.

The intermediate castes, which found political leadership from Dr Lohia and Charan Singh, sought to establish their own political footing. The year 1967 marked the decisive culmination of this process. Under the Samyukta Vidhayak Dal banner, several mutually antagonistic parties, which only had one abiding trait in common—their pathological hatred for the Congress- came together. The aggregation of political parties representing both the Right and the Left of the political spectrum was to have immediate political repercussions, which have been detailed elsewhere. The upshot of all these changes was steady erosion in the Congress support base.

Peasant proprietorship, which roughly accounted for about 12 per cent of farmers in the countryside, acted as an adhesive to Lohia's attempt to cobble together what Indira Gandhi described as the Grand Alliance of reactionary forces out to oust her politically and destabilize the benefits accruing out of new agricultural polices. From a party that had thus far been an acceptable proposition for contending castes and classes, the Congress was now reshaped into a narrow, rich-peasant dominated party. This may not have been entirely true, but the political message of the Green

Revolution alienated the Congress from the middle and lower rungs of rural society. This loss was to prove irretrievable even when seasoned minds like Union agriculture minister C Subramaniam and the pioneering scientist, M.S. Swaminathan had made out a convincing case for broad-basing the gains of the Green Revolution. Unfortunately for the Congress, good economics lost to bad politics.

The Congress tried to approach the Assembly polls in eight states in 1967 as a party that was as much committed to the soundness of Green Revolution as a principle as it was to the needs of those left out of its ambit. However, this appeal became a victim of internal bickering, bad marshalling of existing political resources within the Congress and a general sense of disquiet after two successively bad agricultural years in the preceding phase.

The Indian National Congress had taken several measures in the post-1951 period, which changed its equations with forces in the rural hinterland. Substantive gains were registered in imposing land ceiling and agricultural productivity. However, the Congress failed to cash on the political benefits of agrarian reforms. The gainers in this case were the party's amorphous opponents. Indira Gandhi, by liberalizing farm credit in a sustained drive towards the re-establishment of its lost moorings among those left outside the pale of the reformist drive but could achieve desired results.

The initial fillip to the slow building up of the economic muscle that enabled political assertion on part of newer segments militated against the major thrust of economic policy in the first two and a half decades after Independence which stimulated industrial growth through a programme of massive public sector investment in heavy industry, through strategies which had been meticulously planned. The initial phase of agrarian reform embodied in the Zamindari Abolition Act did not immediately translate into effective political assertion. Forcible dispossession of land was a later phenomenon. The Congress was obviously playing a very shrewd game. Brahmins and Thakurs, the two upper castes in India's most populous state, Uttar Pradesh, were to be administered the pill in small doses, which was a perfect clinical approach.

As for land reforms, the route undertaken was far more complicated—perhaps by design. By the time that the Centre through its agencies such as the Planning Commission began to exert pressure on the states to enforce limitations on ownership, the landowners had mobilized politically. The fact that the legal system had the sophistication that enabled state governments to enact laws formally imposing restrictions on ownership, ceiling laws took time to concretize in actual fact. The ensuing reforms in the structure of land relations were also marred by deliberate obfuscation. Issues like land reforms took the back seat, while the farm lobby within the Congress pushed its agenda towards ensuring more remunerative farm prices. There was a virtual freeze on the prices of agricultural inputs manufactured by the industrial sector. This to a great extent helped avert the possibility of an increased demand for lowering agricultural profitability and farm incomes. The Congress wanted to have its cake, and eat it too.

Until 1975, the Congress policy to appease both the powerful farm lobby on the one hand and the industrial sector on the other ensured the politically necessary status quo. Indira Gandhi's celebrated notions of having distributive justice on the top of her post-1971 political agenda had already been forgotten. It was not until 1977, after the Congress was defeated in the aftermath of the Emergency, that there was a shift in priorities towards the rural sector in general and the agricultural sector in particular. This became possible only because investment in agriculture was sought to be put on par with that in industry, overturning the primacy accorded to the latter in the preceding Congress years.

The radical stirrings of the early Seventies were forgotten barely four years after they had created such a ripple. It was certainly not an accidental lapse due to oversight. Populism being the governing factor behind the new economic thinking, it was only inevitable that most schemes designed to make a dent in the clout wielded by the rich peasant lobby in the Congress were eventually consigned to the dustbin. In subsequent years, even the pretence of agrarian restructuring in favour of the lower rungs of the sector has been given up. Several Congressmen still feel that the failure to energise the economic initiatives mooted in the early Seventies contributed enormously to the Congress party's fading halo.

Since the Avadi session of the Indian National Congress, Charan Singh and other protagonists of a conscious shift in economic priorities were becoming both more restive as well as vocal in their disagreement with the official line. This mismatch between two ideologically opposed camps had been neutralized by powerful personalities like Nehru and Indira Gandhi because they enjoyed mass popularity. The narrow margin given to reforms was largely a political decision, which could work only till the OBC's lacked their own political platform. From the mid-Sixties onwards, Charan Singh was the catalyst striving towards a policy shift in that direction. Lohia's attempts outside the Congress fold were to prove very helpful in creating the basis for the rise of a political counter to the leverage enjoyed by the urban elite.

Till such time that the Congress could prevent the consolidation of a new political alignment emerging against it, the use of the state apparatus came very handy in the process. But the post-Emergency period threw up a set of forces that were clear about their agenda. They wanted a dismantling of the Congress support base in urban India by pitting their perceived softness for the agricultural and rural sector. This was also not so much by design as by chance. The politics of Emergency was defeated, and some of its economics was also dismantled. The fact that the new rulers failed to carry forward their economic agenda to a logical conclusion has been analysed at length by several scholars and academics to need further elaboration.

The first clear indication of changed power equations was visible in the composition of the sixth Lok Sabha in 1977. The representation of rural-based politicians showed a dramatic increase. Complacent in the belief that their hold on power would remain undisturbed, the urban middle class overlooked the potential danger, treating it as just a one-time aberration. They were proved woefully wrong.

The subsequent collapse of the Congress party in the Hindi heartland thus becomes more appreciable. The Congress party, atrophied and clueless at the same time, no longer has had either the programme or the leadership to reconcile hostile class interests. It is because of bad economics that emotive issues like Ayodhya, the Shah Bano case and several other instances, which point to the failure to retain its secular credentials have become such milestones indicating a Congress decline on all fronts. Liberalisation as a palliative for the urban middle class is hardly a potent political weapon in electoral terms. The Congress discovered this through the Eighties and the Nineties. The saffron brigade is discovering this in the subsequent phase, where all the tall talk of disinvestments and globalisation has faced opposition from within the Sangh Parivar itself, leave aside critics outside the saffron pale. Merely reiterating the "irreversibility" of economic reforms makes absolutrly no sense at all.

The Congress and the BJP are fooling not only themselves but also the people at large by trying to ride two horses at the same time. The first generation of economic reforms was ushered in a politically conducive climate; subsequently, both the Congress and the BJP have lost their strongholds because the absence of vision is a malady that affects them alike. There cannot be human face to the reform programme if the market forces drive the economy for they do not recognize human beings and do not have any social obligations. They recognize only consumers and their profits. And if the state retained the power for state intervention, there would be no market forces to take over the economic reforms. So the market forces driven economy can never have a human face and people cannot be taken in by such talks for they have already faced what their plight would be if the economy was fully in hands of the market forces as the liberal economic reforms envisage. The collapse of global economic has already been visible in other parts of the world as John Ralstron Saul says in his book

One reason why Nehru opted for the mixed economy model was his control over the state apparatus ensured a modicum of cooption of market forces as well. Indira Gandhi too spoke of the social obligation of the market forces when she told captains of industry in April 1971 that the GDP did not reflect the correct picture of the development if the GDP was made up or inflated due to increased production of luxury goods that were beyond the reach of the masses. Today the GDP is inflated not by increased production of the items of mass consumption but by the increased production of automobiles and telecom gadgetry. The glitter is there; but at the core, the infrastructure is still too weak to give it a permanent sheen. Neither the BJP nor the Congress seem to have internalized one basic reality: unless the base is made more responsive to changes effected from above, all smart schemes dictated by multilateral bodies will only end up being resounding failures. The Indian capitalist class is 'swadeshi' only to the extent its own profitability-curve keeps going up. Otherwise, for corporate houses, governance only means having the finished product delivered on a platter. The hard work is the responsibility of the state sector.

Party leaders may come and go. But unless there is a level of continuity and clarity in socio-economic policies, the fate of parties will continue to widely fluctuate from election to election. A party like the Congress, which has a history of 120 plus years, cannot be effective in terms of sustained political retention until such time its identity is camouflaged by patterns of expediency.

The Congress party has always avoided a detailed discussion on the causes and reasons for its electoral disasters. The fact that it has substantial presence in several states and controls power in them has obscured a thorough analysis of its overall decline at the national level. The disasters of 1989 and 1999 went unanalyzed because politics was reduced to a game of numbers rather than a matter of conviction and ideology. The BJP is headed for a similar fate, because its narrow support base cannot please large sections of the people who reject majoritarianism and communalism as a matter of their collective intelligence.

Victories in individual states have their own importance. But the continued vacuum at the top reinforces the central thesis of this book. The Congress has always been a personality-driven party. Till such time that Nehru and Indira Gandhi were at the helm, the rot within it was obscured. Rajiv Gandhi was a man imbued with confused but at least fresh ideas, howsoever unrealistic they may have appeared in actual fact. But Rajiv Gandhi represented the last great hope of evolving into an all-encompassing national leader. His blunders and the tragic assassination that followed killed that hope as well.

15
Uncertain Future

> Though, our present life is governed by our past, our future must, by that very law of cause and effect, be affected by what we do now.
> Mahatma Gandhi

On August 21 2004, a day after the 60th birth anniversary of the former prime minister, Rajiv Gandhi, the All India Congress Committee held its session in Delhi— first one after it had emerged as the single largest party in May 2004 parliament elections. The session was convened for the ostensible purpose of commemorating the birth anniversary of its departed leader; but it turned out to be a marathon exercise in sycophancy. The adulation for Sonia Gandhi turned into a deluge as speaker after speaker sang paeans in praise of her. Sonia Gandhi was elevated to the pantheon of Hindu goddesses for her great sacrifice by not accepting the post of prime minister and of instead gifting it to Dr. Manmohan Singh. Priya Ranjan Dasmunshi, a Cabinet Minister outdid every one in lauding the Gandhi's with a remark that the Nehru's and Gandhi's were not a family but a national movement.

The mood during the sessions was gung-ho as the party was returning to power after an exile of eight long years-this was in spite of the fact that Congress was heading a coalition of many small parties with the communists lending support from outside.

Forty carefully selected members participated in debates over seven resolutions including the one that placed on record the services and the sacrifices of the Nehru Gandhi family to the nation and to the Congress Party. This resolution was placed to the assembly w'ithout the permission of the chair. It was an occasion to celebrate the return to power. This was no occasion to introspect as to why the party faired so abysmally in many states and why it could not get more seats for itself. In states after states, Congress's electoral performance was very poor.]n the Hindi heartland, the party's performance was still very bad. Party leadership had little patience for thQse workers who wanted to debate over the shrinking geographical and social vote base of the party .

A similar mood prevailed in the highest decision making body of the party, Congress Working Committee (CWC). It refused to get out of its self destructive mode by refusing to debate on economic and socia] issues. Virtually every meting of the committee ended with adopting a resolution authorizing the party president to take appropriate decision on critical issues.

The mandate for the] 4th Lok Sabha clearly revealed that the Congress vote base had shrunk so much that its immediate recovery was not really possible. Besides, it had been vacillating on what strategy it should adopt for its revival. After refusing to take support from regional parties for four years after the party strategy session at Panchmarhi in 1999, it suddenly did a vo]te face in July 2003 party conclave in Shimla. There it gave a call to like minded parties to come together for the cause of secularism under the leadership of Sonia Gandhi. It was for the first time that the party admitted that it needed help from other parties to come to power.

A cursory look at the electoral statistics of the 2004 polls makes it clear that the Congress had lost substantia] ground to other parties-including its allies. It does not require poring over voting percentages to draw this conclusion. In 1999 elections, Congress won 112 seats on its own. In the 2004 election the number fell to 83 seats. Rest of the seats came its way due to alliance with other regional parties. With the way that party affairs are being conducted these circumstances are unlikely to change soon.

In six states of Himachal, Delhi, Rajasthan, Gujarat, Madhya Pradesh and Chhatisgarh where the Congress was directly in confrontation with the BJP and where there was no third force, the Congress gained 30 seats of 102 seats.

In eight states of Haryana, Punjab, Uttaranchal, Uttar Pradesh, Assam, West Bengal, Orissa and Karnataka where the third force had strong presence but the Congress fought the election without a political or electoral understanding with any regional party, the Congress could win only 47 seats, which is less than one fourth of the total 217 seats.

In seven states with 209 seats in Bihar, Jharkhand, Andhra Pradesh, Tamil Nadu, Kerala, Kashmir and Maharashtra, where the Congress had pre-electoral seat adjustments, the Congress ended up winning 63 seats. It won 30 percent of the seats in these states when it gave primacy to the regional party.

In eight small states with 13 seats, the Congress could win only 3 seats while it bagged three of six seats in the Union territories.

In other words, the Congress could win less than twenty five per cent of 334 seats where it preferred to stand on its own without the support of regional parties. These results conclusively prove that the Congress is in no position to contest elections on its own.

Little away from the stage from where hosannas were being sung in favor of Sonia Gandhi during the congress convention, Chandrajeet Yadav, former general secretary of the party, was telling some media persons about the miserable state of the Congress party in North India. "Not even ten Rahul Gandhi can turn tables for the party in Uttar Pradesh", he claimed authoritatively.

Understandably, Yadav was not in the list of the leaders selected to speak at the Session. Couple of years ago he was hooted out at the Bangalore Session when he had shown the courage to express his views, which were radically different from the ones held by party leadership. He had claimed that the party could not recover the lost ground till it refused to take cognizance of the changing social complexities. He claimed that 58 per cent among the electorate were constituted of the down-trodden including the Dalits, who demanded a proportional share in power. Their economic conditions had improved since the introduction of the Green Revolution in 1966 and they were asking for a share in power.

However, the Congress Party had failed to create space for this aggressive class of voters. It is of no of solace for the Congress party that even other national party Bharatiya Janata Party was not giving them any space in the leadership. Due to this reason, many of these dalits and backward castes have joined regional parties.

The Congress leadership structure seems frozen in time. The same two dozen odd leaders who have been controlling the party since 1986 maintain their stranglehold over the organization even now. Periodically, they are shifted from one post to another, but their essential task remains the same- of managing personnel in the party and controlling the entry to the office of the Congress President. Sycophancy and personal loyalty to the leader are the only criteria for doing well in the party. There is no room in the party for merit or a leader with grass root support. No one really bothers about the fact whether these leaders are corrupt or not.

Things have come to such a pass that party observers dispatched to states for selection of panels of candidates for elections, have been accused of "taking money". In fact there were incidents at the AICC head quarters in 2005 when disappointed aspirants and their supporters had stormed into offices of high functionaries and abused them and charged them of giving nominations to undeserving candidates for a consideration.

All these factors conspired to delay by six months the appointment of President of Gujarat Pradesh Congress Committee. The choice was between Bharatsinh Solanki and Sidhartha Patel- both are sons of former chief ministers: Madhavsinh Solanki and Chimanbhai Patel Their names were short listed not for their ability to build a movement against BJP chief minister Narendra Modi, but because they were considered loyal to the party president. A contractor living off government contracts was made the leader of the legislature party in the state ignoring the fact such a person was vulnerable and could be manipulated by the unscrupulous BIP chieftain. There have been rumors in Congress circles that the party's revival has got stymied due to in appropriate selections for different offices in the state.

This is not one specific example. Similar kind of situation prevails in different states with several factions fighting with each other rather than fighting political opponents outside the party. The high command has been merely formalizing factions by accommodating all factions in the nominated structure in the hope of buying peace. This has made state organizations unwieldy and dysfunctional.

Absence of internal democracy in the organization is having a debilitating impact on the Congress. As many of the top positions in the party are nominated it does not bring out the best person to the top. It gets stuffed by individuals who would be more worried about perpetuating in the office rather than generating new ideas that would inspire people. They would be more interested in managing disorder that prevails rather than engineering solutions that would make disorder vanish. Hence nominated persons take an easy course of not offending the leader by airing unpleasant hard realities on the ground. The functionaries also tend to sterilize the access to the leader for others who would blurt out truth.

The Congress leadership could have taken a bold decision of keeping away from K Karunakaran and his party the Indira Congress that he had formed after breaking away from the Congress in 2005 because the Congress had refused to accommodate his demands for placement for his own children'in the party positions. It would have cost few seats in the Assembly elections in 2006 in the state but the party would have emerged with a new image that it would not compromise with self serving leaders even at the cost of seats to the party. But orthodox minds could not come up with a bold strategy and ended up being thrown out of power corridors.' It is not a matter of consolation that the party improved its performance by few seats in the state assembly polls over its performance in the 2004 Lok Sabha polls. But it exposed its weakness in a large measure by compromising with

Karunakaran. And the party ended up with an image that it was not averse to even bad compromises for the sake of power. The party functionaries from the state agreed that keeping away from Karunakaran would have been a prudent option though they also pleaded their helplessness as cooperation with Karunakaran was ordered from above.

The party also suffers from a lack of two way system of communications within the party. There was no internal communication system so that the party high command would remain aware and apprised immediately of developments in any state. Only in such conditions it can evolve the long term strategies rather than resort to fire fighting operations when bush fires catch up the party. The pathetic was the way in which the party depended on a professional Public Relations company for improving its image and also for providing the party with specific issues in different states during the 2004 Lok Sabha election. Sonia Gandhi's speech writers were supplied detailed analysis of specific problems of places where Sonia Gandhi was scheduled to address the rally in the elections. It ought to have been an internal function of the party as it was expected to remain in touch with the state and district units and understand their specific problems and demands. Instead it had to outsource information about political issues in different states. Even senior party leaders assigned election duties in different states had to be briefed by the agency on what to say and what ought to be avoided at any cost.

An access to the leader for the party workers has become a difficult process for various reasons. Foremost is the security barriers that have now been raised. The second cause is the personal staff of the leader who has no clue who was what in the party. The party men's .reluctance to communicate the hard reality to the leader is yet more problem. Sanat Mehta could easily communicate to Indira Gandhi in September 1977 of an incident involving an Adivasi youth traveling in a bus in Gujarat and Indira Gandhi could visualize the impact her politics had made on Janjati (Tribals) people all over the country. She did ask Sanat Mehta to move the political resolution in the first session of her new party in

January 1978 for his communication had given her new vision of her dormant strength. She also chose "Hand" as an election symbol of her new party in 1979 before the 1980 elections because of that incident.

One cannot expect a political miracle that would put the Ganges on fire but certainly expect more innovative ideas that would generate and build up momentum for the party and attract more of young people. But only dismay is in store as same set of conservative minds have been manning the party. They go in huddle to evolve strategies that would galvanize the party but end up with same old ideas of throwing few crumbs at voters in a belief that it would attract them to the party and vote for it. So the human resources development minister comes up with a proposal for affirmative discrimination in favour of Other Backward Classes in admission to institutes of higher education but without taking the party leadership in confidence. He did not even ponder why the Dalits had run away from the party even after it provided them with benefits of reservations for the past fifty years? He did not even wait to think how his proposal would impact minds of poor among the OBCs who did not get event decent primary education facilities? It is also a matter for debate whether the OBC families whose children could reach to the stage of admission to higher institutes do need the crutch of positive discrimination- reservation for admission?

Another idea which the Prime Minister Manmohan Singh de&cribed as historic scheme was the Employment Guarantee Scheme for selected 200 backward districts in the country - yet another crumb thrown at poor to win their votes. How would it impact on remaining 350 districts of the country? Does the party have a cadre to reap political advantage of the scheme? Only the BJP with cadre and the Left parties that also have cadre would benefit from this 'historic scheme' is patently apparent but the Congress leadership could not see it.

The Party certainly has ambitions of returning to power on its own but without addressing to the question: why its geographical and social vote base has been shrinking? Unless it is understood, evolving the effective strategy to overcome the situation becomes an impossible task. That raises yet another important question. How people perceive the Congress Party? They can identify Mulayam Singh, Laloo Yadav, Chandrababu Naidu, two DMKs as espousing cause of the OBCs. They see in Mayavati a voice of the Dalits and in the BJP as a party that is trying to further the Hindu cause. But what is the Congress identity in general perception? It claims to stand for Aam Adami but the Left parties have,. with their periodic outbursts against the Manmohan Singh government's liberal economic policies, effectively punctured that claim as well and in few cases made the government even to roll back its decisions.

It also claims to stand for secularism and the BJP has successfully driven home a perception and effectively too during the decade that the Congress party's secularism means appeasement of the Muslims but the Muslim masses do not believe it stands for them. Hence they have strayed away to Mulayam Singh and Mayavati.

More than fifty per cent of the electorate in the country is of people below the age of thirty. Their language, their grammar, their idioms, their aspirations and ambitions are totally different from the understanding of the Congress leadership because the Congress has been more or less living in the past as its slogans suggest. For the older generation of people above sixty years of age, the Congress is a living memory but for the new generation below thirty years of age, it has turned into a page of history.

But the party has not made a sincere attempt to address the new generation in its' own language to bring it to the party by espousing their cause before others begin. Dr. Murali Manohar Joshi of the BJP had tried to sell them the dream of the past glory of the Indian civilization but his efforts were to no avail for the party. There are several lessons for the Congress to learn from the defeat of the BJP in the last election despite its six years in power but only if it would make efforts to understand them.

Many in the party believe that arrival of Rahul Gandhi, son of the party chief Sonia Gandhi was the answer to the question of resurgence of the party. They have been clamouring since the Delhi session in 2004 to the Hyderabad session in January 2006 for assignment of party responsibility to Rahul Gandhi. The chant was intensified after the unprecedented margin of votes by which Sonia Gandhi won the Raebareli bye-election in May 2006. The success was attributed to the political acumen and management skills of Rahul Gandhi even though six per cent less of the electorate had participated in the May 2006 voting compared to the May 2004 elections with the weather conditions being more comfortable in 2006 than in 2004.

Can fortunes of a party be identified and subsumed in a single personality without clearly charted out programme for which the party stands? Indira Gandhi had won the 1971 mandate massively as her identity was clearly marked out but had to face the disaster in March 1977. Rajiv Gandhi had won unprecedented numbers in 1984 elections but had lost power in 1989 because his programme had failed to attract votes. Even Sonia Gandhi could bring only 112 members of her party back to the Lok Sabha in the 1999 elections: Why the family charisma did not work on these occasions and why it will work in future are questions that need to be answered fully.

Absence of a clearly identifiable image makes the future uncertain for the Congress Party. The hope for the Congress is harnessing the younger generation by espousing for their cause rather than clinging to the old conservative ideas of depending on the family and dynasty that remained the central thought of the party since Indira Gandhi era as it had nothing tangible to hold for resurgence and a brighter future.

Groups of states for analysis of the Lok Sabha Polls 2004

(A) States where two national Parties confront each other without presence of a third party

State	*Total Seats*	*gained by Congress*
Himachal	4	3
Delhi	7	6
Madhya Pradesh	29	4
Chhatisgarh	11	1
Gujarat	26	12
Rajasthan	25	4
Total	102	30

(B) States with powerful third parties but the Congress fought alone

Haryana	10	9
Punjab	13	2
Karnataka	28	8
Orissa	21	2
Bengal	42	6
Assam	14	9
Uttar Pradesh	80	9
Uttaranchal	5	I
Total	213	47

(C) States where the Congress had seat adjustments with regional parties

Bihar	40	3
Iharkhand	14	6
Maharashtra	48	13
Kerala	20	0
Andhra Pradesh	42	29
Tamilnadu	39	10
Kashmir	6	2
Total	209	63

(D) *Small States and Union Territories*

Goa	2	1
Manipur	2	1
Tripura	2	0
Meghalaya	2	1
Mizoram	1	0
Nagai and	1	0
Arunachal Pradesh	2	0
Sikkim	1	0
Andaman	1	0
Chandigarh	1	1
Daman	1	1
Dadra Nagarhaveli	1	0
Lakshadweep	1	0
Pondichery	1	1
Total	19	6

Number of seats won by the Congress in states Where it had seat adjustments	63
No of seats it won without seat adjustments	83

Sketches of Men at the Top

Brief Sketch of men who were at the helm of affairs as the Party president in order of their tenure till the posts of the party president and the prime minister where held by one person since 1980

K Kamaraj: Canny Giant

With the redoubtable Chakravarti Rajagopalachari as his mentor, K. Kamaraj needed to invest his own effort, ability and understanding to become a key figure at the state level in the Congress. A set of favourable circumstances brought him to the national centre-stage, but the powerful Nadar leader had by then established a strong enough individual mass-base which was to come in handy as he traversed through various lanes and by-lanes of fame. His mentor, who had taken over from Lord Mountbatten as the first (and last) Governor General of Free India, included this unassuming powerful Nader leader in his cabinet; Kamaraj served as an ideal counter to politically engage the powerful Dravid movement led by Periyar and subsequently, C.N. Annadorai. His backward caste clout supplemented Rajaji's sway over the state's upper castes.

Kamaraj became the chief minister of the state after Rajaji left the Congress party to found his own Right-wing political platform called the Swatantra Party. Kamaraj had succeeded in defending the Congress against the onslaught of the Dravid Munnetra Kazhagam, a regional party born out of the Periyar movement. Kamaraj was a powerful speaker in Tamil though he was not well versed in use of other languages. He understood both English and Hindi though he could not speak either language. He gave the evidence of it when he became the Congress president in 1963. Nehru had picked him up to bring him to the national politics when Nehru found himself hard pressed by the political circumstances created by the Chinese Betrayal in September 1962 and by the fact that he was forced to sack the defence minister V K Krishna Menon.

Kamaraj had a solution for Nehru who had felt threatened by the senior leaders. Kamaraj suggested a plan that Nehru ought to get rid of some seniors for the party work and thus eliminate them from a commanding position in the party. Six leaders including chief minister of Uttar Pradesh CB Gupta, a regional satrap in his own right, and who could arguably defy Jawahar Lal Nehru and get away with it. Gupta and several others were instant choices for the chopping board. Morarji Desai was the prime target. Jagjivan Ram was incidental and Lal Bahadur Shashtri was a ploy to justify the action. This was subsequently proved when Shastri was taken back to the Cabinet a few weeks later, as a minister without portfolio.

Kamaraj played a crucial role in the complicated transition after Nehru died. Shastri, too, was destined to meet the same fate soon after he had signed the Tashkent agreement. The sudden flux created a first rate crisis. He had cooperation from other regional bosses like SK Patil of Bombay, Atulya Ghosh of Bengal and S Nijlingappa of Mysore. Between them they decided that Morarji Desai should not be allowed to head the government at New Delhi as it would not be possible for them to manage him for he was too independent minded character. They had cast themselves in a role of kingmakers. Kamaraj maybe quite liked the new role, for he always managed a wry smile when he was referred to as the kingmaker.

Kamaraj was given a second term in 1965 at the Hydrabad session because the then Prime Minister Shastri wanted him to continue though Morarji Desai has expressed his strong reservations over giving him the second term. But by the time of 1967 general election, he had lost touch with his own state where passed on to the Dravida Munnetra Kazhagam. The state never came back to the Congress fold because the Congress could never make an inroad in the OBCs base of the Dravid movement. But that is another story

S Nijlingappa: The Unlikely Executioner

Politics in erstwhile Mysore (now Karnataka) has always been dominated by two castes, Lingayats and Vokkaliga. The Lingayat are basically Shaivites, followers of Lord Shiva, the Great Destroyer and one of the triumvirates who were known to be the originators of the Cosmos of Hindu mythology. Vokkaligas are basically Vaishnavites, followers of lord Vishnu, another of the same triumvirate. S Nijlingappa was a politician who had managed to obtain support from both the communities that were always in opposition in the state politics.

He was considered to be the dominant state boss and had a long and close association with other states bosses who were to play important role in changing the course of Indian politics as the crucial times of two transitions of leadership at New Delhi. When the question came of selecting the leader to replace Kamaraj as the president of the Indian National Congress in 1967, the then Prime Minister Indira Gandhi preferred S. Nijlingappa for he had contributed vastly in her becoming the Prime Minister. But soon enough, she found to her dismay that she had chosen a wrong man for Nijlingappa refused to toe the line.

While Indira Gandhi was driving the party and her government towards a Leftist orientation, he was not too willing to shift the policy stance of the party that quickly, even though the Working Committee had decided on the ten point programme. The high command was also defeated at the June 1967 AICC session by the dramatic move of the Young Turks. Nijlingappa was playing the role of a speed breaker to the vehicle that was being driven by Indira Gandhi.

She confronted him at the Congress Session in April 1969 held at Faridabad when the party had decided to evolve the different political strategy to stem the rot that had set in the party. He had taken over the party reins only after it had suffered heavy jolt in the fourth general elections and had lost power reigns in nine states of the country. The confrontation between Indira Gandhi and Nijlingappa reached a flashpoint after Indira Gandhi ensured the defeat of the official Congress candidate Neelam Sanjiv Reddy in the most controversial Presidential election ever. That was in August1969.

The intense activities in the two opposing camps reached the climax when Nijlingappa prepared his colleagues to punish Indira Gandhi for her acts of indiscipline against the party. He had already prepared a draft enlisting the reasons why she should be expelled from the party. Unfortunately for him, Dr. Shankar Dayal Sharma who was then the party general secretary carried his draft to Indira Gandhi. The untimely exposure of his plan for expulsion caused considerable embarrassment and he was forced to deny the move. However he could not avoid the final confrontation because of the internal pressure from other state bosses who had felt that the party and they would not survive if Indira Gandhi were allowed to get away with her coup against them.

The suave and soft-spoken Nijlingappa had a tremendous sense of humour but he would not compromise on his views, a trait which often proved to be a big handicap during these months of power-struggle. Several meetings with Indira Gandhi during the critical period between June and November 1969 always only ended in failure, because the party chief was quite unwilling to yield even an inch. Thus he became the last President of the (till then) undivided party, which had a vertical split on November 22 1969 after the Congress Working Committee expelled Indira Gandhi from the party on November 11 1969. Thus Nijlingappa became an unwilling, unlikely executioner.

C Subramaniam: Sterling Mind vs. Political Bind

One of the sharpest brains with tonnes of acumen never really fully utilised. That could be just the right description for Chintamani Subramaniam, a leader from Tamilnadu who was brought to the centre by the then Congress president Kamaraj and introduced to Jawahar Lal Nehru. The latter immediately recognized His thorough grasp of economic processes. His stint as the union agriculture minister in the first Indira Gandhi government was memorable, because he provided the political articulation to Green Revolution which revolutionized agrarian practices in parts of the North through improved technological inputs and High Yield Variety (HYV) seeds to improve both production and productivity of food grains in the country. It was in 1966 that he decided to make the change. His programme soon started showing results and India's dependence on the food charity from United States ended in the next two years.

Even as the finance minister in the Indira Gandhi government, he was to introduce many changes in the Indian economy. He was an ardent supporter of Indira Gandhi. He alone was present with Indira Gandhi when she had returned to her room after her defeat at the Parliamentary Board meeting that selected Neelam Sanjiva Reddy as the party candidate for the presidential election at the Bangalore Session. She declared to him that she would send in her resignation as the Prime Minister since she could not have her way in selection of the candidate and was defeated at the Parliamentary Board meeting.

Subramaniam was alarmed, but he also knew that he could not move her in her resolve and from her dejection. He immediately got hold of Chandra Shekhar who was ambling in the nearby park with his friends devising the new strategy for the session that was to be held next day. Chandra Shekhar told Indira Gandhi that there was no need for her to resign. She ought to fight the old generation. Subramaniam took a sigh of relief and flew back to New Delhi with her. Perhaps on the way, they also decided the strategy for the future that was confronting them after the Presidential election.

Indira Gandhi chose him to head the party after the great divide of the Indian National Congress in November 1969. From the lawns of the Constitution Club where the first session of the new party was held, he gave the clarion call for removal of the poverty from the country. The originator of the slogan Remove Poverty was C Subramaniam. He held to the post for one year while consolidating the party base by moving from state to state and winning over many diffident Congress leaders in states. But he was also aware that he was merely a stopgap arrangement and would have to hand over the party reins to some one else. He was also instrumental in selection of Jagjivan Ram a known Dalit leader of long standing years in the party.

Subramaniam was a brilliant academician. He proved by his lectures since his retirement from the national politics. He was appointed as the governor of Maharashtra but he resigned when he developed differences with the government at the centre because his conscience could not allow him to sit on and witness the worst communal carnage that Mumbai had seen in January 1993 after the demolition of the controversial structure known as Babri Masjid at Ayodhya. Subramaniam would be remembered for his major contribution in ending the dependence of India on the food charity from other countries for he had introduced the Green Revolution and was also responsible for the White Revolution that has flooded India with milk production. No other leader has made such a contribution in improving the food grains production in the country as he did. Though Nehru conceived the idea of Agriculture Research Council, Subramaniam was responsible for its activisation and maximum utilization. Incidentally, in contrast to 'Garibi Hatao' (Remove poverty) that became the radical Congress buzzword, Subramaniam preferred the term 'Quit Poverty' (Garibi Chhodo).

Jagjivan Ram: Politician extraordinaire

Post Independence India has seen fewer better exponents of the Art of the Possible than Jagjivan Ram, a Dalit (Chamar by caste) from Saharsa in Bihar who had a longest stint in the Lok Sabha. He was inducted in the Central cabinet as a junior minister in 1938. He continued to be elected to the Lok Sabha from Saharsa, a reserved constituency for the Scheduled castes. He never allowed the constituency to be dereserved though several delimitations were carried out since the first election to the Lok Sabha in 1952.

He was a powerful speaker and it was sheer pleasure reporting his speeches when he participated in Parliamentary debates. Even though he was a dalit leader, he was well versed with Vedas, Ramayana and Mahabharata, and could teach a thing or two to even to those who claimed to know better. His remarks in the Lok Sabha that the Vedas had permitted the consumption of beef, which was the most delicious meat, sparked off a major controversy in the country. It led to a confrontation between the Lok Sabha and the Supreme Court when one of the Shankaracharyas approached the Supreme Court for deletion of the remarks from the records of the Lok Sabha. Jagjivan Ram refused to bow to such pressures, and the Lok Sabha had to stand by him.

He also introduced a path breaking social reform when he abolished the procedure of serving of water on railway stations on the basis of religion. When he became the railway minister in 1963, the practice was prevalent to serve the Hindu paani and the Muslim paani at railway stations. He appointed Dalit women to serve water to all passengers without inviting a protest because few had become aware of or conscious of the transformation he had introduced.

He was removed from the cabinet under the Kamaraj plan and his protests did not elicit any support within the party because the regional bosses who had stood firmly with Nehru did not like him and were against Morarji Desai but Jagjivan Ram could not bring himself to align with Desai. He was taken in at the behest of Prime Minister Shastri. Indira Gandhi persisted with him because there was none to match his stature as a leader of Dalits. Indira Gandhi also chose him for the candidature in the Presidential election in 1969, but she could not push through her proposal at the Parliamentary Board meeting. She was hesitant earlier to choose him as her candidate because of the tax problems that had enveloped Jagjivan Ram. Not only that he had not paid the Income Tax for years but had also not filed the mandatory Tax Returns. Indira Gandhi knew that Morarji Desai was sitting on the files as the finance minister.

The issue came up for the debate in the Lok Sabha after the split in the Indian National Congress and he was chosen to preside the Indira Gandhi Congress party at the Bombay Session in December 1970. He made his famous statement that he knew India and he knew also that the people would forget and forgive him for his lapses in filing the tax returns. But his other statement as the party chief on the eve of the Lok Sabha election results in march 1971 had earned him the ire of Indira Gandhi. When the outcome appeared uncertain with the speculative reports that the Indira Congress might not get a majority on its own and there would be need to have alliance with other parties, he remarked at the press briefing, ' I am not a sleeping president." She had soon replaced him with another Dalit leader D Sanjivaiya from Andhra Pradesh.

Shankar Dayal Sharma: Reluctance personified

Dr. Shankar Dayal Sharma, an expert on Constitutional law, was happy teaching at the Lucknow University when he was picked up to head the government in a small state of Vindhya Pradesh before the formation of states on linguistic basis. He soon joined the government as the cabinet minister when the new state of Madhya Pradesh was formed. Nijlingappa had brought him to the national politics and assigned him the task of handling the party affairs as the party general secretary because Sadiq Ali who had held the post had become too old and had retired.

Dr. Shankar Dayal Sharma had virtually decided to remain with Nijlingappa in case the split in the party became unavoidable. But he changed his mind after he received a dressing down from the revered leader of Bhopal Yusuf sahib, nephew of Maulana Abul Kalam Azad who had introduced Dr. Sharma to Jawahar Lal Nehru and had thus paved his path in the national politics. Dr. Sharma carried with him on October 31 1969, only few days before the scheduled meeting of the Congress Working Committee that was to decide the action against Indira Gandhi for the indiscipline and open defiance of the party high command, and had handed over the draft listing reasons for action against her to Indira Gandhi. She had immediately Jagjivan Ram and Fakhruddin Ali Ahmed, another senior minister to issue a statement condemning Nijlingappa for planning expulsion of Indira Gandhi.

Dr. Sharma was appointed party general secretary of the new party. He was then appointed as the party president in 1972 and continued to hold the office till he handed over the reigns to

Dev Kant Barooah in 1974 and was shifted to the Union cabinet as the communication minister in 1974. He remained loyal to Indira Gandhi. She depended on him was evident from his appointment as the governor of Maharashtra after her dramatic return to power. She shifted him as the governor of Andhra Pradesh in August 1984 where he managed to reinstall the Ramarao government that removed by the earlier governor Ram Lal at the behest of Rajiv Gandhi, then the party general secretary. Dr. Sharma was elevated to the position of the Vice President and then president of India in 1992.

But the Constitutional law expert was not at ease in his relations with Rajiv Gandhi because he could not agree to many a demand that were made on him when he was the Vice President and was presiding over the Upper House. Once Congressmen held up proceedings in such a way that a desperate Dr. Sharma was driven to tears. In private, he often complained about the manners in which Rajiv Gandhi was being pushed into driving the economy into an abyss. But he was too weak to register his protest strongly and publicly.

Dev Kant Barooah: Mediocre supplicant

Indira Gandhi chose a rather unsung 60-year-old Assamese leader Dev Kant Barooah as the successor to Dr. Shankar Dayal Sharma who had completed a two-year term in 1974. Sidhartha Shankar Ray, who was busy pulling strings in the 'kitchen-cabinet' around Indira Gandhi from his safe abode in Calcutta, had introduced Barooah to Indira Gandhi. His loyalty was cited as Barooah's greatest asset. Indira Gandhi had earlier inducted him as the union petroleum minister and was satisfied with his political responses and his advice on occasions when he was summoned to the strategy evolution meets at her residence.

Barooah was no doubt erudite and voracious reader as well as keen television fan that would spend hours watching a wildlife film that the BBC had then produced. Barooah had studied well as evident from the manners he handled leaders and feuds from different states. Haryana chief minister Bansi Lal had come close to him and so also Rajni Patel who had come to the Congress in

1970. The group performed well when the Total Revolution movement led by Jai Prakash Narayan was at its intense best. Bansi Lal had even threatened to break every bone in the body of JP if he dared to step in his state Haryana.

It soon became apparent that Bansi Lal had moved closer to Barooah only as an adept conduit as Sanjay Gandhi virtually ran a parallel government and taking his own independent decisions. Barooah encouraged the rise of the Extra-Constitutional authority from the residence of the Prime Minister in a belief that it would train Sanjay Gandhi and provide experience when he was to eventually take over from Indira Gandhi. He had also initiated actions for review of the constitution. In fact a committee headed by Swaran Singh was preparing a new constitution so that Indira Gandhi rule could be perpetuated. However Indira Gandhi did not fall to such designs and dismissed the effort of the coterie with a single question that was put to her one evening by Bansi Lal.

ev Kant Barooah would always be remembered only because of his (in) famous quote, Indira is India that he had uttered in the Central Hall of parliament when a solidarity meeting was convened after Indira Gandhi was unseated from her Lok Sabha membership by the Court verdict. He did manage to retain his office in December 1975 at the Plenary Session of the Congress party at Chandigarh where Indira Gandhi had planned to hand over the party affairs to PV Narasimha Rao. But Sanjay Gandhi intervened at the last minute and Barooah remained the Congress President for another term.

He took the responsibility for the rout of the party in the March 1977 elections and submitted his resignation at the Working Committee meeting on April 2 but had forgotten to send an invitation to Indira Gandhi to attend the meeting. His action invited ire from other members but Barooah cared less and soon faded out into oblivion. Only trace he left behind him was the quotation that was to be cited on many occasions.

Swaran Singh: Diplomat too far

Swaran Singh took over as an interim arrangement when Barooah had virtually walked out of his post leaving bitter memories all around. Swaran Singn was one of the three senior leaders of the party from Punjab, but devoid of a personal mass following, he could never reach anywhere in state politics. Perhaps his habit of delivering the long winding arguments on any subject had never allowed him to expand his support base in the state politics. However it served him well as the foreign minister. Normally diplomats are supposed to never answer in affirmative tone to any question. However Swaran Singh exemplified the extreme limit; He could exasperate any one with his deadpan silence.

Once at the UN Security Council meeting where the Kashmir issue debate brought India and Pakistan representatives face to face, Zulfiquar Ali Bhutto had the misfortune of facing the Indian foreign minister Swaran Singh. He tried to extract straight answers from Swaran Singh who was India's foreign minister but failed to get any response because Swaran Singh continued his long winding arguments and never come to the point. He could say without a turning a muscle on his face that South Korea is to the south of North Korea. It was obvious that Bhutto had to pull his hairs in desperation and exasperation while Swaran Singh continued on his discourse without getting affected.

Swaran Singh was one of the few men whom Indira Gandhi trusted and had entrusted him with many delicate missions. One such occasion was in July 1973, when tact was required. She sent Swaran Singh to Gujarat to supervise the change of the chief minister in the state after the High command had asked Ghanshyam Oza to hand over his resignation as he had failed to stem the rot that was setting for the party in the state due to rising discontent against him. Swaran Singh created a history by bringing the ballot box to New Delhi instead of counting the votes in Ahmedabad. He counted the votes in his office and declared the winner. Never before or after such a procedure was adopted but Swaran Singh got away with one liner that there was tension in the State Congress Legislature Party so he brought the ballot box to Delhi.

K Brahmanand Reddy: Maverick landlord

Brahmanand Reddy was elected as the party chief who took over from Swaran Singh in October 1977. But his election did not have the approval of Indira Gandhi who had gradually begun to build her base once again by launching direct action. Senior leaders of the party had forgotten the art of coming to the streets to take up public causes and thus mobilize public support. Brahmanand Reddy who was the home minister in the Indira Gandhi government in 1975 was supported by other senior leaders who thought that their role was confined to opposing the Morarji Desai government in two Houses of parliament and not outside.

To protest against the imposition of Reddy on the Congress party, she asked Devraj Urs, chief minister of Karnataka to hold a party workers convention in Delhi and not invite the Congress president Brahmanand Reddy or any senior leader of the party who were taken in the Congress Working Committee by Reddy. Thus his term became the most ineffectual term because Indira Gandhi had separated away from the older generation in the Congress and had set up her own separate party on January 1, 1978. It was a fade out signal to the older generation after the split in the Congress party in parliament.

Those Who Influenced

Mahatma Gandhi and Jawaharlal Nehru defined the broad canvas that gave the Congress its moorings. Sardar Patel gave the vision a concrete shape. From then on, however, successive Congressmen have had to lean on think-tanks, forums and sometimes, armchair analysts to do their thinking.

Indira Gandhi was an exception; she was undoubtedly sharp, but she was too much of a politician to be ponderous and painstaking. She always decided the pace, but she also allowed several people to become her advisers and think-tanks. She was prepared to listen to advice, but often gave the impression that long discourses bored her. She entrusted the task of drafting resolutions, notes and formulations to several liberal-left intellectuals who manned the committees and panels that she constituted. The years during which she grappled with the old guard saw her lean more and more on radicals like the fabled Young Turks.

She encouraged the formation of a Socialist Forum which was distinct from the Young Turks—to give the impression that she was not overly dependant on just one shoulder at the expense of the other. Raghunath Reddy was the prime mover of the Socialist Forum. While other members of the Socialist Forum were dead set against any interaction or cooperation with the Young Turks, Raghunath Reddy was working in cooperation with them behind the scenes because of his personal equation with Chandra Shekhar.

The necessary research and groundwork that led to curbs on the monopolistic practices of big business groups can be attributed to a jointly worked out draft by the Young Turks and the Socialist Forum. Her trusted lieutenant Uma Shankar Dikshit, who was working as the party treasurer for a long time, was instrumental in the formation of the Nehru Forum.

Indira Gandhi relied on a set of brilliant bureaucrats who inter-acted with her at a day-to-day level, and thrashed out several key and tricky issues which gave a certain momentum to her.

Morarji Desai

One of the most acerbic, eccentric but principled politicians of his era, Morarji Desai could celebrate his birthday only once every four years because he was born on 29 February. He was brought up in a prudent Anavil Audichya Brahmin family of Surat district. Repelled from childhood itself by the atrocities committed by drunks on their wives and others, Desai became obsessed against drinking and drunks. His prohibition policy militated against the basics of revenue generation; but he risked personal ridicule to remain a steadfast prohibitionist all his life.

He was the deputy collector of Godhra (made infamous by the ghastly train massacre in 2002) in 1928 when the city was engulfed by severe communal strife. His superior, a British civil servant, asked him to blame a particular community for the riots; Morarji refused to write this, saying he was not into fabricating truth. When adverse remarks were entered into his Confidential Report, he quit the government job and joined the freedom movement.

He became the chief minister of bilingual Bombay state amid intense opposition from both Gujaratis and Maharashtrians. He shifted to New Delhi after many were killed in the police firing both in Maharashtra and Gujarat.

He was a shade too dogmatic for his own good, although as a finance minister(he served under both Nehru and Indira Gandhi), he proved quietly efficient. His success in halting increasing devaluation of the Indian rupee has been widely acknowledged. He shepherded the compulsory deposit scheme as well as the gold control measures, which initially attracted wide criticism but were subsequently accepted as inevitable.

He challenged Indira Gandhi for the election of the Congress parliament party leader in January 1966 because he strongly believed that she was a mere tool in the hands of those who were bent upon trivializing the gains of an earlier generation so that they could remain party bosses.

It was not personal animus against Indira Gandhi but his aversion to Jagjivan Ram that forced Morarji to go along with the old guard in the Parliamentary Board meeting to select the Presidential candidate in 1969. Indira Gandhi had prior information that Morarji had retained the documents regarding Ram's failure to file his tax returns.

Radicalism of any sort was anathema to Morarji. Hence he opposed the nationalization of major banks only due to his firm belief that banks would function inefficiently as government departments once they were nationalized. He favoured social controls over banks to control the credit flows in right directions. But Indira Gandhi was obsessed with her political agenda of teaching a lesson to the old guards by defeating them at their game in the presidential elections. So she forced Morarji to send in his resignation from the cabinet by divesting him of the finance portfolio. Morarji acted in the way he was expected to behave. Indira Gandhi got the approval of the cabinet for nationalization of major banks as her messenger was carrying the resignation letter of Morarji Desai for acceptance by the president on the night of July 19 1969. This was the beginning of a new chapter in Indian politics.

Dr. Ram Manohar Lohia

Perhaps the most brilliant student of the dynamics of caste, the enigmatic Dr. Ram Manohar Lohia could have scaled greater heights in Indian politics if had rid himself of his obsessive and pathological hatred for the Nehru family. He had, in his lengthy correspondence with Dr BR Ambedkar on the caste issue, conclusively established his sharp understanding of social reality.

He had read both Gandhi and Karl Marx and had written an excellent treatise on differences and similarities between the two philosophies and their immediate use for the Indian variety of socialism. He had also predicted that ultimately the backwards, the intermediate castes and the Dalits would combine and consolidate their strength to challenge the dominant upper castes and uproot them from power corridors. His belief was based on the impact of the expansion of higher education in country, especially because it had begun to attract the backward class and the Dalit students. They had begun to question and challenge the dominant castes and their supremacy.

The famous "mink coat" speech he made against "Gungi Gudiya" Indira Gandhi is still recalled; as also his pithy observation, quoted elsewhere in the book, that lively, vibrant nations don't wait five years to effect social change (Zinda Qaumein paanch saal tak intezar nahin kartein). A brilliant man became a victim of his own prejudices and whims.

Piloo Mody

"You would not get an invitation for a dinner at my place that way," Piloo Mody told Indira Gandhi at the reception organized by the Janata Party president Chandra Shekhar for the visiting British play write Noel Coward in the Parliament House canteen in November 1978. Piloo could taunt Indira Gandhi and get away with it, because he bore no personal rancour against her. Once he wore a placard that announced: "I am a CIA agent" and wore it to Parliament.This was his way of ridiculing the general Congress habit of seeing a foreign hand in every inconvenience that visited the party's leader. As for Indira Gandhi, after she had made a sensational comeback through her by-election victory from Chikmagalur, Piloo did invite her for a meal at his house! Only close friends were invited to that dinner and Piloo Mody told her to expect her expulsion from the Lok Sabha by the yearend. He also said that it would do a lot of good for her future. If he were the prime minister he would not act that way, Piloo added, but Charan Singh was from a different stock altogether. He could well have had his way, because Morarji had turned democrat at a wrong time! A great music-buff, he loved western classical music and apart from owning thousands of long-play records, he could also play the piano to great effect. He was a transformed man once he sat on his piano. From his father, he inherited the culinary art. He had done his graduation in architecture from Berkley University. His father was Homi Mody was knighted by the British government. He had worked with Le Carbousier, the architect famous for building Chandigarh. He had designed and constructed several prominent hotels in India and abroad.

A quick-witted Parliamentarian, he served both Houses. Jyotirmoy Basu, Madhu Limaye and Piloo made a scintillating trio. His editorials in his weekly 'March of the Nation' were evidence of his understanding of the Indian politics and also of the Indian psyche.

Madhu Limaye

Madhu Limaye was engrossed in chatting up a senior journalist in Parliament's Central Hall, Lal Krishna Advani walked towards them and innocently asked Madhu: "When did you come back from Paris?" Madhu was perplexed because he had not gone to Paris. He told Advani as much and asked: "Who told you that?" Hiding his mischief well, Advani replied:" I recently read in the newspapers that the Socialist party in France split so I thought that you must be in Paris." Madhu Limaye took the aside in the right spirit and guffawed aloud.

This Chit Pawan Brahmin (pure-hearted, twice-born) from Pune was like Lohia, a brilliant socialist who had all the sophistication necessary to become a top-flight academician. He has left an indelible mark in Indian politics by breaking the Janata Party on the dual membership issue. He was in the forefront against those from the former Jan Sangh who continued to owe their allegiance to the RSS even after becoming members of the Janata Party. His intellect and endearing ways made him popular across the political spectrum.He had evolved the effective strategy to push the government to the wall over the Pondichery License scandal. He knew that Indira Gandhi would never agree for a parliamentary probe into the scandal. So he and Piloo Mody moved a privilege motion against George Fernandes whose weekly 'Pratipaksha" had written a scathing article over the issue describing the Members of parliament whose names were dragged in the scandal as power brokers and corrupt. It was another way of securing a Parliamentary probe. Indira Gandhi was however equal to the challenge and got it nullified. He also lured away George Fernandes out of the Janata Party even after his brilliant defence of the Desai government in the debate over the no confidence motion in the Lok Sabha only forty eight hours earlier. Fernandes was not ready to move out but had ultimately give in.

Jyotirmoy Bosu

Bosu who had worked as a tea taster in the Tea gardens of Assam, had strayed into the Indian politics on a CPI-M ticket. He had three terms beginning 1967. He was a cause of great embarrassment to the Indira Gandhi government because he had unmatched access to the higher echelons of the bureaucracy. He was privy to the Reserve Bank of India report on the generation of black money in the country. When the government refused to confirm or deny the existence of the report, he undertook the responsibility of proving its genuineness and had authenticated before placing it on the table of the House. He came well prepared and asked such searching questions that the concerned ministers did not know where to look. He made ministers work hard to gather information to answer his queries. His interventions in several important and stormy debates in the House were memorable but he always maintained discipline and never behaved in a rowdy manners. In fact he would always ring up the parliamentary affairs minister and inform him of his intentions before hand so that the targeted minister was warned before hand what to expect in the House.

Bhupesh Gupta

'Sir, Can a member switch off his hearing aid when the prime minister is addressing the House?' asked Piloo Mody pointing out to Bhupesh Gupta who had switched off his hearing aid and was seen dozing in the Rajya Sabha. Indira Gandhi who was addressing the House could not suppress her smile because an embarrassed Bhupesh Gupta needed to be woken up by a member sitting next to him. He was very affable character and Indira Gandhi had a great liking for the communist leader who was a fine orator and members were loathe to miss his speech in the House for they all knew that they would learn something when he spoke in the House.

But Bhupesh did not suffer fools gladly. He had a habit of switching off his hearing aid when he was in an unwanted company and would continue to nod his head even if he had not heard a single word. He enjoyed company of Piloo Mody in the Central Hall. Even though he was a harsh critic of the establishment, he was soft on Indira Gandhi because of his liking for her. She also recognized the affection and responded positively to whenever he had made any suggestion.

Controversies

Brief Notes of Vexatious Issues

Himalayan Blunder

Jawahar Lal Nehru has placed a greater stake in cultivating friendship with China on the basis of five principles 'Panch Sheel' as a force against the two super powers, America and Soviet Union. China had also responded to the overtures by Nehru, especially after Nehru decided to prefer silence when China annexed Tibet as its autonomous territory. Yet China decided to send its troops to borders in September 1962 to redraw MacMohan line that was the disputed border between India and China since the British times. The resistance by the Indian Troops turned out to be a disaster with humiliating defeat. Nehru was virtually thrown into a stupor from which he could never recover. The episode has been described as the Himalayan blunder of India

Babri Masjid Controversy

The Mythological Indian epic Ramayana says that lord Rama, the most revered image of Indians ruled from Ayodhya on the banks of the River Sarayu, only 120 kms north of Lucknow, capital of the most populous state Uttar Pradesh some three thousand years ago. It was also believed that a temple stood where Rama was said to have born. No historical or archeological evidence was ever established to prove that there was a temple on the site. The general belief was also that Babar, first Moghul emperor or his Generals had destroyed the ancient temple to construct a Mosque some 455 years ago.

In 1949, some persons had, with the direct and active assistance of the senior police official of the state had installed some idols inside the Mosque and had begun worship. It led to violent reactions from the Muslims. To avoid further confrontation between the two sides, the Indian government had locked up the disputed structure. The structure remained out of bounds of both the sides the period since it was locked up. Though the Hindus claim that they had been regularly performing Puja of idols, the Muslims could not offer namaz prayers inside the Mosque since main gates were locked up.

In 1986, Rajiv Gandhi took a step to throw open doors of the Mosque so that the Hindus could officially enter into the structure and worship the idols. The move was initiated to pander the hurt Hindu feelings over the concessions that Rajiv Gandhi had made to the Muslim clergy in amending the law relating to the maintenance and alimony to divorced Muslim women. For the rabid elements in the majority community this action provided an impetus further their movement for construction of the Ram temple at the controversial site. They wanted an immediate action though the dispute between two communities was with the Court for the four decades.

In subsequent three years, the Vishwa Hindu Parishad, an appendage of the Rashtriya Swayam Sevak Sangh had built a movement over the issue. It forced Rajiv Gandhi to order participation by his home minister Buta Singh in the foundation stone laying ceremony in October 1989 when the country was already in the thick of election campaign for the Lok Sabha. When Vishwanath Pratap Singh introduced the Mandal Commissions recommendations based Reservations in government jobs for the backward classes in the entire country, there was a violent reaction to it from the Upper castes. The Bharatiya Janata Party that had adopted an ambivalent attitude till then seized the opportunity to hijack the temple movement and build its political base on its foundations through a Rath Yatra undertaken by the BJP president Lal Krishna Advani starting in September 1990 from Somnath an ancient temple city in Gujarat that was raided and ravaged by the mad Mohmed Gajhani 11 times in 16th century to Ayodhya. But he was arrested at Sitamarhi in Bihar on October 25 1990 and his Yatra was stopped.

The BJP and its sister organizations made an attempt to force itself for puja known as kar save but they could not succeed because of the police cordon raised by the then chief minister Mulayam Singh Yadav around Ayodhya. In December 1992 the BJP again planned a religious function at the controversial site with assurance that nothing untoward would be allowed to happen. However the situation did not remain in the control of the senior leaders. Vandals climbed on the rooftop of the controversial structure and it was brought down in five hours while the Prime Minister Narasimha Rao remained glued to the television networks that were showing the act of vandalism. Only seven hours after the Rao government dismissed the state government and moved in but by then the vandals had succeeded in building up a ramshackle temple on the site of the demolished structure.

Communal violence erupted with unprecedented force in most northern states, Maharashtra and Gujarat as a sharp reaction when those who had participated in the religious function returned to their home states and were given a heroes welcome for destroying the symbol of shame that the Babri Masjid had become for all of them. The issue remains the root cause of the communal tension in the country and also remains unresolved because both sides have refused to yield in their position and their claims over the site. The Indian governments since the Rao government have declared that either the two communities resolve their differences or wait for the verdict by the Supreme Court. The VHP refuses to abide by the Court verdict with a claim that it was a matter of their faith and the court had no jurisdiction over their faith.

Shahbano Case

A Muslim divorcee Shahbano had sought maintenance from her ex husband so that she could live in decency. She had taken a legal recourse when she was denied her right. She reached up to the Supreme Court to claim her right to a decent maintenance allowance from her former husband and won the case in the Supreme Court. The verdict triggered off a crisis in the country because the Muslim clergy felt that the verdict was against the Shariat and also against the Muslim Personal Law. It demanded a change in the Criminal procedure Code on the basis of which the Supreme Court had delivered its judgment so that the Muslim divorcee women should be treated differently and in consonance with Shariat and the Muslim Personal Law.

The progressives among the Muslims, especially women demanded that if there were to be amendments to the law to treat the Muslim women differently then there should be amendments to the Muslim Marriages law so that men could not get rid easily of their wives by uttering three times a dreaded word Tallaq and throw out their wives without compensating them with resources that would enable them to live decently.

They were able to engage the conservatives among the community when Rajiv Gandhi suddenly decided to amend the law and make a new provision for the divorced Muslim women. His decision was sudden and almost a about turn because he had defended the Supreme Court verdict in a fierce debate in parliament only three months earlier in the Winter Session of 1985. Arif Mohmed Khan had defended the case brilliantly and effectively to silence the conservatives among the Muslims. But Rajiv Gandhi was led to understand that if he agreed to change, he would win over the Muslim community as his permanent vote bank. He agreed to. It was a major political blunder because he did not earn gratitude of Muslim women nor did earn votes of the majority community for his surrender to the conservatives among the Muslims. Both felt let down by Rajiv Gandhi.

His advisers did not tell him that a political short cut was the longest distance between two points the start and the end. He had created an event with intentions but the logic of the event had overtaken his intentions and he turned out to be the loser in the end.

Scandals

Brief details of some of the important controversies and scandals that hit the headlines

Nagarwala case

Jimmy Nagarwala was employed with the Research and Analysis Wing of the cabinet secretariat. He rang up the chief cashier of the State Bank of India, Parliament Street branch, to tell him to keep Rs. 50 lakh in cash ready. He had imitated the voice of Indira Gandhi or so V.K. Malhotra, the chief cashier, told the police. A part of the contingency funds available to the Prime Minister was kept with this SBI branch. Nagarwala reached the bank, collected the cash and then vanished into thin air. Malhotra panicked and rushed to the PMO; police was sent on the Nagarwala trail. The Police nabbed him a short while later from a dharmashala. But he did not have the cash that he had collected earlier in the day.

The unorthodox withdrawal of such a huge sum triggered off a huge din. Indira Gandhi had to answer to several embarrassing questions; she had few answers to convince an excited Opposition. Nagarwala was subsequently lodged in Tihar Jail; he was to complain of a certain uneasiness, but by the time medical assistance could reach him, it was too late. Nagarwala, a few months ago, had faced an attack from unidentified assailants while he was with his family in his car. The mystery further compounded when VK Malhotra, after he retired from the SBI, was hired as the Chief Accounts Officer by Maruti Udyog.

The Pondicherry License Scandal

Till the late seventies, import licenses were issued against export figures. Licensees were permitted to transfer their licenses to others who wanted to import items for their use. This made licenses a high-premium commodity. Traders used whatever means they had to obtain licenses, import items of higher value and subsequently, sell them in 'black' to garner huge profits. The premiums were some times to the tune of three hundred per cent more for items that were just not available in India, but were critical for manufacturing trade in certain items that provided higher profits. Political clout was the decisive factor. A Pondicherry based firm ensnared Tul Mohan Ram, an MP from Bihar, who had claims of being close to the then commerce minister Lalit Narayan Mishra. He obtained letterheads of 19 other MPs and sent letters of recommendation to the Pondichery firm. The business ran into crores of rupees. Amid Parliamentary furore, Indira Gandhi saved Mishra but Tul Mohan Ram was expelled.

The Maruti Land Scandal

An automobile repairs shop owner Arjun Das accidentally met Sanjay Gandhi who was then chasing the dream of manufacturing a "people's car." Das was allotted prime land adjoining an IAF establishment in Gurgaon astride the Delhi Airport. The transaction violated security requirements because the new factory was sought to be premised close to a defence establishment. The debate also focused on the fact that Sanjay Gandhi and Sonia Gandhi were directors in the United Province Road Roller Manufacturing Company founded by someone with suspect credentials. The company had made only one road roller but had sold scores of road rollers to the Border Roads Construction Corporation, a public sector unit owned by the Indian government. The company had collected money but had never dispatched a single road roller. It had receipts from the railways of having loaded the road rollers in wagons that never reached their destinations. The Central Bureau of Investigation was asked to enquire, but could never unravel the truth.

Snam Progetti Connection

The Indira Gandhi government decided to set up two giant fertilizer plants— one at Hazira in Gujarat and the other at Thal Vaishet in Maharashtra. From among various bids, two were short listed for final negotiations. One proposal was from CF Brown and other was from Snam Progetti, an Italian firm.

Snam Progetti had Octavio Quattrochi as its CEO in the Indian operations of the company. Quattrochi had known the Mainos, whose daughter Sonia had married Rajiv Gandhi. Quattrochi befriended the Rajiv-Sonia couple, and gained access to Indira Gandhi's residence. Since Snam Progetti managed to wangle both projects, the usual pandemonium in Parliament was accompanied by allegations of kickbacks paid to the Gandhis. The government refused to order a probe into the deal. However, things became too hot for the Italian businessman after the Bofors deal was clinched, in which Quattrochi was believed to have been involved in receiving a fat commission. While the CBI was closing in on him following letter rogatories being exchanged between Indian agencies and their Swiss counterparts, Quattrochi had by then settled down in in Malaysia. He is believed to be stationed there till date.

Indira Gandhi Pratisthan

Maharashtra chief minister Abdul Rehman Antulay, a Sanjay Gandhi protégé, set up a private Trust in Mumbai with the avowed purpose of helping out poor families from Colaba in particular. He named the ensuing private trust after Indira Gandhi. The charge against Antulay was that he used official power to benefit his private trust. Cement, a scarce commodity available against fixed permits, was readily made available in bulk quantities to the trust. The Essential Commodities Act to harass the shopkeepers through which the food grains were issued through the Public Distribution System. Even minor variations in supply were used to threaten shopkeepers with police action unless they shelled out the specific amount. They were told they would have to make high payments in case a police complaint and an even higher amount if a charge-sheet was filed. It led to panic in Maharashtra; hundreds of shopkeepers turned up to return their licenses. The ensuing political storm subsequently consumed Antulay's chief ministership. Antulay subsequently quit the Congress, fought the Assembly election and won. He returned the Congress later, and won a Lok Sabha seat in 1991.

Bofors Scandal

In April 1987 the Swedish Radio had shaken the Indian polity from its roots with a report of kick backs paid in the defence deal that India had signed with the Swedish firm for purchase of 400 Howitzer 155 guns in March 1986. Few days later the then Defence Minister Vishwanath Pratap Singh found a note in one of the files in which a cable message remained stuck from the German private firm expressing its inability to part with the commission demanded as pay back for the deal for submarines. He ordered a inquiry without consulting the Prime Minister Rajiv Gandhi. It was the beginning of a charade that was to hound India for three decades.

Rajiv Gandhi stood accused only because he was in charge of the defence ministry since he had removed PV Narasimha Rao from Defence Ministry in September 1985. The deal was signed in an apparent hurry after Rajiv Gandhi had attended the funeral of the slain Swedish Prime Minister Olaf Palme only two months before India had signed the contract for purchase of guns.

The government had claimed that it had barred presence of all middle men and agents in defence deals. However the opposition was not willing to accept the claims of innocence by the prime minister even after he made a clear statement in the Lok Sabha that neither he nor his family was involved in accepting any commissions in the deal.

The Parliamentary Committee that was appointed to probe into the deal could not produce any evidence of involvement of any politician in kick backs. Another parliamentary Committee endorsed that the best gun out of three that were short listed for the long range guns, was purchased.

But the opposition would not allow the parliament to function for days for three sessions and the dismissed defence minister was portrayed as the messiah of poor who was out to cleanse the system. The most of the opposition leaders even handed over their resignations in the mid term and the parliament functioned without the true opposition till Rajiv Gandhi dissolved the Lok Sabha in October 1989 to go in for the fresh mandate in December 1989. He could not bring his party back to power as he could get only 212 seats. For the second time a non- Congress government with support from the right wing parties and the left parties came to power in India. But that did not end the shadows of the Bofors scandal over the Indian polity and the Indian National Congress.

The St Kitts Scandal

Controversial god man Chandra Swamy is credited with having faked this scandal to somehow besmirch the reputation of V.P. Singh, then spearheading the anti-corruption agitation against Rajiv. A document was produced to suggest that V.P.'s son Ajeya Singh was holding a numbered bank account with First Trust Corporation Limited at St Kitts, a private bank and had not informed the Reserve Bank of India as required by law. The document pertained to a numbered bank account. The document indicated who the owner of the code numbered bank account was and where he resided. It was a rather odd way of establishing the fact because the code numbered bank accounts do not reveal identity of the account holder. It would render meaningless if identity can be established so easily. It was said that Narasimha Rao, who was then the foreign minister had ordered the Indian diplomat in the island to facilitate Chandra Swamy in his mission. Except one mainline paper from Delhi, none in the media took note of the alleged fraud.

The Securities' Scandal

The late Harshad Mehta, who was in 1990 an enterprising stockbroker in Bombay owed his meteoric rise to certain bullish operations that pushed existing stock prices to unprecedented high levels in a short span of time. His rise was automatically ideal copy for every financial, and even non-financial, periodicals. Called now 'Big Bull,' of Bombay, Mehta became the toast of the power-circuit. Until his arrival on the financial scene, most industrialists mobilized resources through credits or loans from banks or financial institutions at the fixed interest rates. They were obliged to pay back and service the debt obligation. It made many of new projects unviable or uneconomic in the long run and had soon turned into sick industries that locked up crores of rupees as non-performing assets with banks or financial institutions. Harshad Mehta showed them a new route for resource mobilization by proving that they could raise their fund requirements through public issues. There was no obligation to pay dividends or interest because the disorganized small investors could never ask them to account for their investments.

His bullish operations had taken the stock prices to unprecedented and unnatural heights making investments in primary and secondary markets the trend. Overnight, thousands of share broker firms had sprung up all over the country, with millions of families disposing off their other assets in stocks, gold, properties, cars and savings to make a direct investment in primary or secondary markets. Mehta's deeds generated such greed that several thousands were sold to his dreamlike transition. The unnatural rise in stock market prices was short-lived. It was not backed either by industrial production or by other concomitant measures. The resultant crash destroyed several hundreds of smalltime investors. The biggest losers were those who had invested in primary markets as their project sponsors suddenly disappeared without trace.

Parliament gave its attention to the financial crisis thus caused with the opposition trying to pin down finance minister Manmohan Singh, his ministry officials and the Reserve Bank of India as responsible for scandal as they had failed to monitor the development caused by the bullish trends initiated by a single broker. They had reason also to go after the Reserve Bank as one of its subsidiaries National Housing Bank was duped in parking funds to the tune of Rs. 1200 crores in one of the dubious deals of Harshad Mehta. Two more foreign banks and few private banks of Mumbai and Karnataka were also involved in other deals. The opposition forced the government to accept the Joint parliamentary Committee probe into the scandal though the finance minister was on records in parliament that he would not lose his sleep over the ups and downs of the stock markets.

However the JPC concentrated its work on pinning responsibilities of different wings of the union government rather than probing into the enormity and other dimensions of the scandal that had opened the route for unscrupulous elements to exploit the public sentiments, their avarice, their greed to make fast bucks in the quickest possible time and had led to ruin of many million families in bad investments through public issues. In two years time companies promoted by unknown persons mopped up more than 93000 crores through public issues. They had since then vanished in thin air. There was no control over their past or their future. There was no way of monitoring persons sponsoring new companies to know their past and ascertain their future. It was loot that was legitimate in the eyes of law because there were no controls on their moves nor there was any law to hold them accountable to public money invested by small investors. No body was caught or brought to books.

The government admitted indirectly that its law enforcement agencies were not equipped to deal with this kind of offences. Hence it proposed to set up a Bureau against frauds in banks. But there was no proposal to control public issues and prevent frauds through public issues. There was no mechanism to warn public of the fraudulent past and persistent failures of promoters of such companies that vanished in thin air as soon as they led their hands on funds so amassed in merchant banks that acted as the lead managers. They either set up unviable units with nominal infrastructure for new company and most of funds were diverted to their other interests leaving no trace of transactions.

Instead of attending to such dubious dimensions of the scandal, the Bharatiya Janata Party decided to malign Narasimha Rao by putting up Harshad Mehta who was by then already facing a CBI and Income Tax authorities to make accusation against Rao that he had paid Rs. one crores to Narasimha Rao. But he did not explain why he needed to pay such a sum to the Prime Minister and for what services that he expected from the Prime Minister?

Harshad Mehta died of heart failure in 2001 in Mumbai and the scandal remains buried in the annuals of parliament.

Telecom Scandal

The Narasimha Rao government decided, as a part of the economic reform programme to allow private sector operators in basic telecom services. Sukh Ram as the telecom minister decided on private operators for different regions against the license fees that they were to pay. His decision became controversial for the opposition thought that he was too liberal in fixing the license fee amount and the national exchequer stood to a loss of more than Rs. Twenty thousand crores over the years. The opposition barracked the proceedings in both the Houses of parliament for nearly three weeks in 1995 budget session. The BJP and Marxist MPs from Rajya Sabha even went to the Supreme Court to prevent the entry of the private operators because of the involved loss. They did not succeed in preventing the entry of the private operators.

Four years later in 1999 when Vajpayee government a caretaker government, decided to reduce the license fees drastically on plea by private operators that they would go out of business if they were made to pay the fixed license fees of Sukh Ram. When the Congress spokesman protested against the reduction of license fees, the Prime Minister's office promptly sent copies of letters by the Congress leaders supporting reduction in license fees as asked for by the private operators. Sukh Ram story also reflects how politicians and political parties improvise and justify. He was an anathema for the opposition because he was corrupt as long as he was in the Congress party. For the BJP, he was a dartboard for every one to throw their verbal darts at him. When he broke away from the Congress and formed his own regional party and won the elections in Himachal Pradesh assembly, BJP quickly embraced him and hugged him with affection for his votes were needed for formation of the government in the state. How quickly they change their stance?

Individual References

Subhash Chandra Bose

Popularly known as Netaji in Bengal, he won the election to the Congress president against the proposed candidate of Mahatma Gandhi at the Haripura Congress in 1938. He quit as Gandhi refused to cooperate with him as both were diametrically opposed in their methods to win freedom from the British. He left India incognito to seek outside assistance to defeat the British through the armed conflict but never returned to India though his fans believe that he was still alive and somewhere in the world.

Mohammed Ali Jinnah

A prominent lawyer of Bombay who was a forward looking nationalist to the core in the initial stage of his political career, but he turned into a different kind of leader and advocated partition of India on religious grounds for he believed that the Muslims would never be treated differently and as equals. He became the first CEO of Pakistan but ended his career in misery and died unsung in Pakistan though he was hailed as a Quaid-E-Azam.

J B Kripalani

An ardent advocate of nationalism, he was close to Mahatma Gandhi and could question even Jawahar Lal Nehru. Known as Acharya, he was general secretary of the party when India attained freedom. But soon he drifted away from the party due to his differences with the leadership. Though he was a man from Sindh, he settled down in Uttar Pradesh and established an ashram for manufacture of Khadi.

Jai Prakash Narayan - JP

A socialist by conviction, he never accepted a political post either in the party or in the government. The intellectual from Bihar scaled the jail walls to escape to continue his fight against the British. He was invited by Nehru to join his cabinet but he refused the offer. He did attempt to broker a peace between India and insurgents of Nagland. He was also instrumental in surrender of arms by many dacoits in the Chambal valley.

Chandra Bhan Gupta

A politician from Uttar Pradesh, he was an unique character- thoroughly honest but outspoken. He could fight Nehru and hold on to his position. He was denied his due during the times of Nehru but asserted his position even though he was forced to resign under the Kamaraj Plan.

VK Krishna Menon

An intellectual from Kerala, he was close to Nehru since both had met in England when Nehru was studying law there. He became the defence minister in the Nehru cabinet despite his alleged involvement in the Jeep Scandal. He was caught napping when the Chinese troops had advanced to redefine the borders between India and China and was forced to resign under the pressure from the party.

Lal Bahadur Shastri

He had true humble beginning in life. He rose to be the Prime Minister of India. A true Gandhian who rose from the ranks in Allahabad to the level of central politics, he was pitch forked to the top seat before he died in tragic circumstances soon after he signed the Tashkent agreement with Pakistan in January 1966.

SK Patil

Although his political bio-data mentions his role in the freedom struggle, this traditional Congressman from Bombay was better known for his outstanding fund-raising capacity. He was the main fundraiser for the party and adorned the post of the party treasurer for many years. His singular achievement was his disclosure in Parliament that he had sufficient stocks of food grains to meet the entire demand and thus end the psychosis of scarcity in 1966. He was also responsible for getting food aid from United States of America under PL 480 Agreement in 1966.

Atulya Ghosh

A veteran from Bengal, he commanded the state unit of the party after the Congress doyen Bidhan Chandra Roy died. He was mainly responsible for the formation of the group of five state bosses when hold of Jawaharlal Nehru's hold over the party began to slacken in the wake of India's debacle in the war with China.

Neelam Sanjiv Reddy

A strong leader from Andhra Pradesh was made the party chief by Nehru when Indira Gandhi quit the party post. He nominated as the party candidate for the most controversial election for the President of India in 1969 but was defeated. He did become the President in 1977 during the Janata Party government. He helped Indira Gandhi in her game to deprive Jagjivan Ram of becoming the successor to Morarji Desai as the Prime Minister.

EMS Namboodripad

He was one of the most brilliant theoreticians that the India Left has seen. Forsaking ancestral property in Kerala, he rose to become the foremost communist leader in the country. He was controversially ousted after heading the first democratically-elected communist government in the country..

Ashok Mehta

A socialist from Maharashtra though he was a Gujarati by birth has been a prominent leader of the Praja Socialist party and its ideologue. He was offered the post of the deputy chairman of the Planning Commission by Nehru. He was a close advisor to Indira Gandhi but soon drifted after their differences over the Indian stance over the Soviet aggression over Czechoslovakia.

Dr. Ram Subhag Singh

An ardent politician from Bihar was a close supporter of Morarji Desai. He proved his ability as the railway minister and also as parliamentary affairs minister but could not go along with Indira Gandhi when the party was divided in November 1969.

Maharani Gayatri Devi

A royal princess from Cooch Bihar married to the scion of the Jaipur state, she drifted into politics for fun when the Swatantra party was formed. She fought the election in 1967 and had come close to becoming the chief minister.

Mohan Lal Sukhadia

The man from Udaipur was a dominant politician who ruled the state for eighteen years without a challenge from the state party. But he had to step down under pressure as he had criticized the Prime Minister Indira Gandhi in the word's duel between Indira Gandhi and the old guard in 1969 when Indira Gandhi was driving the party towards a split.

Dr. Sarvapalli Radhakrishnan

An educationist and a known philosopher from Tamilnadu was the President of India in 1962. He was grudgingly accepted for many in the Congress wanted dr. Rajendra Prasad for a third term.

Dr. Zakir Hussain

An educationist from Andhra Pradesh was chosen as the President of India in 1967. he was the least controversial personality that had strayed into the Indian politics but unfortunately died in harness on May 3 1969 setting the Indian politics ablaze. Given him, he would have avoided such a catastrophic exit.

Venkta Giri Varaha Giri

A trade union leader from Karnataka rose to occupy the office of the Vice President. Indira Gandhi aroused him to become the independent candidate for the most controversial Presidential election and he took the bait though the victory was uncertain. He lasted the full term.

M. Hidayatulla

A pious Muslim from Nagpur was the Chief Justice of India when he was called up to perform the duties as the acting president in june 1969 since the president had died in harness and the vice president had quirt his office to contest the presidential election. He became the Vice president later but was not given the opportunity to become the president as was the tradition till then.

Dwarika Prasad Mishra

A Brahmin from Kannauj in Uttar Pradesh, he had settled down in Madhya Pradesh for two generations and was the home minister in the Shukla government in CP & Berar province before the State Reorganisation. He had the nerve to abuse Nehru when Nehru ensured departure of Purushottam das Tandon from the post of the party president in 1952, from the floor of the state assembly. After an exile of nearly two decades from the party, he returned to take over the combat of Indira Gandhi against the old guard after having successfully installed her twice as the prime minister.

Fakhruddin Ali Ahmed

A lawyer from Assam, he was inducted as cabinet minister by Indira Gandhi though he was hardly known in other parts of the country as a leader of consequence. He became the President of India in July 1974 and suddenly died on February 11 1977. He had signed on the dotted line when Indira Gandhi had taken the notification for proclaiming Emergency on June 25 1975 after she was unseated from the Lok Sabha by the Allahabad High Court.

Yashwantrao Chavan

He was chosen by Morarji Desai to be his successor as the chief minister of Mumbai state. Nehru brought him to the Union cabinet as the defence minister after Nehru was forced to ask VK Krishna Menon to quit in 1962 after the humiliating defeat India suffered in the border skirmishes with the Chinese troops.

Indira Gandhi did not trust him because he was the leader of the single largest and most organized community of Maharashtra- the Marathas. He became home minister in July 1966 after riots in Delhi near parliament house by demonstrators who had come in a large procession to demand ban on cow slaughter in the country.

Mohan Dharia

A Gujarati settled in Maharashtra for three generation was a leftist who aligned with Chandra Shekhar to take over the anti-establishment role. He was the minister in the Indira Gandhi government and was a cabinet minister in the Morarji Desai government as well because Chandra Shekhar refused to join and nominated Dharia.

Krishna Kant

A son of freedom fighter from Haryana, he was in a league to the Young Turks but drifted away when VP. Singh became the Prime Minister to obtain an office. He became the governor of and later the Vice president of India. He was denied the opportunity to become the President of India in 2002 and died in 2002.

Chimanbhai Patel

A son of a farmer, Chimanbhai was a postgraduate in Economics from MS University of Baroda and started his career as the university teacher in Economics but soon joined the Congress party. He was an astute and consummate politician who could recall the antecedents of every party worker he came in touch with. Given a rare ability to foresee the oncoming events,

he was a also a capable administrator. But he had to pay the price for falling out with Indira Gandhi.
Ghanshyam Oza

A Brahmin leader from Gujarat was the minister of state in the Indira Gandhi government when he was chosen to be the chief minister of Gujarat only because he did not have support in the state assembly party on his own. He was challenged to identify even six MLAs by name after seeing them. Lack of base in the state was his qualification to become the chief minister.

Dr. Amul Desai

A socialist from Gujarat shot up to fame when he had defeated the Bombay chief minister Morarji Desai in the assembly election. He was the finance minister in the Chimanbhai Patel government in Gujarat.

Jaswant Mehta

Another Socialist from Gujarat shot up to fame because of improvement he had affected in Mahuva when he was the chairman of Mahuva Municipal Committee. He was the finance minister in Ghanshyam Oza government.

Chhabil Mehta

A socialist from Gujarat was chosen by Chimanbhai Patel for his ministry as a counter weight to Jaswant Mehta who was a power to reckon with. Both hailed from Mahuva that the stronghold of the Praja Socialist Party in the state

Zinabhai Daraji

A powerful backward class leader in Gujarat was the main architect of social engineering for the electoral purpose when he devised the combination of backward and the dalits against the dominant upper castes to win a two thirds majority in the assembly elections for the Congress. Indira Gandhi depended on him for her state politics for he was a good organisor.

Sanat Mehta

Another socialist and active trade union leader was the real architect of the social engineering by combining caste composition. He was the main organizer of the combination of KHAM that won a clear edge over others in Gujarat. He was the brilliant finance minister in Gujarat and introduced many fiscal reforms to put the state finances on sound footing. He also put the Narmada River Project on a sound footing and accelerated the pace of construction for five years. As his claims for his place in the state unit of the party were ignored in preference to others, he was disenchanted with the Congress after Sonia Gandhi took over and left to join Sharad Pawar.

Madhavsinh Solanki

A journalist who entered into the political arena at young age had derived benefits and offices merely because he belonged to the backward classes. He was the chief minister for 100 days during the emergency. He was forced to resign in the wake of violent eruption in the state against his policies of pampering the backward classes. The strong aversions that his policies caused have been responsible for the rout of the party in the state and for emergence of the saffron brigade in the state

Laloo Prasad Yadav

A student leader of Bihar who caused several sleepless nights to Indira Gandhi during his days as student leader of the Bihar movement.. An able communicator, he can mesmerize his audience with earthy idioms. Despite the alleged involvement in a massive fodder scandal, he has overcome the anti incumbency factor in Bihar politics.

Lalit Narayan Mishra

He got into the Council of Ministers because of the confusion in the Prime Minister's Office. The invitation for the ministerial intended for LN Misra of Orissa was delivered to him. He became the main fund raiser for Indira Gandhi and died as a consequence in a bizarre rail accident near Patna, his home state- Bihar.

Uma Shankar Dikshit

Another Brahmin leader from Kannauj in Uttar Pradesh who started his career as a secretary to the Commerce Chamber in Bombay soon moved closer to Indira Gandhi as her advisor and keeper of party funds. He alone could maintain detachment from power though he helped Indira Gandhi in all her games.

Kamla Pati Tripathi

A Brahmin leader from Varanasi was removed as the chief minister of Uttar Pradesh after a revolt in the state's armed constabulary. He again resigned in a huff after Indira Gandhi had publicly criticised his performance as the rail minister. He was accommodated by Rajiv Gandhi in the party post without giving him any authority.

Hemvati Nanda Bahuguna

Another Brahmin leader from Uttar Pradesh came to forefronts as the general secretary of the Congress during the period immediately after the great divide. His brilliance made Indira Gandhi weary of him though she did allow him to succeed Tripathi as the chief minister of the state. She never trusted him. He left the Congress along with Jagjivan Ram at the crucial stage.

Narayan Dutt Tiwari

A Brahmin from Uttar Pradesh hill region is considered to be the most malleable politician who occupied several offices both in the state and also at the center. He broke away from the Congress during the Narasimha Rao regime but could achieve little. He was close to Sanjay Gandhi and succeeded Bahuguna as the chief minister.

Nandini Satpathy

A fellow traveler from Orissa came to the Congress immediately after the split in the party and wormed up herself in the proximity to Indira Gandhi. She was sent to Orissa as the chief minister in 1972. However she was disappointed with Indira Gandhi and left the Congress to join the new party formed by Jagjivan Ram in February 1977.

AK Anthony

A serious person from Kerala is known to be honest politician. He is respected character but cannot mobilize a large support for the party, as he is not a mass leader. He had nerve to tell publicly that traces of corruption had reached to the doorsteps of the Prime Minister when Indira Gandhi was ruling supreme.

Rajni Patel

A flamboyant lawyer from Bombay, he was a man of many parts. At the critical time he became a hatchet man for Indira Gandhi providing her crucial logistics and inputs. He forced the then Maharashtra chief minister V P Naik to sell off the reclaimed land at Nariman Point in Bombay that raised considerable funds and furore.

Siddartha Shankar Ray

He joined the Congress Party after Indira Gandhi had brought about the great divide of the Congress in November 1969. He became the law minister in 1971 and was considered to be a close advisor to Indira Gandhi. He was shifted to Bengal as the chief minister in 1972. He was one of the main architects\advisors for imposition of the Emergency after Indira Gandhi had lost her seat in the Lok Sabha due to the Court verdict. He deserted Indira Gandhi after the electoral debacle of 1977 and was rehabilitated only by Rajiv Gandhi by assigning him the governor's post.

Bansi Lal

Bansi Lal rose to fame by his rule termed misrule byhis opponents) in Haryana state as the chief minister. He has transformed the face of the state and also made it a state for tourism even though the state did not have a single resort before.

He moved closer to Sanjiv Gandhi in 1974 when Indira Gandhi was facing political flak due to the increasing discontent against her government. He was made defence minister in 1976. he was the main votary of a new constitution so that the country could have the Gandhi family domination in perpetuity.

Hari Krishna Shastri

The eldest son of late Prime Minister Lal Bahadur Shastri, he opted to remain with the old guard at the time of the great divide. He soon joined Indira Gandhi camp and was rewarded with the post of secretary in the Congress party. He later became a minister of state in the Rajiv Gandhi government and was popular among the party MPs because of his suave nature.

Charan Singh

He was a unrivalled leader of the Jats and the kulak lobby. He had the nerve to oppose Nehru at the Avadi Congress session over the issue of making agriculture a co-operative enterprise. He defected from the Congress in February 1967 to become the chief minister of Uttar Pradesh. He joined the Morarji cabinet as the Union home minister but was soon evicted from the office. He split the Janata party to become the Prime Minister with assistance from Indira Gandhi.

Ravindra Verma

A Gandhian from Kerala was the parliamentary affairs minister in the Morarji Desai government. His calculations went awry in handling Indira Gandhi games in the parliament and the Desai government was embarrassed for it had to appoint an Inquiry Commission for corruption charges against son of the Prime Minister and daughter of the home minister Chavan Singh.
NKP Salve

A chartered accountant by profession he was the Rajya Sabha member from Maharashtra for several terms. A refined orator he moved the resolution seeking the Inquiry Commission.

Vasant Sathe

He came to the Lok Sabha through a bye-election from Maharashtra in 1969. A socialist, he has been known for proposal for converting the Indian democracy into a presidential form of government.

Shashi Bhushan

A known supporter of Indira Gandhi had defeated the powerful Jan Sangh leader Balraj Madhok in 1971 election in South Delhi though he did not belong to Delhi. He also forced the government to take over the part of Birla Bhavan where Mahatma Gandhi used to hold his prayer meetings and where he was assassinated.

ML Fotedar

A small time politician in Kashmir acquired the political clout beyond his own imagination due to his proximity to Indira Gandhi when he was appointed as her political advisor in 1980. He aligned with Arjun Singh in battle against Narasimha Rao.

Arjun Singh

Some consider him to be a wily Thakur from Madhya Pradesh. He had a successful tenure as the state chief minister between 1980 and 1985. He was abruptly shifted to be governor of Punjab where he worked out an accord with the Akali Dal. He strived constantly to remain closer to Sonia Gandhi after Narasimha Rao gave him his due.

Arun Nehru

A senior executive with a multinational firm, Arun Nehru, a cousin of Indira Gandhi stepped into the political arena to help out Indira Gandhi. He broke away from Rajiv Gandhi because of the constant suspicion in Rajiv's mind about his ambitions. He propped up VP Singh as a leader against Rajiv Gandhi.

Arif Mohammad Khan

A student leader from Aligarh University, Arif Khan began his political career as the Swatantra party member but joined the Congress in 1978 and soon moved closer to Indira Gandhi because of his abilities. He took a bold step of opposing the Rajiv Gandhi government on the Shah Bano issue. He was also instrumental in propping up the Jan Morcha against the Rajiv Gandhi government.

VC Shukla

The young son of the late chief minister Ravi Shankar Shukla of Madhya Bharat has been most flamboyant political character. VC Shukla was dropped in 1983 by Indira Gandhi as the cabinet minister for no reason. He joined Jan Morcha when he failed to gain any office in the Congress. Even VP Singh also did not accommodate him in his cabinet though Shukla has joined his Jan Morcha. He broke away from VP Singh to go with Chandra Shekhar but lost his membership as his change had invited a disqualification as his change was treated as defection.

G Kurup Moopanar

Moopanar, a big landlord in Tamilnadu joined the Congress on invitation of Kamaraj and soon moved closer to Indira Gandhi after Indira and Kamaraj fell out. He was general secretary of the party since the Indira Gandhi. But he could not countenance Narasimha Rao's agreement for coalition with Jailalitha for the 1996 elections and left the Congress to form a state party.

Ram Dhan

One of the Young Turks has traveled long to gain his moorings but ultimately was stranded with no party. He was member of the Lok Sabha since 1967. he became the chairman of the Backward Classes Commission during the Narasimha Rao period.

George Fernandes

A fiery orator and trade union leader of Bombay shot up to fames when he defeated the uncrowned King of Bombay SK Patil in February 1967 elections with a comfortable majority. He has been against the foreign multinationals as a socialist leader but has undergone a complete change since he became a part of the National Democratic Alliance.

Zail Singh

An Indira loyalist was preferred as the chief minister of Punjab to Darbara Singh because he was known to be down to earth politician. However he messed up politics of Indira Gandhi by triggering off the Punjab problem. He was home minister in the Indira Gandhi government and was later elevated to be the President of India.

Darbara Singh

He was the only politician of Punjab whose vision extended beyond Punjab. He did not get the enough backing from the Union government to translate some of his political moves into reality that could have averted the crisis in its final form.

R. Venkataraman

He was a technocrat from Tamilnadu who had reached New Delhi through efforts of the then Congress president K. Kamaraj. He held several offices at the center though his political reach in the state was limited. He was elevated to the post of the President by Rajiv Gandhi.

Farooq Abdulla

His only claim to fame was that he was son of dr. Abdulla known as lion of Kashmir. He was flamboyant with a gift of gab though his words did not add any meaning to them.

NT Ramarao

A matinee idol of Telugu film world, he believed that he was destined to be a new avatar in the state. He loved to play a role of elder statesman to the United Front that was formed in 1988 as a front against Rajiv Gandhi. He succeeded because Rajiv Gandhi had publicly humiliated the Congress chief minister of the state. But he was betrayed by his son in law to virtually usurped power from his hands.

Atal Behari Vajpayee

A Brahmin leader from Madhya Pradesh has been a member of the RSS since early age. He has been a powerful orator and has mesmerized audiences with his words though he hardly gave a copy to media persons. He ventured to form the government even though he did not have the requisite majority in the Lok Sabha after May 1996 elections. He bowed out in thirteen days though he later became the Prime Minister. He has got himself elected from outside Madhya Pradesh since he twice lost election from Madhya Pradesh.

HD Devegowda

A farmer from Karnataka was the chief minister of Karnataka when the national Front decided to prop him up as the prime minister after the Vajpayee government bowed out. He was a surprise choice by the coterie in the National Front.

Inder Gujral

Inder Gujral a leftist who moved to the Congress much before his other fellow travelers had a successful stint in the Indira Gandhi government but fell from grace because he had chosen to oppose Sanjay Gandhi. He succeeded Devegowda as the Prime Minister

Harkishen Surajeet

A diehard Communist known for his behind-the- scenes maneuverings, he has been holding the reins of party power for a long period. He has been instrumental in selection of candidates for high posts. But he committed a historic blunder when he proposed name of Devegowda instead of sponsoring the name of Jyoti Basu as the Prime Minister in May 1996.

Jyoti Basu

He was considered to be one of most effective and successful chief ministers who emerged from outside the Congress party and managed the coalition politics in Bengal for twenty-three years. He has been a revered figure; suave and well-spoken, who was denied an opportunity to adorn the highest executive office by young turks within his own party and also Sonia Gandhi.

MK Karunanidhi

A cinema scriptwriter from Tamil Cinema, he entered into the political arena from an early age and became a powerful chief minister of Tamil Nadu. His government was dismissed because he continued to assist the Tamil Tigers of Sri Lanka despite the specific instructions from the Union government.

J Jayalalitha

Her phenomenal rise in the Tamil politics was through her ability and her understanding of the human nature. She could be suave as well as a ruthless person depending with whom she was dealing. She has faced several cases of corruption and was even convicted in one case though she remained in the office because of stay granted by the superior courts.

Sharad Pawar

The Maratha leader from Maharashtra could never rise above the state politics though he had several opportunities to make his mark in the national politics. He made a cardinal mistake of returning to Maharashtra when he was the defence minister of India. However he had shown courage in questioning the credentials of Sonia Gandhi for stacking claims to become the Prime Minister. He formed a new party Nationalist Congress party in 1999.

Dr. Najma Heptulla

She is the grand niece of Maulana Abul Kalam Azad though she has never flouted her ancestry to demand any position in the party. Indira Gandhi brought her to the Upper House in 1980 from

Bombay and Rajiv Gandhi made her the Deputy Chairman of the Rajya Sabha. She became the first woman to be the President of the Inter Parliamentary Union. She has been the longest serving deputy chairman of the Upper House.

Mayavati

An educated dalit woman from Uttar Pradesh has expanded her political base through organising the dalits through a hate campaign against the upper castes. She has been the chief minister of Uttar Pradesh through politics of coalition with BJP.

Mulayam Singh Yadav

A socialist from Uttar Pradesh has been a fire brand politician who has at last succeeded in mobilizing the support from the backward classes. He was antagonistic to VP Singh and could not trust him but he could not remain with any other national leader. He was the defence minister in Devegowda and Gujarat cabinets.

Sant Longowal

A priest who took keen interest in politics because he wanted to preserve the hegemony of jat Sikhs in the state politics. He signed an Accord with Rajiv Gandhi to settle the Punjab problem even when he was not vested with authority by the entire state. He paid the price for settlement with New Delhi.

Prakash Singh Badal

Prakash Singh Badal was twice chief minister of Punjab but could complete full term only once. He tried to establish the supremacy of his family in state politics but could not

Chronology

1962	
January	Third General Elections held.
October 20	China launches offensive against India on western and eastern borders.
November 7	Nehru accepts resignation of defence minister VK Krishna Menon.
1963	
August	Six union ministers including the UP chief minister resign to take up government work under the Kamaraj Plan.
1964	
January	Jawaharlal Nehru suffers his first stroke.
May 10	Last AICC Session that Nehru attended held in Bombay
May 27	Death of Jawaharlal Nehru and Shastri elected as the Prime Minister.
1965	
August	Kamaraj was given another term as the party chief at Hyderabad Session.
September 1	Indo Pak war that lasted 22 days leading to a decisive victory for India: Bangladesh liberated
1966	
January 11	Prime Minister LB Shashtri dies after signing the Tashkent peace Agreement with Pakistan's President Gen. Ayub Khan
January 17	Indira Gandhi defeats Morarji Desai in the election of the leader of the Congress party in parliament
January 24	Indira Gandhi becomes Prime Minister.
June 6	Indira Gandhi government devalues the Indian rupee by 35.5 per cent.
1967	
February	The fourth General elections held. Congress majority reduced and several states lost to the party
May	The Congress Working Committee adopts ten-point economic rejuvenation programme

June 22	The Congress high command defeated over two amendments to the economic resolution seeking bank nationalisation and abolition of the privy purses
1968	
August	Ashok Mehta forced to resign after the party refuses to endorse his demand for condemnation of the USSR for its use of brutal force and occupation of Czechoslovakia
1969	
April	The rift emerges in the Congress at the Faridabad session where the idea mooted to seek co-operation and alliance with like-minded parties in future
May 3	The President of India Dr. Zakir Hussain dies in harness
June 24	Indira Gandhi defeated in the Congress Parliamentary Board on selection of the candidate for the Presidential election.
July 19	Indira Gandhi virtually sacks Morarji Desai and nationalizes 20 major private banks.
August 17	The official Congress candidate is defeated and V V Giri independent, candidate becomes the president of India.
November 9	Indira Gandhi expelled from the Indian National Congress for her defiance of the party high command
November 22	The Indian National Congress is split vertically
1970	
December	Indira Gandhi defeated in the Rajya Sabha on the Bill seeking end to privy purses by a fraction of vote
December 3C	Indira Gandhi dissolves the Lok Sabha to seek a mid term poll
1971	
March 12	Indira Gandhi wins 352 seats in the Lok Sabha with 43.7 per cent votes.
March 25	Pakistani Army begins operations in East Pakistan
August 11	India signs Indo friendship Treaty with USSR

October	Indira Gandhi fails to prevent Chandra Shekhar from getting elected to the Central Congress Election Committee.
December 3	Pakistan Air Force attack several Indian military airports.
December 17	India declared unilateral ceasefire after Pakistan's Maj General Niazi surrenders in Dhaka.
1972	
June	Indira Gandhi and Pakistan prime minister Z A Bhutto sign the peace agreement at Simla.
1973	
April	Three senior judges of the Supreme Court superseded in appointment of Justice AN Ray as the Chief Justice. Three judges resign.
July 14	Chimanbhai Patel of Gujarat challenges Indira Gandhi over the election of a new leader of the Gujarat Congress legislature party.
October 10	Nav Nirman movement launched in Gujarat.
1974	
February 9	Chimanbhai Patel forced to resign.
February 17	Gujarat assembly dissolved and central rule imposed.
March	Bihar movement launched.
May 8	Railway strike begins. Main leaders arrested.
May 28	The rail strike withdrawn.
May 28	Nuclear fusion experiment carried out at Pokharan in Rajasthan.
1975	
March 6	Jai Prakash Narayan leads a long march from the Ramlila grounds to the Parliament House in Delhi and gives a call to armed forces.
March 25	The election scheduled for the Gujarat assembly polls announced.
June 12	Indira Gandhi unseated by the Allahabad High Court for corrupt practices in her election in 1971 from Rae Bareli.
June 12	The Congress fails to win a clear mandate in the Gujarat assembly polls.
June 25\26	Indira Gandhi imposes the Emergency and imprisons the most opposition leaders.

July 2	Indira Gandhi announces new economic programme.
August 15	Bangladesh president Mujibur Rehman assassinated.
December 18	Lok Sabha term extended by a year. Assemblies also follow.
1976	
December 18	Indira Gandhi expands her cabinet, installs Madhavsinh Solanki as the Gujarat chief minister and extends the term of the Lok Sabha by one more year.
1977	
January 18	Indira Gandhi addresses the chief ministers' conference on land reforms.
	Indira Gandhi dissolves the Lok Sabha and opts for the poles in March.
March 24	Indira Gandhi personally defeated, her party routed in the entire north. The Janata Party government came to power to be the first non-Congress government.
May 29	Polls held for nine state assemblies and the Congress again routed.
May 31	Indira Gandhi visits Belchi in Bihar where Harijans families were massacred.
October 12	Indira faction holds its separate conclave.
November	Indira Gandhi wins the by-election to the Lok Sabha from Chikmagalur.
December	Indira Gandhi expelled from the Lok Sabha.
1979	
July 15	Indira Gandhi faction moves a no confidence motion against the Morarji Desai government that results in a split in the Janata Party with Charan Singh straying away
July 25	Morarji Desai resigns. and Indira Gandhi decides to support Charan Singh to form the government.
August 3	Charan Singh seeks to dissolve the Lok Sabha even before facing it.
1980	
January 11	Indira Gandhi wins a landslide victory.
June 23	Sanjay Gandhi dies in a plane crash.

July	Her elder son Rajiv Gandhi is brought in politics.
1981	
September	Sant Jarnail Singh Bhindranwale arrested but released.
1982	
September	Sheikh Abdullah of Kashmir dies and son is anointed as the new leader.
November	Asian Games become a political issue because of a ban on entry of Sikhs to stadia.
1983	
February	Nellie massacre catches world attention just before the NAM conference at Delhi.
April	A senor Punjab police official SS Atwal was assassinated outside the Golden Temple steps.
1984	
June 6	Operation Blue Star was carried out to flush out terrorists holed up in the holy shrine.
July	The reaction spreads in several units of the Armed Forces and strict security laws come into operations.
October 31	Indira Gandhi assassinated. and Rajiv Gandhi takes over.
December 31	The Rajiv Gandhi government wins unprecedented victory.
1985	
August	Rajiv Gandhi signs the Punjab Accord.
August 14	Rajiv signs Assam Accord.
September	The Shah Bano verdict by the Supreme Court.
1986	
Feb	Babri Masjid doors thrown open.
March 12	Rajiv signs the contract for the Swedish Bofors guns.
1987	
March	Kashmir assembly elections.
April 17	Swedish Radio allegations on kickbacks in the Bofors Gun deal.
April	Defence minister VP Singh sacked.
October	Jan Morcha formed.
1988	
June	By-election to Allahabad constituency VP Singh wins.

October 12	Janata Dal formed.
October	Nation Front comes in existence with VP Singh presiding.
1989	
July	Opposition quits Lok Sabha.
October	Rajiv Gandhi dissolves Lok Sabha and seeks fresh elections.
December 2	The National Front government headed by V P Singh in place.
1990	
August 7	The Prime Minister VP Singh announces acceptance of the Mandal Commission recommendations.
September	Lal Krishna Advani starts Rath yatra from Somnath to Ayodhya.
October 24	Advani arrested and BJP withdraws support to the government.
November 7	VP Singh defeated in the Lok Sabha.
November 10	Chandra Shekhar sworn in as Prime Minister.
1991	
March 8	Chandra Shekhar resigns and dissolves Lok Sabha.
May 16	Lok Sabha elections.
May 21	Rajiv Gandhi assassinated.
June 21	Narasimha Rao sworn in as Prime Minister.
1992	
Dec 6	Babri Masjid demolished.
Dec 8	Three BJP leaders arrested.
1993	
January	Sharad Pawar shifted to Maharashtra.
March 12	Bombay rocked by a series of bomb blasts.
1994	
	Securities scandal.
1996	
May	Lok Sabha elections.
May 13	Atal Behari Vajpayee sworn in as Prime Minister.
May 28	Vajpayee resigns.
June	HD Devegowda sworn in as the Prime Minister Sitaram Kesri takes over as Congress president.

1997	
March 30	The Congress president Sitaram Kesri withdraws support to the United Front government.
April	Devegowda resigns after defeat in Lok Sabha.
April	IK Gujral new Prime Minister.
1998	
April	Gujral resigns and dissolves the Lok Sabha Vajpayee sworn in as Prime Minister. Sonia Gandhi takes over the Congress chief and also as the leader of the Congress party in Parliament.
November	BJP defeated in assembly elections in 3 state.
1999	
April	Jaylalitha withdraws support. Sonia Gandhi stakes claims to form the government but does prove majority support. Elections ordered.
May	Shard Pawar and two other seniors thrown out of the Congress party for raising the issue of Sonia Gandhi's foreign origins.
May	The Kargil Operations.
October	Vajpayee heads the NDA government after the elections.
2001	
January	Earth quake rocks entire north India.
December 13	Indian parliament house under the militant attack Kaluchak incident leads to offensive diplomacy against Pakistan.
2002	
February 27	The Sarvodaya Express train burning at Godhra in Gujarat.
February 28	The unprecedented communal carnage in Gujarat
April 10	The Prime Minister changes his stance but the Congress is silent.
October	Kashmir assembly elections. National Conference defeated. Sayeed Mohammed Mufti becomes chief minister.
2002	
October	Uttar Pradesh Assembly elections held and the BJP went out of power.

December	BJP returns to power in the Gujarat Assembly elections with two thirds majorityState Assembly Polls. The Congress ousted in Rajasthan, Madhya Pradesh and Chhatisgarh however it returns to power in Delhi.
2004	
February	Lok Sabha dissolved as National Democratic Alliance seeks fresh mandate.
May	NDA defeated. The Congress stakes claim after formation of United Progressive Alliance. The Congress forms alliance governments in Andhra Pradesh and Karnataka. Orissa remains with Biju Janata Dal. Sonia Gandhi declines to be prime minister. Instead names Manmohan Singh for the post.
August	All India Congress Committee meet at Delhi.
October	Assembly polls in Maharashtra with Nationalist Congress emerging as single largest party replacing the Congress in the state assembly.
2005	
October	Assembly polls in Bihar, Jharkhand and Haryana. The Congress wins Haryana but has to retrace its move in Jharkhand. Bihar goes to Janata Dal BJP combine.
December	Lal Krishna Advani steps down as the president of Bharatiya Janata Party.
2006	
January	The Congress Session at Hyderabad. Demand for a prominent role to Rahul Gandhi, son of Sonia Gandhi was raised again.
May	Assembly held polls in Assam, Bengal, Kerala, Tamilnadu and Union Territory of Pondicherry. The Congress routed in Bengal and Kerala. It scrapped through in Assam and Pondicherry
May 8	Sonia Gandhi re-enters Lok Sabha after winning bye-election from Raebareli with record margin.

Confession

In October 2002, Pradyut Lal formerely of Patriot suggested that I should write a book on the Indian National Congress as I had been covering the party for more than forty years. I accepted the suggestion and immediately gave him the time division of developments in the Congress affairs. I delivered a chapter each day for twenty days which was merely a down-load from my memory. While he worked on what I had written, I got to check facts and events by verification from records and interaction with others to confirm the events.

Pradyut turned the book into a narration in Marxist jargon that was not approved by many other friends who had seen the first script. Particularly they had disapproved of the chapter The Slide as they felt that it was too heavy to read but Pradyut had set his heart so much on his work that I decided to retain it as it were though for life of mine I can never present it in the language and construct that Lal has given to it for I am a simple person not given the gift of gab or flourish of language.

Readers might find different styles and constructs in few other chapters. It is only because many friends and well wishers have lent their support to make the book readable and also valuable. While their attempts were to make it more comprehensive, I own up for all mistakes that have crept into the book.

But I would like to thank all friends, particularly Sanjay Kapoor, Om Gupta and Thomas J Mathew for the assistance they rendered to make the book possible. I am thankful to P. Lal for his efforts and his help. I must contain this not a historical account but personal observations based on interactions.

Vijay Sanghvi

New Delhi June 15, 2006

Bibliography

Acharya, K R - *The Critical Elections* (Hyderabad,1979).

Aggarwala, Satish; Aggarwala Adish -*Legacy of Indira Gandhi* (Socialist Age Publications).

Ali, Tariq - *The Nehrus And the Gandhis: An Indian Dynasty* (Picador).

Baxter, Craig - *The Jana Sangh* (Philadelphia).

Blair, Harry - *Voting Caste, Community Society* (Young Asia Publication).

Bose, N K - *Culture and Society in India* (Asia).

Brass, Paul R - *Factional Politics In An Indian State* (OUP): *Faction And Party* (Chankya).

Brecher, Michael - *Nehru's Mantle: Politics of Succession in India* (New York 1966).

Brown, J M - *Modern India: The Origins of an Asian Democracy* (OUP).

Carras, Mary C -*Indira Gandhi: In The Crucible of Leadership* (Jaico 1980).

Chandra, Bipin -*The Rise and Growth of Economic Nationalism in India* (People's Publishing House).

Chandra, Shekhar - *Zindagi ka Caravan:Dynamics of Indian Politics.*

Desai, A R - *Social Background of Indian Nationalism* (Popular Prakashan).

David, Shulman *Orthodoxy, Heterodoxy and Dissent in India* (Mouton Publishers).

Edwardes, Michael -*Nehru A Political Biography* (Penguin Books).

Ghosh, Atulya - *The Split in The Indian National Congress* (Calcutta).

Hangen, Welles - *After Nehru, Who?* (Rupert Hart Davis London)

Harry, Henry C - *Indira Gandhi's India* (Westview Press).

Healy, Kathleen - *Rajiv Gandhi: The Years of Power* (Vikas Publishing House).

Jagannathan, N S - *A Revolution in Making* (New Delhi People's Action).

Jain, Meenakshi - *The Congress Party* (Vikas Publishing House).

Kochneck, Stanley A -*The Congress Party of India.*

Mathai, M O - *Reminiscenes of the Nehru Age* (Vikas Publishing House).

Mathew, George - *Shift in Indian Politics* (Delhi Concept).

Narain Iqbal - *Twilight or Dawn- Political Change in India.*

Narasimhan, V K - *Democracy Redeemed* (S Chand & Company).

Nayar, Kuldip -*India, Critical Years:The Judgment.*

Nigam, Raj K - *Indira Gandhi's Legacy to the Indian Nation* (Doc Centre).

Puri, Rajinder - *Crisis of Conscience.*

Ralhan, O P - *Indira Gandhi: The Champion of Secularism* (India Integration Movement).

Roy, Ramashray - *The Uncertain Verdict* (Orient Longman).

Sengupta, Barun - *Last Days of the Morarji Raj* (Ananda Publishers).

Singh, Mahendra Prasad - *Split In A Predominant Party* (Abhinav Publiciations).

Vasudev, Uma - *Two Faces of Indira Gandhi* (Vikas Publishing House).

Viet, Lawrence - *India's Second Revolution* (Tata Macgrew).

Weiner, Myron - *Party Politics in India (Princeton)*: *States Politics in India* (Princeton): *India at the Polls: Parliamentary Elections of 1977* (Washington).

Wood, John - *State Politics in Contemporary India* (Westview Press).

Zaidi, A M - *The Great Upheaval* (Oriental India).

Index